T0252333

Bioinformatics and
Medical Applications

Scrivener Publishing
100 Cummings Center, Suite 541J
Beverly, MA 01915-6106

Publishers at Scrivener
Martin Scrivener (martin@scrivenerpublishing.com)
Phillip Carmical (pcarmical@scrivenerpublishing.com)

Bioinformatics and Medical Applications

Big Data Using Deep Learning Algorithms

Edited by

A. Suresh
S. Vimal
Y. Harold Robinson
Dhinesh Kumar Ramaswami
and
R. Udendhran

Scrivener
Publishing

WILEY

This edition first published 2022 by John Wiley & Sons, Inc., 111 River Street, Hoboken, NJ 07030, USA and Scrivener Publishing LLC, 100 Cummings Center, Suite 541J, Beverly, MA 01915, USA
© 2022 Scrivener Publishing LLC
For more information about Scrivener publications please visit www.scrivenerpublishing.com.

Wiley Global Headquarters
111 River Street, Hoboken, NJ 07030, USA

For details of our global editorial offices, customer services, and more information about Wiley products visit us at www.wiley.com.

Limit of Liability/Disclaimer of Warranty
While the publisher and authors have used their best efforts in preparing this work, they make no representations or warranties with respect to the accuracy or completeness of the contents of this work and specifically disclaim all warranties, including without limitation any implied warranties of merchantability or fitness for a particular purpose. No warranty may be created or extended by sales representatives, written sales materials, or promotional statements for this work. The fact that an organization, website, or product is referred to in this work as a citation and/or potential source of further information does not mean that the publisher and authors endorse the information or services the organization, website, or product may provide or recommendations it may make. This work is sold with the understanding that the publisher is not engaged in rendering professional services. The advice and strategies contained herein may not be suitable for your situation. You should consult with a specialist where appropriate. Neither the publisher nor authors shall be liable for any loss of profit or any other commercial damages, including but not limited to special, incidental, consequential, or other damages. Further, readers should be aware that websites listed in this work may have changed or disappeared between when this work was written and when it is read.

Library of Congress Cataloging-in-Publication Data

ISBN 978-1-119-79183-6

Cover image: Pixabay.Com
Cover design by Russell Richardson

Set in size of 11pt and Minion Pro by Manila Typesetting Company, Makati, Philippines

10 9 8 7 6 5 4 3 2 1

Contents

Preface

This book features bioinformatics applications in the medical field that employ deep learning algorithms to analyze massive biological datasets using computational approaches and the latest cutting-edge technologies to capture and interpret biological data. In addition to delivering the various bioinformatics computational methods used to identify diseases at an early stage, it also collects cutting-edge resources in a single source designed to enlighten the reader with topics centered on computer science, mathematics, and biology. Since bioinformatics is critical for data management in the current fields of biology and medicine, this book explains the important tools used by bioinformaticians and examines how they are used to evaluate biological data in order to advance disease knowledge.

As shown in the chapter-by-chapter synopsis that follows, the editors of this book have curated a distinguished group of perceptive and concise chapters that reflect the current state of medical treatments and systems and offer emerging solutions for a more personalized approach to the healthcare field. Since applying deep learning techniques for data-driven solutions in health information allows automated analysis, this method can be more advantageous in addressing the problems arising from medical- and health-related information.

- Chapter 1, "Probabilistic Optimization of Machine Learning Algorithms for Heart Disease Prediction," discusses the ensemble learning that overcomes the limitations of a single algorithm, such as bias and variance, by using a multitude of algorithms. It highlights the importance of ensemble techniques in improving the forecast accuracy and displaying an acceptable performance in disease prediction. Additionally, the authors have worked on a procedure to further improve the accuracy of the ensemble method post application by focusing on the wrongly classified records and using probabilistic optimization to select pertinent columns by increasing their weight and doing a reclassification which would result in further improved accuracy.

- Chapter 2, "Cancerous Cells Detection in Lung Organs of the Human Body: IoT-Based Healthcare 4.0 Approach," analyzes three types of cancer—squamous cell carcinoma, adenocarcinoma, and large cell carcinoma—derived from lung tissue, and investigates how AI can customize treatment choices for lung cancer patients.

- Chapter 3, "Computational Predictors of the Predominant Protein Function: SARS-CoV-2 Case," describes the main molecular features of SARS-CoV-2 that cause COVID-19 disease, as well as a high-efficiency computational prediction called the polarity index method. Furthermore, it presents a molecular classification of the RNA-virus and DNA-virus families with results obtained by the proposed non-supervised method focusing on the linear representation of proteins.

- Chapter 4, "Deep Learning in Gait Abnormality Detection: Principles and Illustrations," discusses cerebral palsy, a medical condition which is marked by weakened muscle coordination and other dysfunctions. This chapter proposes a deep learning technique, including support vector machines, multilayer perceptron, vanilla long short-term memory, and bi-directional LSTM, to diagnose cerebral palsy gait.

- Chapter 5, "Broad Applications of Network Embeddings in Computational Biology, Genomics, Medicine, and Health," mainly focuses on the current traditional development of network or graph embedding and its application in computational biology, genomics, and healthcare. As biological networks are very complex and hard to interpret, a significant amount of progress is being made towards a graph or network embedding paradigm that can be used for visualization, representation, interpretation, and their correlation. Finally, to gain more biological insight, further quantification and evaluation of the network embedding technique and the key challenges are addressed.

- Chapter 6, "Heart Disease Classification Using Regional Wall Thickness by Ensemble Classifier," focuses on the cardiac magnetic resonance images that are formed using radio waves and an influential magnetic field to produce images showing detailed structure within and around the heart.

These images can be used to identify cardiac disease through various learning techniques employed to evaluate the heart's anatomy and function in patients. In this chapter, an ensemble classification model is used to classify the type of heart disease.

- Chapter 7, "Deep Learning for Medical Informatics and Public Health," highlights deep learning drawbacks related to data (higher number of features, dissimilar data, reliance on time, unsupervised data, etc.) and model (dependability, understandability, likelihood, scalability) for real-world applications. It emphasizes the DL techniques applied in medical informatics and recent public health case studies related to the application of deep learning and certain critical research questions.

- Chapter 8, "An Insight into Human Pose Estimation and Its Applications," discusses human pose estimation and examines potential deep learning algorithms in great detail, as well as the benchmarking datasets. Recent important deep learning-based models are also investigated.

- Chapter 9, "Brain Tumor Analysis Using Deep Learning: Sensor and IoT-Based Approach for Futuristic Healthcare," proposes an approach for the prediction of brain tumors.

- Chapter 10, "Study of Emission from Medicinal Woods to Curb Threats of Pollution and Diseases: Global Healthcare Paradigm Shift in the 21st Century," focuses on techniques to prevent pollution-related diseases.

- Chapter 11, "An Economical Machine Learning Approach for Anomaly Detection in IoT Environment," presents an improved version of the previous machine learning architecture for ransomware assault in the IoT since it could be more destructive and hence might influence the entire security administration scenario. Therefore, precautions are to be taken to secure the devices as well as data that is being transmitted among themselves, and threats have to be detected at an earlier stage to ensure complete security of the communication. The work proposed in this chapter analyzes the communicating data between these devices and aids in choosing an economically appropriate measure to secure the system.

- Chapter 12, "Indian Science of Yajna and Mantra to Cure Different Diseases: An Analysis Amidst Pandemic with a

Simulated Approach," discusses deep Yagya training, which is an amazingly practical application that is easy to use and exciting, and has a great impact on delicate thinking and emotions.

- Chapter 13, "Collection and Analysis of Big Data from Emerging Technologies in Healthcare," discusses the fact that new diseases, such as COVID-19, are constantly being discovered. Since this results in a tremendous surge in data being generated and a huge burden falling on medical personnel, this is an area in which automation and emerging technologies can contribute significantly. Since combining big data with emerging healthcare technologies is the need of the hour, this chapter focuses on the collection of big data using emerging technologies like radio frequency identification (RFID), wireless sensor networks (WSN), and the internet of things (IoT), and their applications in the medical field. After discussing different data analysis approaches, the challenges and issues that arise during data analysis are explored and current research trends in the field are summarized.

- Chapter 14, "A Complete Overview of Sign Language Recognition and Translation Systems," discusses the use of human body pose and hand pose estimation. Sign language recognition has been conventionally performed by some preliminary sensors and later evolved to various advanced deep learning-based computer vision systems. This chapter deals with the past, present, and future of sign language recognition systems. Sign language translation is also briefly discussed, providing insights into the natural language processing techniques used to accurately convert sign language to translated sentences.

The editors thank the contributors most profoundly for their time and effort.

A. Suresh
S. Vimal
Y. Harold Robinson
Dhinesh Kumar Ramaswami
R. Udendhran
February 2022

1

Probabilistic Optimization of Machine Learning Algorithms for Heart Disease Prediction

Jaspreet Kaur[1]*, Bharti Joshi[2] and Rajashree Shedge[2]

[1]Ramrao Adik Institute of Technology, Nerul, Navi Mumbai, India
[2]Department of Computer Engineering Ramrao, Adik Institute of Technology Nerul, Navi Mumbai, India

Abstract

Big Data and Machine Learning have been effectively used in medical management leading to cost reduction in treatment, predicting the outbreak of epidemics, avoiding preventable diseases, and, improving the quality of life.

Prediction begins with the machine learning patterns from several existing known datasets and then applying something very similar to an obscure dataset to check the result. In this chapter, we investigate Ensemble Learning which overcomes the limitations of a single algorithm such as bias and variance by using a multitude of algorithms. The focus is not solely increasing the accuracy of weak classification algorithmic programs however additionally implementing the algorithm on a medical dataset wherever it is effectively used for analysis, prediction, and treatment. The consequence of the investigation indicates that ensemble techniques are powerful in improving the forecast accuracy and displaying an acceptable performance in disease prediction. Additionally, we have worked on a procedure to further improve the accuracy post applying ensemble method by focusing on the wrongly classified records and using probabilistic optimization to select pertinent columns by increasing their weight and doing a reclassification which would result in further improved accuracy. The accuracy hence achieved by our proposed method is, by far, quite competitive.

Keywords: Kaggle dataset, machine learning, probabilistic optimization, decision tree, random forest, Naive Bayes, K means, ensemble method, confusion matrix, probability, Euclidean distance

Corresponding author: jaspreetseera@gmail.com

A. Suresh, S. Vimal, Y. Harold Robinson, Dhinesh Kumar Ramaswami and R. Udendhran (eds.)
Bioinformatics and Medical Applications: Big Data Using Deep Learning Algorithms, (1–28)
© 2022 Scrivener Publishing LLC

1.1   Introduction

Healthcare and biomedicine are increasingly using big data technologies for research and development. Mammoth amount of clinical data have been generated and collected at an unparalleled scale and speed. Electronic health records (EHR) store large amounts of patient data. The quality of healthcare can be greatly improved by employing big data applications to identify trends and discover knowledge. Details generated in the hospitals fall in the following categories.

- Clinical data: Doctor's notes, prescription data, medical imaging reports, laboratory, pharmacy, and insurance related data.
- Patient data: EHRs related to patient admission details, diagnosis, and treatment.
- Machine generated/sensor data: Data obtained from monitoring critical symptoms, emergency care data, web-based media posts, news feeds, and medical journal articles.

The pharmaceutical companies, for example, can effectively utilize this data to identify new potential drug candidates and predictive data modeling can substantially decrease the expenses on drug discovery and improve the decision-making process in healthcare. Predictive modeling helps in producing a faster and more targeted research with respect to drugs and medical devices.

AI depends on calculations that can gain from information without depending on rule-based programming while big data is the type of data that can be supplied to analytical systems so that a machine learning model could learn or, in other words, improve the accuracy of its predictions. Machine learning algorithms is classified in three sorts, particularly supervised, unsupervised, and reinforcement learning.

Perhaps, the most famous procedure in information mining is clustering which is the method of identifying similar groups of data. The groups are created in a manner wherein entities in one group are more similar to each other than to those belonging to the other groups. Although it is an unsupervised machine learning technique, such collections can be used as features in supervised AI model.

Coronary illness, the primary reason behind morbidness and fatality globally, was responsible for more deaths annually compared to any other cause [1]. Fortunately, cardiovascular failures are exceptionally preventable and straightforward way of life alterations alongside early treatment incredibly improves the prognosis. It is, nonetheless, hard to recognize high-risk patients because of the presence of different factors that add to the danger of coronary illness like diabetes, hypertension, and elevated cholesterol. This is where information mining and AI have acted the hero by creating screening devices. These devices are helpful on account of their predominance in pattern recognition and classification when contrasted with other conventional statistical methodologies.

For exploring this with the assistance of machine learning algorithms, we gathered a dataset of vascular heart disease from Kaggle [3]. It consists of three categories of input features, namely, objective consisting of real statistics, examination comprising of results of clinical assessment, and subjective handling patient related information.

Based on this information, we applied various machine learning algorithms and analyzed the accuracy achieved by each of the methods. For this report, we have used Naive Bayes, Decision Tree, Random Forest, and various combinations of using these algorithms in order to further improve the accuracy. Numerous scientists have just utilized this dataset for their examination and delivered their individual outcomes. The target of gathering and applying methods on this dataset is to improve the precision of our model. For this reason, we gave different algorithms a shot on this dataset and successfully improved the accuracy of our model.

We suggested using the ensemble method [2] which is the process of solving a particular computer intelligence problem by strategically combining multiple models, such as classifiers or experts. Additionally, we have take the wrongly classified records by all the methods and tried to understand the reason for wrong classification and modify it mathematically in order to give accurate results and improve model performance continuously.

1.1.1 Scope and Motivation

Exploring different classification and integration algorithms to perceive teams in an exceedingly real-world health record data stored electronically having high dimension capacity and find algorithms that detect clusters within reasonable computation time and ability to scale with increasing data size/features while giving the highest possible accuracy. Diagnosis is a challenging process that, as of today, involves many human-to-human interactions. A machine would increase the speed of giving a diagnosis and lead to a more rapid treatment decision and would be able to detect rare events easier than humans.

1.2   Literature Review

Over the years, many strategies have been used regarding data processing and model variability in the field of cardiovascular diagnostics. Authors in [4] show that splitting the data into 70:30 ratio using for tutoring and examination purpose and 10-fold cross proofing putting logistic regression into operation improved the accuracy of the UCI dataset to 87%.

Authors in [5] have used ensemble classification techniques using multiple classifiers followed by score level ensemble for improving the prediction accuracy. They pointed out that maximum voting produces the highest level of development. This functionality is enhanced by using feature selection.

Hybrid approach has been proposed in [6] by consolidating Random Forest along with Linear method leading to a precision of around 90%. In [7], Vertical Hoeffding Decision Tree (VHDT) was used accuracy of 85.43% using 10-fold cross-validation.

Authors in [8] outline a multi-faceted voting system that can anticipate the conceivable presence of coronary illness in humans. It employs four classifiers which are SGD, KNN, Random Forest, and Logistic Regression and joins them in a consolidated way where group formation is performed by a large vote of the species making 90% accuracy.

The strategy utilized in [9] finds these features by way of correlation which can help enhanced prediction results. UCI coronary illness dataset is used to evaluate the result with [6]. Their proposed model accomplished precision of 86.94% which outflanks Hoeffding tree technique which reported accuracy of 85.43%.

Different classifiers, mainly, Decision Tree, NB, MLP, KNN, SCRL, RBF, and SVM have been utilized in [10]. Moreover, integrated methods of bagging, boosting, and stacking have been applied to the database. The results of the examination demonstrate that the SVM strategy utilizing the boosting procedure outflanks the other previously mentioned techniques.

It was exhibited in [11] after various analyses that, if we increase the feature space of RF algorithm while using forecasts and probability of a tuple to belong to a particular class from Naive Bayes model, then we could increase the precision achieved in identifying the categories, by and large.

Studies in [12] suggested that Naive Bayes gives best result when combined with Random Forest. Also, when KNN is combined with RF or RF+NB, the errors remain same suggesting that it is the dominating method.

Authors in [13] compared the precision of various models in classification of coronary disease taking Kaggle dataset of 70,000 records as input. The algorithms used were Random Forest, Naive Bayes, Logistic Regression, and KNN among whom Random Forest was the winner with an accuracy of 73%.

Creators in [14] have fused the results of the AI examination applied on different informational collections focusing on the CAD illness. Common features are compared and extracted from different datasets, and advanced concepts such as fast decision trees and pruned C4.5 tree are administered on it resulting in higher classification accuracy.

Ensemble Optimization is applied in [15] wherein fuzzy logic is used for extraction of features, Genetic Algorithm for reducing them and Neural Network for classifying them. The results have been tested on a sample of size 30 and accuracy achieved is 99.97%

Based on the detailed research discussed above, we analyze by comparing different strategies suggested by different authors in their respective papers. This helps us to quickly understand where we stand presently with respect to these techniques and how they need to mature further.

1.2.1   Comparative Analysis

Please refer to Table 1.1 to get a comparative study of the methods and understand the strengths and weakness of each. This helped us immensely in designing our prototype.

1.2.2   Survey Analysis

Analyzing the literature, we came to know the scope and limitations of prediction techniques. In present days, heart disease rate has significantly increased and the reason behind deaths in the United States. National Heart, Lung, and Blood Institute states that cardiovascular breakdown is a problem in the typical electrical circuit of the heart and siphoning power.

The incorporation of methodologies with respect to information enhancement and model variability has been coordinating preparing and testing of AI model, Cleveland dataset from the UCI file utilized a ton of time since that is a checked dataset and is generally utilized in the preparation and testing of ML models. It has 303 tuples and 14 attributes that depend on the factors that are believed to be associated with an increased risk of cardiovascular illness. Additionally, the Kaggle dataset of coronary illness containing records of 70,000 and 12 patient attributes is also used for the purpose of training and assessment.

Table 1.1 Comparative analysis of prediction techniques.

Title	Problem	Solution	Result
"Machine Learning Algorithms with ROC Curve for Predicting and Diagnosing the Heart Disease" [4]	Inspect and look at the precision of four diverse AI calculations which take ROC curve for anticipating and diagnosing cardiovascular ailment analyzing the 14 indicators of the UCI Cardiac Dataset.	Logistic regression, support vector machine, stochastic gradient boosting, and random forest are applied on UCI dataset and accuracy was compared using ROC curve.	Ten-fold cross-validation applied to maximize ROC. Logistic regression performs the best with 87% accuracy.
"Improving the accuracy of prediction of heart disease risk based on ensemble classification techniques" [5]	1. Increase the efficiency of weak classification algorithms. 2. Usage on clinical dataset to show utility to foresee illness at beginning stage.	Research is done on ensemble techniques such as bagging, boosting, majority vote, and stacking, and results are assessed. They are further upgraded by using feature selection.	1. Majority voting produces highest improvement in accuracy. 2. Feature FS2 along with majority voting yields best results.
"Effective heart disease prediction using hybrid machine learning techniques" [6]	Improve precision in forecast of cardiovascular illness	Presented a method called the Hybrid Random forest with Linear Model (HRFLM). It utilizes ANN with back propagation taking as input 13 clinical features	HRFLM ended up being quite precise in the prediction of heart illness.

(Continued)

Table 1.1 Comparative analysis of prediction techniques. (*Continued*)

Title	Problem	Solution	Result
"A classification for patients with heart disease based on Hoeffding tree" [7]	Characterize information for patients with coronary sickness and assessment of models used to foresee coronary disease patients.	Hoeffding tree deals with increasing tree proofs and the capacity to gain from steam of huge information assuming that the distribution sample remains constant with time.	Results exhibit an accuracy of around 85% and the processing error value of 14%.
"Heart Disease Detection Using Machine Learning Majority Voting Ensemble Method" [8]	Give more certainty and precision to the Specialist's analysis considering the face that the model is prepared using real information of healthy and sick patients.	Data was divided in 80:20 ratio for training and testing and a combination of four algorithms (SGD, KNN, RF, and LR) was used by majority voting method.	A precision of 90% was achieved based on the hard voting ensemble model.
"Robust Heart Disease Prediction: A Novel Approach based on Significant Feature and Ensemble Learning Model" [9]	Coronary illness prediction with accessible clinical information is one of the huge difficulties for scientists.	Selected significant attributes by using correlation accompanied with RF and Stratified K-fold cross-validation.	Achieved accuracy of 86.94% which outperforms the 85% precision reported by Hoeffding tree method.

(*Continued*)

Table 1.1 Comparative analysis of prediction techniques. (*Continued*)

Title	Problem	Solution	Result
"A Comprehensive Investigation and Comparison of Machine Learning Techniques in the Domain of Heart Disease" [10]	Compare the accuracy of different data mining classification schemes, employing Ensemble Machine Learning Techniques, for forecasting heart ailments.	Various classifiers, namely, DT, NB, MLP, KNN, SCRL, RBF, and SVM, have been employed.	SVM method using the boosting technique outperforms the other aforementioned methods.
"Increasing Diversity in Random Forests Using Naive Bayes" [11]	Improve the classification accuracy.	Enhanced variety of Random Forests put forward that was constructed by pseudo randomly picking up certain attributes and incorporating Naive Bayes estimation into the training and segregation category.	Proposed method works more efficiently in comparison to other advanced ensemble methods.
"Improved Classification Techniques by Combining KNN and Random Forest with Naive Bayesian Classifier" [12]	Increase classification accuracy.	Utilized average class probabilities to concatenate Naive Bayes, KNN, and Random Forest.	Naive Bayes combined with Random Forest has ended up being the ideal blend.

(Continued)

Table 1.1 Comparative analysis of prediction techniques. (*Continued*)

Title	Problem	Solution	Result
"Comparison of Machine Learning Models in Prediction of Cardiovascular Disease Using Health Record Data" [13]	Examination of ML models on forecast of cardiovascular illness utilizing patients' cardiovascular hazard factors.	Used Cross Industry Standard Process for Data Mining and four algorithms, namely, RF, NB, LR, and KNN, were used.	Random Forest outperforms other models by achieving an accuracy of 73%, sensitivity of 65%, and specificity of 80%.
"Feature Analysis of Coronary Artery Heart Disease Data Sets" [14]	Combine results of the AI examination applied on various datasets centering on CAD.	Common features are compared and extracted from different datasets and fast decision trees and pruned C4.5 tree are administered on it.	Precision of the collected dataset is around 80%.
"Cardio Vascular Disease Classification Ensemble Optimization Using Genetic Algorithm and Neural Network"[15]	To construct the detection system based on fuzzy logic algorithm for extraction of features making use of neural network classifier of heart disease.	Dataset is categorized via the usage of fuzzy logic, genetic algorithm, and, moreover, training is performed by neural network by the extracting features.	The accuracy is elevated up to 99.97% and the error rate is decreased to 0.987%.

Experimental testing and the use of AI indicate that supervised learning is certain calculation exceeds an alternate calculation for a particular issue or for a specific section of the input dataset; however, it is not phenomenal to discover an independent classifier that accomplishes excellent performance the domain of common problems.

Ensembles of classifiers are therefore produced using many techniques such as the use of separate subset of coaching dataset in a sole coaching algorithm, utilizing distinctive coaching on a solitary coaching algorithm or utilizing multiple coaching strategies. We learnt about the various techniques employed in ensemble method like bagging, boosting, stacking, and majority voting and their affect on the performance improvement.

We also learned about Hoeffding Tree which is the first distributed algorithm for studying decision trees. It incorporates a novel way of dissecting decision trees with vertical parallelism. The development of effective integration methods is an effective research field in AI. Classifier ensembles are by and large more precise than the individual hidden classifiers. This is given the fact that several learning algorithms use local optimization methods that can be traced to local optima.

A few methodologies find those features by relationship which can help successful predictive results. This used in combination with ensemble techniques achieves best results. Various combinations have been tried and tested and none is the standardized/best approach. Each technique tries to achieve a better accuracy than the previous one and the race continues.

1.3   Tools and Techniques

Machine learning and information gathering utilizes ensembles on one or more learning algorithms to get different arrangement of classifiers with the ability to improve performance. Experimental studies have time and again proven that it is unusual to get one classifier which will perform the best on the general problem domain. Hence, ensemble of classifiers is often produced using any of the subsequent methods.

- Splitting the data and using various chunks of the training data for single machine learning algorithm.
- Training one learning algorithm using multiple training parameters.
- Using multiple learning algorithms.

Key ideas such as the data setup, data classification, data mining models, and techniques are described below.

1.3.1   Description of Dataset

The source of data is Kaggle dataset for cardiovascular diseases which contains 70,000 records with patient information. The attributes include objective information, subjective information, and results of medical examination. Table 1.2 enumerates the 12 attributes.

A heatmap is a clear representation of data where data values are represented as colors. It is used to get a clear view of the relationship between the features. The coefficient of relationship is a factual proportion of the strength of the association between the general developments of two factors with values going between −1.0 and 1.0. A determined number more prominent than 1.0 or less than −1.0 indicates a slip-up in the relationship estimation. Figure 1.1 represents the heat map for the input parameters of the defined dataset.

Table 1.2 Dataset attributes.

Feature name	Variable name	Value type
Age	Age	No. of days
Height	Height	Centimeters
Weight	Weight	Kilograms
Gender	Gender	Categories
Systolic blood pressure	Ap_hi	Integer
Diastolic blood pressure	Ap_lo	Integer
Cholesterol	Cholesterol	1: Standard; 2: Above standard; 3: Well above standard.
Glucose	Glu	1: Standard; 2: Above standard; 3: Well above standard.
Smoking	Smoke	Dual
Alcohol intake	Alco	Dual
Physical activity	Active	Dual
Presence or absence of CVDs	cardio	Dual

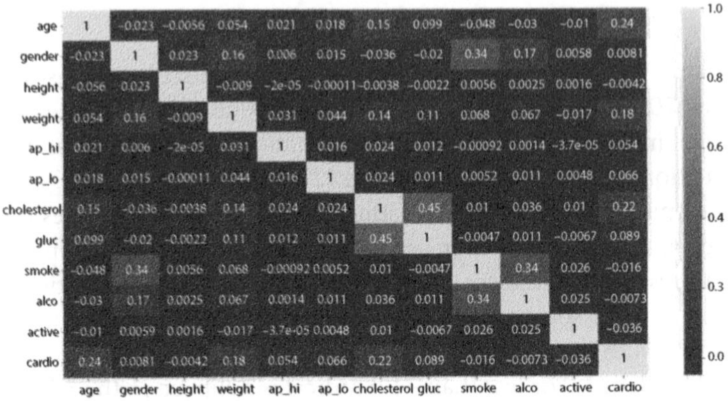

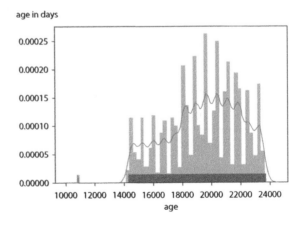

Figure 1.1 Heatmap of input attributes.

Figures 1.2, 1.3, 1.4, and 1.5 display the distribution of some of the input values such as age, gender, presence of cardiovascular disease, and cholesterol type.

1.3.2   Machine Learning Algorithm

Post analysis of the data, it was broken up into training (80%) and testing (20%) sets, respectively. This is necessary to accept the power of the model to summarize new details. A few classifier models have been tested which have been explained as follows.

Figure 1.2 Age distribution.

```
0.0      35014
1.0      34977
Name:  cardio, dtype:  int64
```

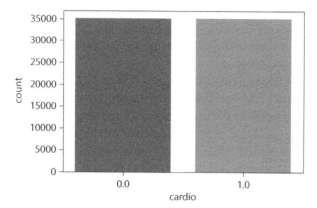

Figure 1.3 Presence of cardiovascular disease.

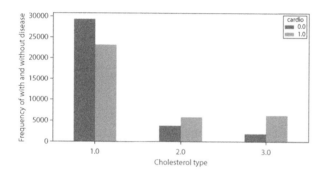

Figure 1.4 Cholesterol type distribution.

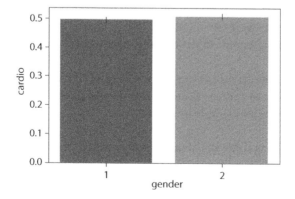

Figure 1.5 Gender distribution.

1.3.3   Decision Tree

Decision Trees are amazing and well-known devices which are used for classification and forecasting. It is a tree based classifier wherein nodes represent a test on one attribute, leaves indicate the worth of the target attribute, edge represents split of 1 attribute and path is a dis junction of test to form the ultimate decision.

The current implementation offers two stages of impurity (Gini impurity and entropy) and one impurity measure for regression (variability). Gini's impurity refers to the probability of a misdiagnosis of a replacement variate, if that condition is new organized randomly in accordance with the distribution of class labels from the information set. Bound by 0 occurs when data contains only one category. Gini Index is defined by the formula

$$I_G = 1 - \sum_{j=1}^{c} p_j^2$$

Entropy is defined as

$$I_H = -\sum_{j=1}^{c} P_j \log_2 p_j$$

where p_j is the proportion of samples that belong to class c for a specific node.

Gini impurity and entropy are used as selection criterion for decision trees. Basically, they assist us with figuring out what is a decent split point for root/decision nodes on classification/regression trees. Decision trees utilizes the split point to split on the feature resulting in the highest information gain (IG) for a given criteria which is referred to as Gini or entropy. It is based on the decrease in entropy after a dataset is split on an attribute. A number of the benefits of decision tree are as follows:

- It requires less effort to process data while it is done in advance.
- It does not require standardization and data scaling.
- Intuitive and simple to clarify.

However, it has some disadvantages too, as follows:

- Minor changes in the data can cause major structural changes leading to instability.

- Sometimes math can be very difficult in some algorithms.
- It usually involves more time for training.
- It is very expensive as the complexity and time taken is too much.
- Not adequate on regression and predicting continuous values.

1.3.4   Random Forest

The Random Forest, just as its name infers, increases the number of individual decision trees that work in conjunction. The main idea behind a random forest is the wisdom of the masses. An enormous number of moderately unrelated trees functioning as a council will surpass any existing models. Random Forest allows us to change the contributions by tuning the boundaries like basis, depth of tree, and maximum and minimum leaf. It is a supervised machine learning algorithm, used for both classification and regression. It makes use of bagging and feature randomness while assembling each singular tree to try to make an uncorrelated forest whose expectation is to be more precise than that of any individual tree. The numerical clarification of the model is as given:

1. Let D be a collection of dataset used for purpose of training $D = (x_1, y_1) \ldots (x_n, y_n)$.
2. Let $w = w_1(x); w_2(x) \ldots w_k(x)$ be an ensemble of weak classifiers.
3. If every w_k is a decision tree, then the parameters of the tree are described as

$$\theta = \theta_k^1, \theta_k^2, \cdots \theta_k^p$$

4. Output of each decision tree is a classifier $w_k(x) = w(x|\theta_k)$.
5. Hence, Final Classification $f(x) = $ Majority Voting of $w_k(X)$.

Figure 1.6 gives a pictorial representation of the working of random forest.

Some of the advantages of Random Forest algorithm are as follows:

- Reduces overfitting problem.
- Solves both clasification and regression problems.
- Handles missing values automatically.
- Stable and robust to outliers.

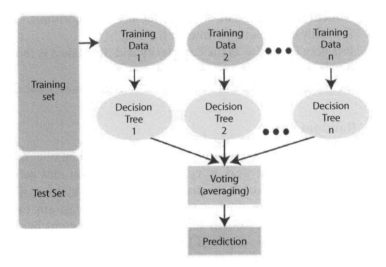

Figure 1.6 Random forest algorithm.

Some of the disadvantages are as follows:
- Complexity
- Longer training period.

1.3.5   Naive Bayes Algorithm

Naive Bayes is a fantastic AI calculation utilized for prediction which depends on Bayes Theorem. Bayes Theorem expresses that given a theory H and proof E, the relationship between possibility of pre-proof likelihood P(H) and the possibility of the following theoretical evidence P (H|E) is

$$P(H|E) = \frac{P(E|H) * P(H)}{P(E)}$$

Assumption behind Naive Bayes classifiers is that the estimation of a unique element is not dependent on the estimation of some different element taking the class variable into consideration. For instance, a product may be regarded as an apple if possibly it is red in color, round in shape, and around 10 cm wide.

A Naive Bayes classifier looks at all these highlights to offer independently to the chances that this product is an apple, although there is a potential relationship between shading, roundness, and dimension highlights. They are probabilistic classifiers and, subsequently, will compute the likelihood of every classification utilizing Bayes' hypothesis, and the classification with the most elevated likelihood will be the yield.

Let D be the training dataset, y be the variable for class and the attributes represented as X hence according to Bayes theorem

$$P(y|X) = \frac{P(X|y) * P(y)}{P(X)}$$

where

$$X = (x_1, x_2, \dots x_n)$$

So, replacing the X and applying the chain rule, we get

$$P(y|X) = \frac{P(x_1|y) * P(x_2|y) * \dots * P(x_n|y) * P(y)}{P(X)}$$

Since the denominator remains same, removing it from the dependency

$$P(y|x_1, x_2, \dots x_n) \alpha\ P(y) \prod_{i=1}^{n} P(x_i|y)$$

Therefore, to find the category y with high probability, we use the following function:

$$y = \arg\max P(y) \prod_{i=1}^{n} P(x_i|y)$$

Some of the advantages of Naive Bayes algorithm are as follows:

- Easy to execute.
- Requires a limited amount of training data to measure parameters.
- High computational efficiency.

However, there are some disadvantages too, as follows:

- It is thought that all aspects are independent and equally important which is virtually impossible in real applications.
- The tendency to bias when increasing the number of training sets.

1.3.6   K Means Algorithm

K means, an unsupervised algorithm, endeavors to iteratively segment the dataset into K pre-characterized and nonoverlapping data groups with the end goal that one data point can have a place with just one bunch. It attempts to make the intra-group data as similar as could reasonably be expected while keeping the bunches as various (far) as could be expected under the circumstances. It appoints data points to a cluster with the end goal that the entirety of the squared separation between the data points and the group's centroid is at the minimum. The less variety we have inside bunches, the more homogeneous the data points are inside a similar group.

1.3.7   Ensemble Method

Ensemble method is the process by which various models are created and consolidated in order to understand a specific computer intelligence problem. This prompts better prescient performance than could be acquired from any of the constituent learning models alone. Fundamentally, an ensemble is a supervised learning method for joining various weak learners/ models to deliver a strong learner. Ensemble model works better, when we group models with low correlation. Figure 1.7 gives the various ensemble methods which are in use. Following are some of the techniques used for ensemble.

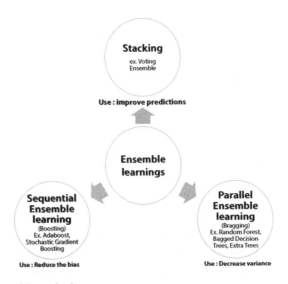

Figure 1.7 Ensemble methods.

1.3.7.1   Bagging

Bagging or bootstrap aggregation assigns equal weights to each model in the ensemble. It trains each model of the ensemble separately using random subset of training data in order to promote variance. Random Forest is a classical example of bagging technique where multiple random decision trees are combined to achieve high accuracy. Samples are generated in such a manner that the samples are different from each other and replacement is permitted.

1.3.7.2   Boosting

The term "Boosting" implies a gathering of calculations which changes a weak learner to strong learner. It is an ensemble technique for improving the model predictions of some random learning algorithm. It trains weak learners consecutively, each attempting to address its predecessor. There are three kinds of boosting in particular, namely, AdaBoost that assigns more weight to the incorrectly classified data that would be passed on to the next model, Gradient Boosting which uses the residual errors made by previous predictor to fit the new predictor, and Extreme Gradient Boosting which overcomes drawbacks of Gradient Boosting by using parallelization, distributed computing, out-of-core computing, and cache optimization.

1.3.7.3   Stacking

It utilizes meta-learning calculations to discover how to join the forecasts more readily from at least two basic algorithms. A meta model is a two-level engineering with Level 0 models which are alluded to as base models and Level 1 model which are alluded to as Meta model. Meta-model depends on forecasts made by basic models on out of sample data. The yields from the base models utilized as contribution to the meta-model might be in the form of real values in the case of regression and probability values in the case of classification. A standard method for setting up a meta-model training database is with k-fold cross-validation of basic models.

1.3.7.4   Majority Vote

Each model makes a forecast (votes) in favor of each test occurrence and the final output prediction is the one that gets the greater part of the votes. Suppose for a specific order issue we are given three diverse classification rules, $c_1(X)$; $c_2(X)$; $c_3(X)$, we join these rules by majority voting as

$$C(X) = \text{mode}(c_1(X); c_2(X); c_3(X))$$

1.4   Proposed Method

1.4.1   Experiment and Analysis

Naive Bayes multi-model decision-making system, which is our proposed method uses ensemble method of type majority voting using a combination of Naive Bayes, Decision Tree, and Random Forest for analytics in the database of heart disease patients and attains an accuracy that outperforms any of the individual methods. Additionally, it uses K means along with the combination of the above methods for further increase the accuracy.

The data pertains to Kaggle dataset for cardiovascular disease which contains 12 attributes. Whether or not cardiovascular disease is present is contained in column carrying target value which is a binary type having values 0 and 1 indicating absence or presence respectively. There are a total of 70,000 records having attributes for age, tallness, weight, gender, systolic and diastolic blood pressure, cholesterol, glucose, smoking, alcohol intake, and physical activity.

Training and testing data is divided in the ratio 70:30. During training and testing, we tried various combinations to see their effect of accuracy of predictions. Also, we took data in chunks of 1000, 5000, 10,000, 50,000 and 70,000, respectively, and observed the change in patterns. We tried various combinations to check on the accuracy.

- NB: Only Naive Bayes algorithm is applied.
- DT: Only Decision Tree algorithm is applied.
- RF: Only Random Forest algorithm is applied.
- Serial: Naive Bayes followed by Random Forest followed by Decision tree (in increasing order of individual accuracy).
- Parallel: All three algorithms are applied in parallel and maximum voting is used.
- Prob 60 SP: If probability calculated by Naive Bayes is greater than 60% apply serial method else apply parallel.
- PLS: First parallel then serial is applied for wrong classified records.
- SKmeans: Combination of Serial along with K means.
- PKmeans: Combination of Parallel along with K means.

From this analysis, we found the PKmeans method to be the most efficient. Though serial along with K means achieves the best accuracy for training data, it is not feasible for real data where target column is not present. The reliability on any single algorithm is not possible for correctly classifying all the records; hence, we use more suitable ensemble method which utilizes the wisdom of the crowd. It uses the ensemble method of the type majority voting which includes adding the decisions in favor of crisp class labels from different models and foreseeing the class with the most votes.

Our goal is to achieve the best possible accuracy which surpasses the accuracy achieved by the individual methods. Figures 1.8 to 1.11 show the confusion matrix plotted by Naive Bayes, Random Forest, and Decision Tree individually as well as their ROC curve.

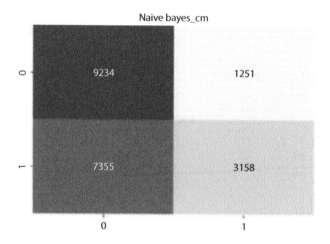

Figure 1.8 NB confusion matrix.

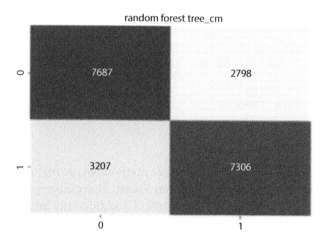

Figure 1.9 RF confusion matrix.

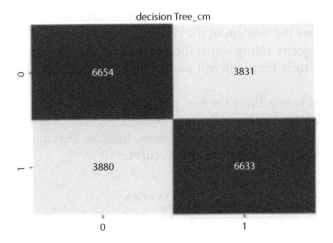

Figure 1.10 DT confusion matrix.

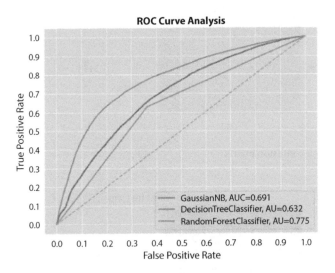

Figure 1.11 ROC curve analysis.

1.4.2   Method

We observed that by applying ensemble method of type majority voting on the algorithms Decision tree, Random Forest, Naive Bayes, and K means, we could achieve an accuracy of 91.56%. To additionally improve the precision, we proposed the following algorithm. The design of the proposed method is as given in Figure 1.12.

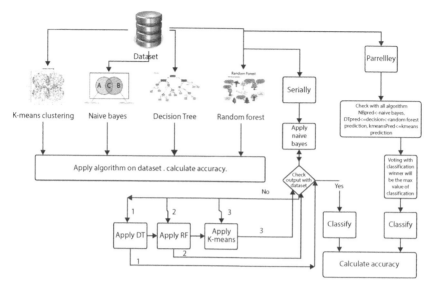

Figure 1.12 Proposed architecture.

Algorithm 1.1 Probabilistic optimization.

---

initialization
$d \leftarrow dataset$
$a1 \leftarrow Naive\_Bayes\_output \leftarrow ApplyNaiveBayes(d)$
$a2 \leftarrow Decision\_tree\_output \leftarrow ApplyDesisionTree(d)$
$a3 \leftarrow Random\_tree\_output \leftarrow ApplyRandomForest(d)$
$a4 \leftarrow K\_Means\_output \leftarrow ApplyKmeans(d)$
$winner(0,1) \leftarrow Voting(a1, a2, a3, a4)$
$op \leftarrow winner\_of\_max\_count(0,1)$
if op ≠ desired_output then
    Probability_calculation of each column with output 0 or 1

$$c_i \leftarrow probability(0,1)$$
end

For each value in c_i
$count \leftarrow c_i/2$
For k to count
    Add the probability (Find the max column with which proba-
    bility matches)
    Number of columns selected as t_i

w_i ← *Weightage of selected columns*
a_i ← *Append the weightage with the input of data*

Find mean square error with the training and find lowest (MSE) parameter. Calculate the Euclidean distance

$$\sqrt{(x_i - x_j)^2 + (z_i - z_j)^2}$$

Find the minimum distance using this formula.
If probability of data > 0.5 and MSE < 0.5 and ED < 0.2
    Classify as 1
else
    Classify as 0

The following block diagram explains the flow of Algorithm 1.1.

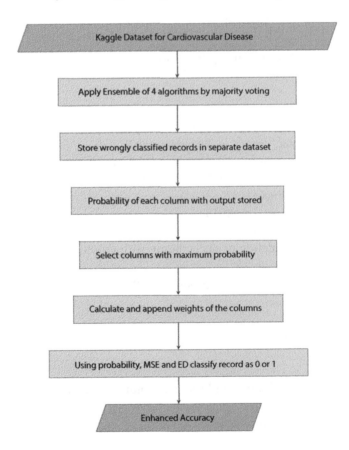

The working of the algorithm is explained briefly as follows.

1. The ensemble method of the four algorithms (Decision Tree, Random Forest, Naive Bayes, and K Means) is applied by majority voting and classification is obtained on presence or absence of cardiopathy.
2. The wrongly classified records are stored in a separate dataset.
3. The probability of each column with output is calculated and stored. For example, considering age, the probability of heart disease for age greater than 45 is more than otherwise.
4. We calculate those columns for which probability is maximum.
5. Only select these columns for further analysis.
6. Calculate the weights of these columns using formula $y = mx + c$ for linear data using Multiple linear regression.
7. For non-linear data wherein the chances of misclassification are more, more complex functions such as tanh, sigmoid, and relu are used for calculating the weights.
8. Append the weights to the column at the time of classification.
9. Calculate the mean square error and Euclidean distance.
10. Finally, based on probability, mean square error and Euclidean distance, we classify the records as 1 or 0 which indicates presence/absence of heart disease.
11. Hence, accuracy achieved is higher than using the classical ensemble method.

Hence, our proposed methodology achieves a precision that not only surpasses the individual methods but also overshoots the combination method and the precision achieved thus is quite competitive.

1.5   Conclusion

An ensemble of classifiers is a collection of classification models whose singular forecasts are joined, by means of weighted or unweighted casting a ballot to dole out a classification mark to each new pattern. There is no single best method of creating successful ensemble methods and is being actively researched. Predicting heart disease has been a topic of interest for researchers for a long time. We therefore check the accuracy of the heart disease prediction using an ensemble of classifiers. For our study, we chose the best performing algorithms whose individual predictions made them classify as strong classifiers. We used a combination of Decision Tree, Naive Bayes, Random Forest, and K means algorithm. Since no single algorithm can guarantee maximum performance under all circumstances, we use the majority voting method to best classify the records. The dataset used for this purpose was Kaggle dataset for cardiovascular disease which has 70,000 records on which we achieved an accuracy of 91.56%.

However, we realized the potential of further increasing the accuracy by analyzing those records which were wrongly classified by all/most of the algorithms. The reason for it could be high bias, high variance, low precision, or low recall. So, we identified those columns/attributes which were causing the data to be misclassified by assigning probabilities to each tuple in the column and combining those probabilities by using conditional probability. Hence, we focused only on those columns which would result in accurate prediction by increasing the weight of those columns and feature reduction. Hence, by using the probabilistic approach, we could effectively remove the anomalies and increase the prediction accuracy.

References

1. Heart Disease Facts Statistics, Centers for Disease Control and Prevention, [Online], Available: https://www.cdc.gov/heartdisease/facts.htm. [Accessed: 27-Apr-2019].
2. Thenmozhi, K. and Deepika, P., Heart disease prediction using classification with different decision tree techniques. *Int. J. Eng. Res. Gen. Sci.*, 2, 6, 6–11, 2014.
3. Kaggle Dataset, Cardiovascular Disease dataset, Available: https://www.kaggle.com/sulianova/cardiovascular-disease-dataset.
4. Kannan, R. and Vasanthi, V., Machine learning algorithms with ROC curve for predicting and diagnosing the heart disease, in: *Soft Computing and Medical Bioinformatics*, pp. 63–72, Springer Singapore, Jun 2018.
5. Latha, C.B.C. and Jeeva, S.C., Improving the accuracy of prediction of heart disease risk based on ensemble classification techniques. *Inform. Med. Unlocked*, 16, 100203, 2019.
6. Mohan, S., Thirumalai, C., Srivastava, G., Effective heart disease prediction using hybrid machine learning techniques. *IEEE Access*, 7, 81542–81554, 2019.
7. Thaiparnit, S., Kritsanasung, S., Chumuang, N., A classification for patients with heart disease based on hoeffding tree, in: *2019 16th International Joint Conference on Computer Science and Software Engineering (JCSSE)*, Jul 2019, IEEE.

8. Atallah, R. and Al-Mousa, A., Heart Disease Detection Using Machine Learning Majority Voting Ensemble Method. *2019 2nd International Conference on new Trends in Computing Sciences (ICTCS)*, 9-11 Oct. 2019.

9. Alim, M.A. and Habib, S., Robust Heart Disease Prediction: A Novel Approach based on Significant Feature and Ensemble learning Model. *2020 3rd International Conference on Computing, Mathematics and Engineering Technologies (iCoMET)*.

10. Pouriyeh, S., A Comprehensive Investigation and Comparison of Machine Learning Techniques in the Domain of Heart Disease. *22nd IEEE Symposium on Computers and Communication (ISCC 2017): Workshops - ICTS4eHealth*, 2017.

11. Aridas, C., Kotsiantis, S., Vrahatis, M., Increasing Diversity in Random Forests Using Naive Bayes. *IFIP International Conference on Artificial Intelligence Applications and Innovations*, September 2016.

12. Gayathri Devi, R. and Sumanjani, P., Improved classification techniques by combining KNN and Random Forest with Naive Bayesian Classifier. *IEEE International Conference on Engineering and Technology (ICETECH)*, 20th March 2015.

13. Maiga, J., Hungilo, G.G., Pranowo, Comparison of Machine Learning Models in Prediction of Cardiovascular Disease Using Health Record Data. *2019 International Conference on Informatics, Multimedia, Cyber and Information System (ICIM-CIS)*.

14. El-Bialy, R., Salamay, M.A., Karam, O.H., Khalifa, M.E., Feature analysis of coronary artery heart disease data sets. *Proc. Comput. Sci.*, 65, 459–68, 2015.

15. Jagwant, S. and Rajinder, K., Cardiovascular disease classification ensemble optimization using genetic algorithm and neural network. *Indian J. Sci. Technol.*, 9, S1, 2016.

Cancerous Cells Detection in Lung Organs of Human Body: IoT-Based Healthcare 4.0 Approach

Rohit Rastogi[1]*, D.K. Chaturvedi[2], Sheelu Sagar[3], Neeti Tandon[4] and Mukund Rastogi[5]

[1]*Department of CSE, ABES Engineering College Ghaziabad, U.P., India*
[2]*Dept. of Electrical Engineering, Dayalbagh Educational Institute, Agra, India*
[3]*Amity International Business School, Amity Univ., Noida, U.P., India*
[4]*Vikram University, Ujjain, M.P., India*
[5]*BTech CSE Third Year, Department of CSE, ABES Engineering College Ghaziabad, U.P., India*

Abstract

Old age cancer was the cause of death. Forty percent of cancers are found in people over the age of 65. Lung cancer is one of these potentially deadly cancers. Young-, middle-, and old-aged patients, men who are chronic smokers or women who have never smoked are all victims of the disease. Therefore, a classification of lung cancer based on the associated risks (high risk, low risk, high risk) is required.

The study was conducted using a lung cancer classification scheme by studying micrographs and classifying them into a deep neural network using machine learning (ML) framework. Tissue microscopy images are based on the risk of using deep concealed neural networks. Neural Networks–Deep Conversion Deep Neural Networks are only used for classification (photo search) based on primary image (for example, displayed name) and similarity.

After that, scene recognition is performed on the stage. These algorithms help to recognize faces, tumors, people, road signs, plastics, and different perspective of visual information. The productivity of circular networks in image detection is one of the primary causes why the world has stirred to proficiency. Their in-depth learning is a major advance in computer vision (CV) that has important

Corresponding author: rohit.rastogi@abes.ac.in

A. Suresh, S. Vimal, Y. Harold Robinson, Dhinesh Kumar Ramaswami and R. Udendhran (eds.)
Bioinformatics and Medical Applications: Big Data Using Deep Learning Algorithms, (29–46)
© 2022 Scrivener Publishing LLC

applications in car driving, robotics, drones, security, medical diagnostics, and treatment of blindness.

Keywords: Deep neural network, lung cancer, CellProfiler, CADe Server, big data analytics in healthcare

2.1   Introduction

NSCLC includes three types of cancer: squamous cell carcinoma, adenocarcinoma, and large cell carcinoma derived from lung tissue. Adenocarcinoma is a slow-growing cancer that first appears in the outer region of the lung. Lung cancer is more common in smokers, but the most well-known sort of lung cancer in nonsmokers. Squamous cell carcinoma is more normal in the focal point of the lung and all the more generally in smokers, but large cell carcinoma can be found anywhere in the lung tissue and grows faster than adenomas and lung cancer [9, 20].

According to Choi, H. and his team members, lung cancer risk classification models with gene expression function are very interesting. Change previous models based on individual symptomatic genes.

They have revealed that the aim to develop a risk classification model was developed based on a novel level of gene expression network that was performed using multiple microarrays of lung adenocarcinoma, and gene convergence network investigation was carried out to recognize endurance networks. Genes representing these networks have been used to develop depth-based risk classification models. This model has been approved in two test sets. The efficiency of the model was strongly related to patient survival in the two sets of experiments and training. In multivariate analysis, this model was related with persistent anticipation and autonomous of other clinical and neurotic highlights.

The researchers have shown that how the gene structures and expressions can be useful in early detection of the cancer and suitable steps can be taken to cure the patients with higher probability of saving the lives [4].

2.1.1   Motivation of the Study

The medical service industry is confronted with the test of the quick improvement of a lot of medical services data. The field of big data investigation is extending—you can leverage your healthcare system to provide valuable insights. As mentioned above, most of the data produced by this system is digitally printed and stored.

The principle distinction between customary well-being analysis and big data well-being is the live programming component. In customary frameworks, the medical service industry depends on different ventures to examine big data. Many healthcare professionals rely on IT industry due to its huge impact. Their operating system is functional and capable of processing data in standard formats.

2.1.1.1 Problem Statements

Malignant lung tumor portrayed by sporadic development of lung tissue is known as lung cancer. Metastases can spread past the lungs to encompassing tissues and different pieces of the human body. Most cancers of the lung are called primary lung cancer, carcinoma. Small-cell lung cancer (SCLC) and non–small cell lung cancer (NSCLC) are the important types of lung cancer. The most common symptoms of pesticides (including coughing blood) are fatigue, emphysema, and angina (coronary thrombosis). NSCLC accounts for approximately 81% to 86% of lung cancers. By this study, we are classifying the lung cancer cases as per their medical parameters.

2.1.1.2 Authors' Contributions

Mr. Rohit Rastogi was team lead and executed experiment. Dr. DK Chaturvedi created the design of the experiment, Ms. Sheelu and Ms. Neeti did experiments and Mr. Mukund did analysis and all contributed in manuscript formation.

2.1.1.3 Research Manuscript Organization

Chapter has been started with abstract and followed by Introduction which contains short literature review then motivation of study. After the problem statement and definition have been introduced, authors' contribution and chapter organization are followed.

After this, literature survey contains latest relevant papers and followed by proposed systems and experimental setup and analysis. After this, results and discussions have been presented which is succeeded by recommendations and considerations, then future research directions, limitations of our study, and conclusions have been established.

It is followed by acknowledgements and refe rences. At last in annex, experimental dataset images and experimental snapshots have been given for readers.

2.1.1.4 Definitions

Some important terminologies and key components are being explained here in the light of our experimental work.

2.1.2 Computer-Aided Diagnosis System (CADe or CADx)

CADe or Computer-Aided Diagnosis (CADx) is a type of system software that has been shown to be very helpful to physicians in the recent microscopic interpretation of medical images. X-ray diagnostics, MRI, and ultrasound imaging technologies provide a wealth of information to help medical professionals to make comprehensive analyzes and assessments in the short term. The CAD system processes the digital image to highlight the normal display or obvious areas such as possible illnesses and provide input to support a particular expert decision [14].

With the help of computers, all-slide imaging algorithms and ML have potential future plans for digital pathology. So far, the program has been limited to physical safety but is now being studied for standard spots. CAD is an interdisciplinary technology with artificial intelligence (AI) computer elements with radiation and pathological imaging. A common program is tumor diagnosis.

2.1.3 Sensors for the Internet of Things

The Internet of Things (IoT) encourages our lives by associating electronic gadgets and sensors through interior networks. IoT utilizes smart gadgets and the Internet to give inventive answers for different difficulties and issues identified with different business, public, and private enterprises around the world. IoT has become a significant part of our daily life that we can look about us. When all is said in done, IoT is an advancement that coordinates different savvy frameworks, systems, shrewd gadgets, and sensors. We also use quantum and nanotechnology in terms of memory, measurement, and unimaginable speeds. This can be seen as a prerequisite for creating an innovative business plan with security, reliability, and collaboration [2, 21].

Here are 9 of the most popular IoT sensors:

1. Temperature
2. Moisture
3. Pressure
4. Adjacent

5. Surface
6. Accelerometer
7. Gyroscope
8. Gas
9. Infrared [2].

2.1.4   Wireless and Wearable Sensors for Health Informatics

IoT is a new concept that enables wearable devices to control healthcare. The IoT supports embedded technologies and is supported as a network of physical objects that connect data and sensors to communicate with the internal and external states of the object and its environment. Over the last decade, wearable have attracted the attention of many researchers and industries and have become very popular recently [7, 19].

2.1.5   Remote Human's Health and Activity Monitoring

Remote monitoring of healthcare allows you to stay at home instead of expensive medical centers like hospitals and nursing homes. Accordingly, it gives a proficient and practical option in contrast to clinical checking here. With a non-invasive, invisible, and visible wearable sensor, such a system is an excellent diagnostic tool for healthcare professionals to diagnose physiologic critical conditions and real-time patient activity from remote centers. In this way, it is intelligible that handheld sensors assume a significant part in such observation frameworks. These reconnaissance frameworks have pulled in the consideration of numerous specialists, business visionaries, and goliath engineers [11].

Handheld sensor-based health monitoring systems include textile fibers, fabrics, elastic bands, or several kinds of adaptable sensors that can be straightforwardly associated to the human body. These sensors measure physiology such as electromyography, body temperature, electromy activity, arterial oxygen saturation, heart rate, blood pressure, electrocardiogram, and respiratory rate and can measure physical symptoms [5].

2.1.6   Decision-Making Systems for Sensor Data

Management decisions are very basic and are widely used in economics. It relies upon the information and experience of the administrator, however increasingly more on target data. There are advance tools available for demographical data measurement like wet land detection and real time monitoring of mountains, rivers and forests [15, 18].

Until now, management has focused only on intuitive facts from checking data, for example, the overall status of water quality pointers, cases without accurate secondary analysis, and for effective management and decision-making [10, 22].

2.1.7   Artificial Intelligence and Machine Learning for Health Informatics

AI showed up in medical services during the 1970s. The main AI frameworks are basically information-based decision support systems, and the principal AI methods are utilized to foresee the classification standards of label sets. These first frameworks function admirably. Nevertheless, it is not commonly used in real patients. One of the reasons is that these systems are independent and have nothing to do with the patient's electronic medical records. Another reason is that the skill communicated in the information on these master frameworks shows that the created framework is not worthy here [13].

After winning several championships in focusing on artificial neural networks and improving complex learning, substance abuse became a new learning method. In May 2019, a team from Google and New York University announced that deep learning models used to analyze lung cancer could improve precision, and the investigation immediately covered numerous newspaper and magazine title texts.

2.1.8   Health Sensor Data Management

Trendsetting innovations, for example, cloud computing, wearable sensor gadgets, and big data will affect individuals' day-to-day life and have extraordinary potential in Internet-based biological systems. It provides personal and shared consumption and information on the development of the health and welfare sector. These apparatuses give numerous better approaches to gather data physically and consequently. Many modern smart phones have some internal sensors such as a microphone, camera, gyroscope, accelerometer, compass, proximity sensor, GPS, and ambient light [12].

You can easily connect the new generation of wearable medical sensors to your smart phone and send the measurement results directly. This set is more effective and convenient than individual health measurement like BP, oxygen content in blood, and heart rate variability. Different sensors can be used for analysis and visualizations of the patient details with accurate and fast speed. This dramatic development enables both data management and collaboration [12].

2.1.9   Multimodal Data Fusion for Healthcare

Given the proliferation of IoT techniques can be used to help the critical functions of healthcare management. In this way, traditional hospitals with large-scale interconnected sensor systems and extensive data collection and collection technology have become the next generation of smart digital environments. From this point of view, intelligent health supports a complex ecosystem of intelligent spaces such as hospitals, ambulances, and pharmacies supported by powerful infrastructure stacks such as edge devices and sensor networks and use new business models and rules [3].

2.1.10   Heterogeneous Data Fusion and Context-Aware Systems: A Context-Aware Data Fusion Approach for Health-IoT

The improvement of inexpensive sensor gadgets and correspondence advancements is quickening the improvement of elegant homes and conditions. With the development of human body networks, wireless sensor networks, big data technologies, and cloud computing, the healthcare industry is growing rapidly and uses IoT, There are numerous difficulties, for example, heterogeneous data blending, text recognition, complex question preparing, unwavering quality, and exactness.

From this point of view, intelligent health supports a complex ecosystem of intelligent spaces such as hospitals, ambulances, and pharmacies supported by powerful infrastructure stacks such as edge devices and sensor networks and use new business models and rules [8].

2.2   Literature Review

According to Timor Kadir and his team members, that machine-based lung cancer prediction model was developed to help undiagnosed lung nodules and assist physicians on-screen. Such systems can reduce the number of node classifications, improve decision-making, and ultimately reduce the number of benign nodules that are tracked or manipulated unnecessarily [9].

This article outlines the main approaches to lung cancer prediction to date and highlights some of the relative strengths and weaknesses. They discuss some of the challenges of developing and validating such technologies, as well as clinical acceptance strategies. They review the main approaches used to classify lymph nodes and predict lung cancer from CT imaging data. In our experience, using the right training data and using a comprehensive CNN, achieving classification performance in regions with low 90s AUC points and sufficient training data [9].

According to Choi H. and Na KJ in this study, a gene correlation network, we created a risk classification model for lung adenocarcinoma. An extension of future research is the use of this method in concurrent networks of cancer progression. Advances in technology change the DL design and the way toward choosing delegate qualities to improve expectation exactness. They found that NetScore was related with sex, status of smoking, phase, and sub-atomic subtype. In summary, a high NetScore trend in men, smokers, and KRAS mutants was delayed and observed to be positive [6].

Finally, they expected future clinical trials designed with all around controlled clinical and obsessive factors to help find clinical applications for their new danger grouping models.

Yin Li and his team members have predicted the risk of lung adenocarcinoma (LUAD) is important in determining subsequent treatment strategies. Molecular biomarkers may improve risk classification for LUAD [11].

Yin Li *et al.* analyzed the gene expression profile of LUAD patients by atlas cancer genome (TCGA) and omnibus gene expression (GEO) analysis. They first evaluated the prognostic relationship for each gene using three separate algorithms: Notable Function, Random Forest, and Variable Coke Regression. Next, survival-related genes were included in the LASSO minimum and selection function models to create a LUAD risk prediction model [17].

They initially identified large dataset significant survival-related genes. A hybrid strategy was used to identify key genes associated with survival in large datasets. Enhancement analysis showed an association of these genes with tumor development and progression. A risk prediction model was created using the LASSO method. The risk model was approved with two outside sets and one free set. Patients in the high-hazard bunch had a lower danger of repeat (RFS) and in general endurance (OS) than patients at low risk. We also created a registry that predicts LUAD patient operating systems, including models and risk stages.

Hence, they conclude risk models may serve as a pragmatic and reliable predictor of LUAD and may provide new experiences into the atomic instruments of infection [11, 16].

The paper was written by Francisco Azuaje titled as "Artificial intelligence for precision oncology: beyond patient stratification" [1].

Francisco Azuaje described axial data from medical conditions and treatment options as a key challenge for accurate oncology. AI offers an unparalleled opportunity to enhance such predictive capabilities in laboratories and clinics. AI, including ML, which is the most well-known area of research, has been able to accurately identify tumors beyond relatively well-known detection patterns such as single-source omics and supervised classification of imaging datasets.

According to him, this perspective, major developments, and challenges in this regard argue that the scope and depth of AI research should be expanded in order to achieve geological advances in accurate oncology [1].

According to Xu J [20] in a large era of data on cancer genetics, wide availability of genetic information provided by next-generation sequencing techniques and rapid development of medical journals integrates AI approaches such as ML, detailed learning, and natural language processing to challenge big data and high-dimensional scalability and uses this method to process clinical data to handle big data. It brings the knowledge that you have. It is bent, using the base. Open and lie down, it is really medicine.

In this paper, they reviewed the current status and future guideline for using AI in cancer genomics in the field of workflow is genomic analysis for accurate cancer treatment. Existing AI solutions and their limitations in genetic testing for cancer and its diagnosis, including various contacts and interpretations, are being considered.

The tools or common algorithms available for the leading NLP technologies in literature extraction are reviewed and compared to evidence-based clinical recommendations.

According to him, this paper deals with data needs and algorithm transparency, the importance of preparing patients and physicians for real-time reproduction and assessment, and modern digital healthcare. They believe that AI is the main factor in the evolution of healthcare into a precise drug but of the precedent that needs to be created to ensure safety and beneficial effects on healthcare [20].

2.3 Proposed Systems

Based on histo-pathological image input, there are two steps:

- Model building: The shape of this model is based on the extraction function.
- Model Evaluation: Form biological communication.

Modeling attempts to preserve the extracted shape by extracting shape-based features with full focus on the shape of the model. The fixed size is considered a constraint, and it focuses on all other faces found to achieve that form of the constraint, making it easy to extract the entire model.

2.3.1 Framework or Architecture of the Work

However, model evaluation includes some of the biological significance of the form, which requires the physician to have the precise and accurate information needed to evaluate the form.

2.3.2 Model Steps and Parameters

Here, we will focus more on size-based clinical models. There are several steps like segmentation, dimension reduction, sampling, enhancement, and active contour mapping and classification of the objects which are involved that help you to design your model in a very efficient way (as per Figure 2.1).

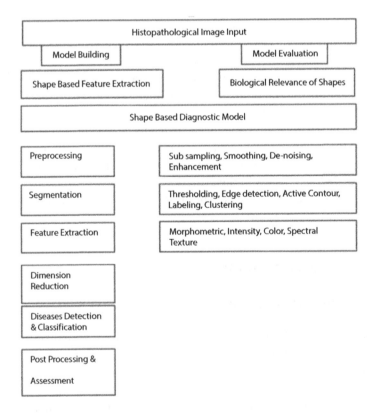

Figure 2.1 Framework of the experimental study of lung cancer stratification.

2.3.3 Discussions

Cancer has been the reason for death for a very long time. A little less than half of the cancer happens in individuals matured ≤70 to 85 years. The maximum death prone cancer is lung cancer where it threatens the all type of aged persons from adolescents to middle age to adults. Those who are addicted with drinking alcohol or smoking or females who were nonsmoking, all type of subjects were included in the list of casualties unfortunately from this illness.

Thus, it is needed to separate lung cancer based on risk included (high-risk, okay, and rising-risk). This investigation depends on building up an arrangement conspire for lung cancers through examining minuscule images and ordering them utilizing Deep Convolution Neural Network (DCNN), which is an AI (ML) structure.

Microscopic images of tissues will be characterized on the basis of risk involved using DCNN. Convolution neural networks are deep artificial neural networks that are utilized fundamentally for ordering images, group them by likenesses (photograph search), and perform object recognition inside the scenes. They are the calculations that can recognize faces, tumors, people, road signs, and numerous different parts of the graphic information.

The effectiveness of convolution networks in image recognition is one of the main reasons why the world has woken up for the productivity of deep learning. They are fueling significant progress in computer vision (CV), which has clear applications for self-driving vehicles, mechanical technology, security, clinical judgments, and medicines for the outwardly impaired.

2.4 Experimental Results and Analysis

The term "tissue characteristics" covers a wide range of meanings, from qualitative assessment to various scientific measurements. In the extensive literature available, we expand the definition of terms, show the relationship between tissue features and images, identify some relevant physical parameters, and briefly describe the subject's medical history. Excerpts are provided to explain how.

2.4.1 Tissue Characterization and Risk Stratification

According to an article titled "Automatic classification of lung cancer from cellular images using deep symmetric neural networks", we evaluated three types of cancer and trained for classification. However, pictures from the same sample belonged to the same group.

While executing cross-validation algorithm in different sets of images, we found that, in Set 1, there are 28 items and respective cross-validation score is 5,280 for adenocarcinoma. There are 42 items and cross-validation score is 5478 for squamous cell carcinoma. For small cell carcinoma, there are 26 images and cross-validation score is 5,070.

In Set 2, there are 28 items and respective cross-validation score is 5,184 for adenocarcinoma. There are 37 items and cross-validation score is 5,220 for squamous cell carcinoma. For small cell carcinoma, there are 33 images and cross-validation score is 5,280.

In Set 2, there are 26 items and respective cross-validation score is 5,040 for adenocarcinoma. There are 46 items and cross-validation score is 5,310 for squamous cell carcinoma. For small cell carcinoma, there are 32 images and cross-validation score is 5,214.

2.4.2   Samples of Cancer Data and Analysis

Figures 2.2 and 2.3 show a sample of cancer types correctly classified and classified using the data amplification method. The classification confusion matrix. Squamous cell carcinoma is often mistaken for adenocarcinoma.

After successfully applying classification model in this dataset, we have to test the accuracy, precision, and recall of the model. So, we observed the confusion matrix whose results are as follows: actual and predicted value of adenocarcinoma is 89% matched and only 11% items are not predicted correctly. Squamous cell carcinoma is predicted correctly 60% which is less as compared to adenocarcinoma. Actual and predicted value of small cell carcinoma is 70% matched and only 30% items are not predicted correctly.

It shows the original image classification and the wide range of image accuracy, respectively. Results obtained using magnification images show that the classification accuracy for adenocarcinoma, squamous cell carcinoma, and small cell cancer is 89.0%, 60.0% and 70.3%, respectively, and the overall corrected rate is 71.1%. In addition, apply plug-in to improve the classification.

Finally, we improved our classification model and accuracy score of trained set and augmented sets are given below:

Adenocarcinoma predicted 73% original images of lung cancer, whereas 89% for augmented images. We found that 45% original images are correctly classified and 60% augmented images are classified for squamous cell carcinoma. Small cell carcinoma is classified correctly 75% for original images and 70% for augmented images.

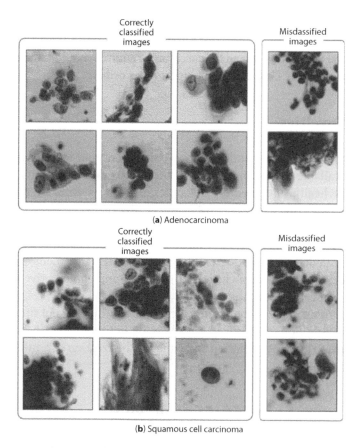

Figure 2.2 Sample images of correctly classified and misclassified carcinoma.

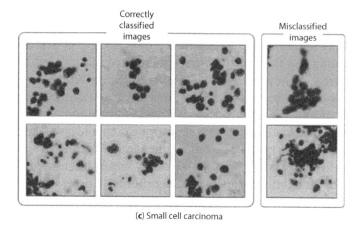

Figure 2.3 More sample images of correctly classified and misclassified carcinoma.

In the three types of lung cancer, the efficiency of the unsupervised clustering was maximum in adenocarcinoma and minimum in squamous cell carcinoma. Squamous cell adenocarcinoma requires more images. DCNN helped to correctly classify 70% of lung cancer cells.

2.5 Novelties

AI will not only identify and predict at-risk patients but will also be a large dataset available to hospitals and healthcare providers to identify changes in patient health and medical outcomes, as well as accurate diagnoses. There are cases that use faster and personal support.

Treatment plan especially is provided in the manuscript for patients suffering with chronic diseases. AI information on infection states depends on learning calculations and doctor experienced in the treatment of patients with indications, signs, conclusions, medicines, and comparative results.

Most clinical data fall into a wide range of limited categories, although they are distant and may be limited by potential sampling, but future studies on the adoption of approved standards are not required. This allows AI algorithms to learn information and enhance the creation of reinforcement learning loops.

2.6 Future Scope, Limitations, and Possible Applications

The forthcoming examination is required to investigate how AI can customize treatment choices for singular patients to a clinician. The nature of data that AI gains from is likewise significant and an expected boundary to the far-reaching selection of exactness medication. The size of data needed for deep learning and the variety of strategies utilized makes it hard to obtain an away from of how precisely AI frameworks may function in genuine practice or how reproducible they might be in various clinical contexts.

Forthcoming exploration openings are necessary to address "social inclination" in AI calculations and sufficient advances should be taken to abstain from compounding medical care differences when utilizing AI apparatuses to save patients are famous. Tolerant security should be ensured and more noteworthy straightforwardness into algorithmic. Fairness is expected to guarantee acknowledgment of AI by suppliers and patients.

IoT solutions for healthcare that collect, transmit, and visualize data in complex intelligent systems via wearable and field sensor networks can facilitate analytics, activity detection, and decision-making. AI and ML technologies play a significant role in this transition, but their implementation requires computational power. It is often only available using cloud services.

In fact, with the increasing amount of data generated by sensors, the performance of ML-based cloud processing has several weaknesses for various reasons.

2.7   Recommendations and Consideration

AI in healthcare is ready to bring change and disrupt medical care. While not giving up marketing and profitability of drug addiction is the wisest guide, it balances AI, the need for comprehensive healthcare to plan and manage and reduce potential unexpected consequences.

It is wise to take. For AI, the best solution is to start with a real healthcare issue, involving the relevant stakeholders, first-line users, patients, and their families (including artificial and non-AI options). You need to find a solution and work on it. It is implemented and extended by our five goals: better health, better care experience, doctor health, lower cost, and common rights.

2.8   Conclusions

The nature of administration is significantly influenced by the nature of your internet association, making it difficult to use. Healthcare providers require shorter response times to address potential health risks, especially when performance such as early detection, risk prevention, and activity diagnosis is guaranteed in real time.

Because of the huge measure of individual data that should be overseen, data stockpiling and security are additionally vital when managing medical care. For all of this, choosing purely local administration, especially for mobility, is not yet practical due to limited processing and storage capabilities.

References

1. Azuaje, F., Artificial intelligence for precision oncology: beyond patient stratification. *NPJ Precis. Oncol.*, 3, 6, 2019, https://doi.org/10.1038/s41698-019-0078-1.

2. Bauer, H., Patel, M., Veira, J., *The Internet of Things: sizing up the opportunity*, McKinsey & Company, New York (NY), 2016, Available from: http://www.mckinsey.com/industries/high-tech/our-insights/the-internet-of-things-sizing-up-the-opportunity.

3. Baloch, Z., Shaikh, F., Unar, M., A context-aware data fusion approach for health-IoT. *Int. J. Inf. Technol.*, 10, 241–245, 2018, 10. 10.1007/s41870-018-0116-1.

4. Choi, H., A Risk Stratification Model for Lung Cancer Based on Gene Coexpression Network and Deep Learning. Applications of Bioinformatics and Systems Biology in Precision Medicine and Immuno Oncology, Research Article | Open Access, BioMed Research International, 2018, 2914280, 11, 2018. 2018 |Article ID 2914280, 11 pages, 2018, https://doi.org/10.1155/2018/2914280, Received 13 Oct 2017| Revised 07 Dec 2017 | Accepted 11 Dec 2017 |Published 16 Jan.\.

5. Deen, M.J., Information and communications technologies for elderly ubiquitous healthcare in a smart home. *Pers. Ubiquitous Comput.*, 19, 573–599, 2015.

6. Gao, W. *et al.*, Fully integrated wearable sensor arrays for multiplexed *in situ* perspiration analysis. *Nature*, 529, 7587, 509–514, 2016.

7. Gyllensten, I.C. *et al.*, A novel wearable vest for tracking pulmonary congestion in acutely decompensated heart failure. *Int. J. Cardiol.*, 177, 1, 199–201, 2014.

8. Haghighat, M., Abdel-Mottaleb, M., Alhalabi, W., Discriminant correlation analysis: real-time feature level fusion for multimodal biometric recognition. *IEEE Trans. Inf. Forensics Secur.*, 11, 9, 1984–96, 2016.

9. Kadir, T. and Gleeson, F., Lung cancer prediction using machine learning and advanced imaging techniques. *Transl. Lung Cancer Res.*, 7, 3, 304–312, 2018, Retrieved from http://tlcr.amegroups.com/article/view/21998.

10. Kumar, S. and Maninder, S., Big data analytics for healthcare industry: impact, applications, and tools. *Big Data Min. Anal.*, 2, 48–57, 2019, 10.26599/BDMA.2018.9020031.

11. Li, Y., Ge, D., Gu, J. *et al.*, A large cohort study identifying a novel prognosis prediction model for lung adenocarcinoma through machine learning strategies. *BMC Cancer*, 19, 886, 2019, https://doi.org/10.1186/s12885-019-6101-7.

12. Li, Y., Wu, *et al.*, Wiki-Health: A Big Data Platform for Health Sensor Data Management. in: Cloud Computing Applications for Quality Healthcare Delivery, A. Moumtzoglou, A. Kastania (Ed.), pp. 59–77, IGI Global, 2014, 10.4018/978-1-4666-6118-9.ch004, 2014.

13. Lisa, A. and Gustafson, D.H., The Role of Technology in Healthcare Innovation. A Commentary. *J. Dual Diagn.* Author manuscript; available PMC 2014 Jan 1. 2013, 9, 1, 101–103, 2013, J Dual Diagn. Published online 2012 Nov 27.

14. Macedo, F. *et al.*, Computer-aided detection (CADe) and diagnosis (CADx) system for lung cancer with likelihood of malignancy. *Biomed. Eng. Online*, 2, 15, 2016.

15. Mike, Hoover, W., Strome, T., Kanwal, S., Transforming healthcare through big data strategies for leveraging big data in the healthcare industry, Health IT Outcomes, USA, 2013, http://ihealthtran.com/iHT2 BigData 2013.pdf.

16. Rastogi, R., Chaturvedi, D.K., Satya, S., Arora, N., Trivedi, P., Gupta, M., Singhal, P., Gulati, M., *MM Big Data Applications: Statistical Resultant Analysis of Psychosomatic Survey on Various Human Personality Indicators*, ICICI 2018 Paper as Book Chapter, Chapter 25, © Springer Nature Singapore Pte Ltd, Singapore, 2020, Book Subtitle: Proceedings of Second International Conference on Computational Intelligence, 2018, https://doi.org/10.1007/978-981-13-8222-2_25.

17. Singh, Y. and Chauhan, A.S., Neural Networks in Data Mining. *J. Theor. Appl. Inf. Technol.*, 5, 6, 37–42, 14, 2005.

18. Sun, and Reddy, C.K., Big data analytics for healthcare, in: *Proc. 19th ACM SIGKDD International Conference on Knowledge Discovery and Data Mining*, pp. 1525–1525, 2013.

19. Wu, M. and Luo, J., Wearable technology applications in healthcare: A literature review. Online. *J. Nurs. Inform. (OJNI)*, 23, 3, 1, Fall. 2019, Available at http://www.himss.org/ojn.

20. Xu, J., Yang, P., Xue, S. *et al.*, Translating cancer genomics into precision medicine with artificial intelligence: applications, challenges and future perspectives. *Hum. Genet.*, 138, 109–124, https://doi.org/10.1007/s00439-019-01970-5, 2019.

21. Zanella, A., Bui, N., Castellani, A., Vangelista, L., Zorzi, M., Internet of things for smart cities. *IEEE Internet Things J.*, 1, 1, 22–32, 2014.

22. Zhao, W. and Wang, H., Strategic decision-making learning from label distributions: an approach for facial age estimation. *Sensors*, 16, 994–1013, 2016.

Computational Predictors of the Predominant Protein Function: SARS-CoV-2 Case

Carlos Polanco[1,2]*, Manlio F. Márquez[3] and Gilberto Vargas-Alarcón[4]

[1]*Department of Electromechanical Instrumentation, Instituto Nacional de Cardiología "Ignacio Chávez", México City, México*
[2]*Department of Mathematics, Faculty of Sciences, Universidad Nacional Autónoma de México, México City, México*
[3]*Clinical Research Center, Instituto Nacional de Cardiología "Ignacio Chávez", México City, México*
[4]*Research Center, Instituto Nacional de Cardiología "Ignacio Chávez", México City, México*

Abstract

In this chapter, we describe the main molecular features of SARS-CoV-2 that cause COVID-19 disease, as well as a high-efficiency computational prediction called Polarity Index Method®. We also introduce a molecular classification of the RNA virus and DNA virus families and two main classifications: supervised and non-supervised algorithms of the predictions of the predominant function of proteins. Finally, some results obtained by the proposed non-supervised method are given, as well as some particularities found about the linear representation of proteins.

Keywords: Adenoviridae, advantages, algorithms, Anelloviridae, Arenaviridae, Caliciviridae, computational predictions, Coronaviridae family, disadvantages, DNA virus, Herpesviridae, Herpesviridae, linear representation, non-supervised algorithms, Papillomaviridae, Parvoviridae, Picornaviridae, PIM® profile, Polarity Index Method®, Poxviridae, putative proteins, Reoviridae, Rhabdoviridae, RNA virus, SARS-CoV-2, supervised algorithms

**Corresponding author*: polanco@unam.mx

A. Suresh, S. Vimal, Y. Harold Robinson, Dhinesh Kumar Ramaswami and R. Udendhran (eds.) *Bioinformatics and Medical Applications: Big Data Using Deep Learning Algorithms*, (47–62)
© 2022 Scrivener Publishing LLC

3.1 Introduction

The discipline called Proteomics focuses, among other things, on the prediction of the predominant function of proteins, since this enables their construction by alteration or removal of their amino acids, either in its linear or in its three-dimensional representation.

This means some benefits for scholars of this discipline; since from these modifications, it is possible to obtain, mostly by accident, proteins with improved toxic action toward some pathogen.

Of course, it does not mean that there are no proteins or peptides in nature that have the toxic action we are looking for, it is just that in most cases, it is less expensive to try to manufacture one than to find it among the many organisms in nature.

The proteins expressing the SARS-CoV-2 that caused the COVID-19 pandemic have the particularity that their linear representation, i.e., their sequence, has a large number of amino acids, approximately 2,400 amino acids (aa). To give the reader an idea of the complexity and dimension of it, let us consider that some short peptides with antibacterial action have an average of 9aa.

Now, the capacity and robustness of the SARS-CoV-2 and all the regulatory processes can be dimensioned. Viruses, in general, have not simple mechanisms; they occupy some microns in length (a micron equals a thousand of a millimeters), but they are specialized organisms with multiple properly regulated functions that are characterized, among other things, for completing themselves when they are in contact with the RNA or DNA of the host.

This particularity suggests that they are not living organisms if we compare them with other living organisms whose species are known. Living organisms are born complete and do not get completed at birth; they have everything to reproduce themselves. This is not so with viruses; in any case, we can say that viruses are another type of life.

The SARS-CoV-2 is a virus of the group of coronaviruses, whose particularity and strength is the possibility of reproducing in any living organism. This feature is not shared by all viruses, e.g., the Ebola virus only passes to certain species, despite its lethality that is greater than 60%, it is less dangerous to our species because, when it kills its host, the virus dies with it and the damage is so fast that the number of deaths is small.

This does not occur with SARS-CoV-2 that can spread rapidly and the infected subject does not show any symptoms (asymptomatic) for 4 or up to 7 days, despite its lethality rate that is no higher than 2%.

From the above, it is clear that the definition of the lethality rate is not just a quotient, but multiple variables have to be considered. Almost as many as asking us about the lethality of a human being.

The review of the basic concepts related to viruses and particularly the SARS-CoV-2, make us think about the complexity of these organisms, not as organisms that by their small size are simple and potentially fragile, but as organisms with an auto-regulatory capacity as complex as the human species but in a few microns.

3.2 Human Coronavirus Types

Coronaviruses feature the crown-like spikes on their surface; they were first identified in the 1960s and there are seven types of coronavirus that infect people [1]:

1. 229E alpha coronavirus causes the common cold; it infects the upper respiratory tract, i.e., nose, throat, sinuses, and larynx. The subject presents symptoms within a couple of days of being in contact with the virus; these can be headache, runny nose, coughing, sore throat, and fever. The illness lasts a week or 10 days, but it can be extended up to three weeks. Sometimes, subjects with other health problems develop pneumonia [2].

2. OC43 beta coronavirus is also the cause of common cold, and just like the 229E, it infects the upper respiratory tract and affects the same organs. The symptoms are also the same as well as the recovery time. Subjects with other health problems can develop pneumonia too [2].

3. NL63 alpha coronavirus causes many common symptoms and diseases; it infects the upper and lower tract and can cause croup and bronchiolitis [3].

4. MERS-CoV, the beta coronavirus, is the cause of Middle East Respiratory Syndrome or MERS; the symptoms are coughing, shortness of breath, and fever. Sometimes, the subject can also present pneumonia and gastrointestinal symptoms, such as diarrhoea. Some laboratory-confirmed cases of MERS-CoV are reported asymptomatic, i.e., the subjects do not present symptoms. Most of these cases are detected after a thorough tracing of laboratory-confirmed cases [4].

5. HKU1 beta coronavirus causes upper respiratory diseases with common cold symptoms and the subject can develop pneumonia and bronchiolitis [5].

6. SARS-CoV, the beta coronavirus, causes severe acute respiratory syndrome (SARS), it starts with a high fever, more than 38°C, the subject presents chills, headache, and muscle pain; some cases have mild respiratory symptoms, and some patients have diarrhoea.

7. Within a week, the subject presents a dry cough or dyspnoea that can progress to hypoxemia. Some cases even require intubation and mechanical ventilation. The white blood cell count decreases and many people have low platelet counts [6].

8. SARS-CoV-2, the novel coronavirus which is the cause of COVID-19, affects people in different ways. In most cases a moderate illness is present and the subject recovers without hospitalization. The symptoms are fever, tiredness, dry coughing, aches and pains, diarrhoea, headaches, conjunctivitis, rash on the skin, and loss of taste or smell. There could also be difficulty breathing, chest pain, and loss of speech or movement [7].

3.3 The SARS-CoV-2 Pandemic Impact

The SARS-CoV-2 and the COVID-19 disease impact is a multifactorial phenomenon to measure it we have to take into account some factors (Section 3.1), so let us only take two of them for the moment; its dissemination capacity and its capacity to kill a human being.

The propagation of viruses has to do with the possibility of passing to any organism and the SARS-CoV-2 virus gets this feature from the Coronaviridae family (Section 3.3.2), which can be considered very high; on the other hand, the lethality of the SARS-CoV-2 is no higher than 2% (Section 3.1), which is low.

However, both factors together create a combination that strongly impacts humans, as their propagation and lethality take on a large number of lives, given the permanence of the virus in human beings.

In this sense, the impact is very high since this coronavirus has a very similar spread to any flu; however, its lethality is very high compared to this disease, as up to date there is no effective treatment or vaccine available; unlike the A H1N1 influenza pandemic in 2009 that had an effective treatment and the vaccine was available few months later.

In this regard, any alert or official warning that the population is facing an epidemic process or a pandemic, in general, has to do with a minimum number of people infected that have had a microbiological corroboration.

In the case of an unknown illness, this verification can take days or even weeks; this is a limitation that defers the notification. So, once this alert has been issued, the authorities should state it is a pandemic and not an epidemic event, according to the definition that at least two continents present infected cases, regardless of the number of them.

From the epidemiological point of view, there should be an algorithm that not only considers the number of confirmed cases, as continuous improvement of the means of transport makes contagion and dissemination of illness much faster nowadays.

3.3.1   RNA Virus vs DNA Virus

There are two main groups in the classification of viruses and they are related to the genetic material a virus uses to replicate, whether it is in a DNA or an RNA host.

DNA viruses are formed by the families (Source: [8]; change family by the corresponding family name): *Adenoviridae, Papillomaviridae, Parvoviridae, Herpesviridae, Poxviridae,* and *Anelloviridae.*

While RNA viruses are formed by the families (Source: [8]; change family by the corresponding family name): *Reoviridae, Picornaviridae, Caliciviridae, Arenaviridae, Rhabdoviridae, Coronaviridae,* and *Herpesviridae.*

Given the purpose of this chapter, the reader is invited to consult the source cited in each of the classifications, if he/she wants to delve into this topic.

3.3.2   The *Coronaviridae* Family

Coronaviruses are transmitted by respiratory secretion sprays, with different incubation periods estimated between 2 days and a week, after these 2 weeks, the virus is eliminated from the body. The virus replicates in the host cell, passing to the Golgi apparatus until they are finally released by exocytosis. In general, coronaviruses induce 15% of colds and flu, and their effect intensifies in winter and early spring.

Coronaviruses infect a large number of birds and mammals, particularly the SARS CoV-2-index-SARS-CoV-2; they are responsible for severe respiratory diseases, which can be spread even to babies; and in few cases, they are responsible for neurologic syndromes.

The virus remains in the upper respiratory tract and exhibits minimal immune response. Due to its mutation capacity, it persists in the invaded species.

3.3.3   The SARS-CoV-2 Structural Proteins

Four structural proteins form the SARS-CoV-2, the Spike, Membrane, Envelope, and Nucleocapsid proteins; there are other groups related to SARS-CoV-2 like the non-structural proteins, and SARS-CoV-2 putative accessory factors; although, there are also protein groups with important structural differences related to it, such as those of the MERS, and SARS-CoV proteins.

3.3.4   Protein Representations

Proteins are formed by amino acids; they are the fundamental units of every living organism; they are transformed into tissues, muscles, skin, or nails, but they can also be converted into accelerators or retardants of chemical or physiological processes. Life could not be understood without them.

The first representation of a protein is a succession of amino acids; it is like placing one amino acid after another, this representation is called linear representation or sequence. Then, three representations take place in the three-dimensional space that are related to the form the amino acids settle.

When protein amino acids cluster, they take forms like alpha helices and beta sheets, this is called a secondary representation. When these small structures bind together, the protein has a tertiary representation. Finally, if the protein is so large that it is made up of two or more tertiary structures, then it is said to be a protein with a quaternary structure.

A protein may be made up of few amino acids or thousands of them; however, their number has nothing to do with the size it adopts but with its regulation. Suffice it to say that as an example the SARS-CoV-2 structural protein (Spike) has 1283aa and yet it only has few microns.

Note 3.1 Here, it is important to mention that viruses are formed by proteins, and although at the time being, it is still discussed whether they are living organisms or not, they are also formed by proteins.

3.4   Computational Predictors

There is a practical interest, besides the scientific interest, in aiming efforts to determine the predominant function of a protein. Let us start by saying that proteins do not have a single action on a pathogen; on the contrary, all proteins have action on several pathogens. For this reason, when examining a database specialized in proteins, it is common to find that the same protein is reported several times, with a different predisposition.

On the other hand, determining the action or function of a protein involves costly experiments and/or clinical trials, without mentioning that there are proteins with pathogenic action that are increasingly difficult to find in nature; as in the case of SCAAPs (selective cationic amphipathic antibacterial peptides) that are highly toxic to bacterial membrane and harmless to erythrocytes.

SCAAPs are also very short 6aa proteins – 14aa; for all these characteristics, they are very valuable in the production of pharmaceutical drugs; however, it is increasingly difficult to find them in nature.

In this scenario, it is very useful to have computational mathematical predictions that can identify the preponderant function of a protein only by taking its sequence. This enables the inspection of databases to search peptides with a specific function. Of course, this will not prevent experimental testing, but it will substantively reduce the proteins tested.

There are several types of classification for prediction algorithms of the protein predominant function, such as the representation of proteins in three-dimensional space rather than in linear representation. Others use stochastic algorithms instead of deterministic algorithms that may or may not evaluate physico-chemical properties.

In this work, we used two main divisions: the supervised algorithms and the non-supervised algorithms, both classifications are discussed below.

3.4.1   Supervised Algorithms

A supervised algorithm is a particular computational code that requires calibration or training to know what to look for. This makes them programmer-dependent codes as, at a first stage, it is calibrated and, at a second stage, when they are already calibrated, they can search a particular profile.

In the proteomics and genomics fields, there are many different algorithms designed under this assumption.

3.4.2 Non-Supervised Algorithms

A non-supervised algorithm is a computational code that does not require calibration or training to know what to look for and, if it requires it, it is only a part of the code and it modifies itself to adjust the search criteria. The running of these codes does not depend on the programmer as they are independent.

In the proteomics and genomics fields, there are also these types of algorithms and although they are less, they are very useful.

In this chapter, we will use an algorithm of this type named Polarity Index Method®, to explore SARS-CoV-2 structural proteins.

3.5 Polarity Index Method®

The non-supervised algorithm named Polarity Index Method® (PIM®) is a system programmed in FORTRAN 77 and Linux. It calculates and compares the PIM® protein profile of the target group with other groups, modifying the PIM® profile of the target group to make it representative and discriminant of the other protein groups it is compared with.

3.5.1 The PIM® Profile

The metrics of the PIM® profile consist to evaluate the 16 charge/polarity interactions identified by reading the sequence of a protein by pairs of residues, from left to right. The PIM® system has three stages:

1. The amino acid sequence is converted to the numeric charge/polarity-related annotations P⁺, P⁻, N, and NP, where P⁺ are H, His; K, Lys; and R, Arg; P⁻ are D, Asp; and E, Glu; N are C, Cys; G, Gly; N, Asp; Q, Gln; S, Ser; T, Thr; and Y, Tyr; and NP are A, Ala; F, Phe; I, Ile; L, Leu; M, Met; P, Pro; V, Val; and W, Trp.

2. The sequence is expressed in FASTA format; all the incidences of these pairs of amino acids are registered in a 4 × 4 algebraic matrix where its rows and columns are the four PIM® profile groups. Once all amino acid pairs are recorded, the incidence matrix is normalized.

3. Create a 16-element vector putting, from left to right, the 16 possible positions from the incidence matrix in increasing or decreasing order. Two proteins are equal if their 16-element vectors are the same.

Two proteins are equal if their 16-element vectors shared the same preponderant function.

3.5.2   Advantages

The main advantage of this method is that the metric acts on the linear representation of the protein and not in the three-dimensional representation of it, making possible a simple analysis. On the other hand, only one physico-chemical property is evaluated, the polarity/charge of the protein.

The analysis is comprehensive as the full spectrum of PIM® profile incidents is examined; in other words, the PIM® profile is not a number but a 16-element vector. Thus, two proteins have the same PIM® profile if their 16-element vectors are equal.

3.5.3   Disadvantages

Its use as part of a biochip is not yet completed; this restricts its use only to determine the predominant function of a protein; however, nowadays, it is not enough to identify the function/structure of a protein but to identify it in the blood of an organism and determine its number.

This will enable the PIM R profile as a rapid detection test.

3.5.4   SARS-CoV-2 Recognition Using PIM® Profile

The PIM® system (Section 3.5.1) was determined in the four SARS-CoV-2 structural proteins: spike, membrane, envelope, and nucleocapsid (Section 3.3.3), and their smooth curves (Figure 3.1) were plotted, it was observed that there is a similarity in these PIM® profiles, except for the region between the polar interactions [P⁻, P⁻] and [N, P⁻] see (Figure 3.2).

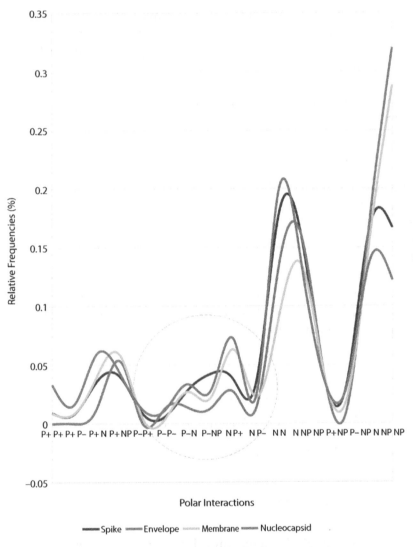

Figure 3.1 Relative frequency distribution of proteins that express the four SARS-CoV-2 structural viral protein group represented by "smooth curves". Graphs were produced using EXCEL software. The X-axis represents the 16 charge/polarity interactions. The ellipse shows the region where curves do not match the trend.

Figure 3.2 shows the PIM® profile of the spike and envelope proteins behaving particularly differently, while the membrane is the translation of nucleocapsid.

A revision of the histograms (Figure 3.3) of the relative frequency distribution of the residues in the sequences of the SARS-CoV-2

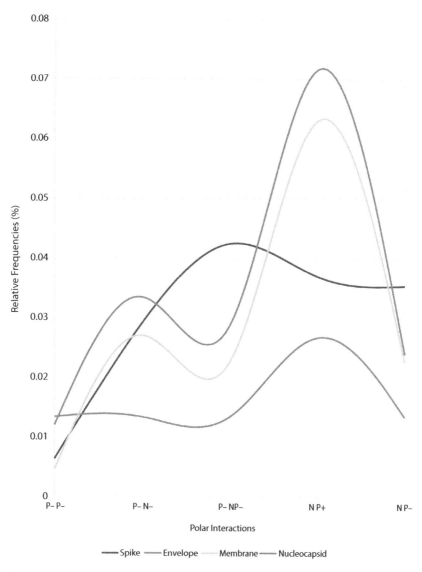

Figure 3.2 Zoom over the Figure 3.1. The X-axis represents the five polar interactions from [P⁻, P⁻] and [N, P⁻]. See (Section 2.5.4).

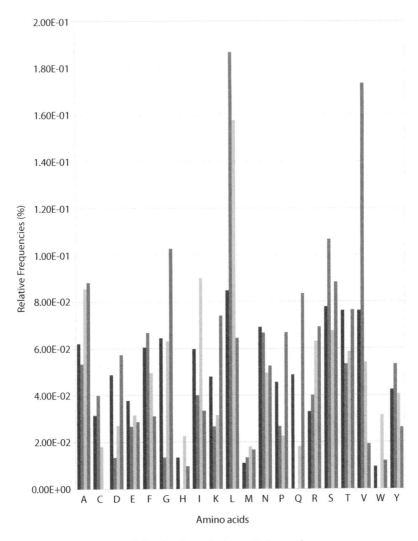

Figure 3.3 Histograms SARS-CoV-2 structural proteins.

structural proteins (spike, envelope, membrane, and nucleocapsid) shows that any of them are similar. When in general, this behavior does not necessarily depend on the length of the sequence.

3.6   Future Implications

Non-supervised algorithms will play a major role in proteomics and genomics applications, as they can be run regardless of the time consumed in the computational platform; we have to bear in mind that, in most cases, the time they will take to search a specific pattern is unknown since the algorithms are non-linear metrics, and therefore, it is not possible to scale the processing time.

All non-supervised algorithms do not depend on any human intervention, so they run freely on a platform until they cast some conclusion. These processes may well be supported by a Hidden Markov Model (HMM) that enables the total control of all processes.

On the other hand, we consider that it will be necessary to reassess the metrics of the prediction programs, to explore differently the evaluation of proteins, both those stored in databases, and those identified in organic fluids that require a quick evaluation.

Metrics may also thoroughly explore only one characteristic and not several, like the method here presented, as we think it will be essential in the analysis of the new generation of algorithms, i.e., if the metric yields a number, it is very little information it provides; however, if it gives a vector, or a matrix, then the information can be considered exhaustive.

The proteomic and genomic for the production of pharmaceutical drugs will rapidly change to the design of biochips that will assess the proteins in organic fluids; this is a very important task, particularly for the latent threat the Coronaviridae family represents to humans due to its ability to disseminate and mutate.

A final observation about this subject is the advantage of the stochastic algorithm over the deterministic algorithm. Although the latter is more precise, they hardly offer any practical solution when the number of factors is large since the prediction of a biological microorganism is a multifactorial phenomenon, a deterministic algorithm will require huge memory and processing speed. Therefore, they will hardly provide a practical solution, as they will face the limitations of any computational architecture.

On the other hand, the stochastic functions are linear, which means that when evaluating multiple variables, the complexity will not increase, so these functions only give a probability value associated with the result, i.e., the associated value will be in the range between 0% a 100%.

3.7 Acknowledgments

The authors thank C. Celis-Juárez and L. Anderson-Coe for proof-reading. Funding: None. Contributions: Theoretical conceptualization and design: CP. Performance: CP. Data analysis: CP, GVA, and MFM. Discussion: CP, GVA, and MFM. Competing interests: We declare there are no financial and personal interests with other people or organizations that could inappropriately influence this work. Data availability: Copyright & Trademark. All rights reserved (México), 2018: Polarity Index Method®. Software and Hardware: Hardware: The computational platform used was two HP Workstations z21400 — CMT — 4 x Intel Xeon E3-1270/3.4 GHz (Quad-Core) — RAM 8/4 GB — SSD 1 x 160 GB — DVD SuperMulti — Quadro 2000 — Gigabit LAN, Linux Fedora 64-bits. Cache Memory 8 MB. Cache Per Processor 8 MB. RAM 8/4. Software: Polarity Index Method (PIM®). Supplementary Materials can be asked to (polanco@unam.mx).

References

1. CDC, Human coronavirus types, National Center for Immunization and Respiratory Diseases (NCIRD), Division of Viral Diseases, Human coronarivus types section. Available at: https://www.cdc.gov/coronavirus/types.html. Last Updated February 15, 2020. Accessed November 22, 2021. 2020, https://www.cdc.gov/coronavirus/types.html.
2. Wikipedia contributors. Coronavirus. Wikipedia, The Free Encyclopedia. November 20, 2021, 05:45 UTC. Available at: https://en.wikipedia.org/w/index.php?title=Coronavirus&oldid=1056173146. Accessed November 22, 2021.
3. Wikipedia contributors. Human coronavirus NL63. Wikipedia, The Free Encyclopedia. August 22, 2021, 00:48 UTC. Available at: https://en.wikipedia.org/w/index.php?title=Human_coronavirus_NL63&oldid=1039988099. Accessed November 22, 2021.
4. World Health Organizacion, Middle East respiratory syndrome coronavirus (MERS-CoV) section, Available at: https://www.who.int/news-room/fact-sheets/detail/middle-east-respiratory-syndrome-coronavirus-(mers-cov). March 11, 2019. Accessed: November 22, 2021.
5. Wikipedia contributors. Human coronavirus HKU1 [Internet]. Wikipedia, The Free Encyclopedia; 2021 Nov 17, 12:27 UTC [cited 2021 Nov 22]. Available from: https://en.wikipedia.org/w/index.php?title=Human_coronavirus_HKU1&oldid=1055721823. Accessed: November 22, 2022.
6. World Health Organizacion, Severe Acute Respiratory Syndrome (SARS) section, Available at: https://www.who.int/health-topics/

severe-acute-respiratory-syndrome#tab=tab_1. March 11, 2019. Accessed: November 22, 2021.

7. National Center for Immunization and Respiratory Diseases (NCIRD), Division of Viral Diseases, Coronavirus disease (COVID-19) section. Available at: https://www.who.int/health- topics/coronavirus#tab=tab3. Last Updated February 15, 2020. Accessed November 22, 2021.

8. The UniProt Consortium UniProt: the universal protein knowledgebase in 2021 Nucleic Acids Res. 49:D1 (2021). Available at: https://www.uniprot.org/proteomes/-query=adenoviridae&fil=reference%3Ayes&sort=score. Accessed: November 22, 2021.

4

Deep Learning in Gait Abnormality Detection: Principles and Illustrations

Saikat Chakraborty[1,2]*, Sruti Sambhavi[2] and Anup Nandy[2]

[1]School of Computer Engineering, Kalinga Institute of Industrial Technology (KIIT), Bhubaneswar, Odisha, India
[2]Machine Intelligence Bio-Motion Research Laboratory, Computer Science & Engineering Dept., National Institute of Technology Rourkela, Rourkela, India

Abstract

Cerebral palsy (CP) is a medical condition which is marked by weakened muscle coordination and other dysfunctions. The root cause for this condition is brain damage in prenatal state. This population experiences musculoskeletal disabilities that bring about abnormalities in some form which affect the gait pattern. We propose various machine learning and deep learning techniques including support vector machines (SVM), multilayer perceptron (MLP), Vanilla long short-term memory (LSTM), and Bidirectional LSTM to diagnose CP gait. The gait dataset consists of linear velocity of seven body joints. All the methods have been deployed by taking each time instant as a data point. LSTM demonstrated to be competing in detecting CP gait.

Keywords: LSTM, cerebral palsy 2, deep learning, SVM

4.1 Introduction

Gait analysis is the study of human locomotion, improved via necessary instrumentation for measuring bio mechanics of movements and muscle activities. Gait analysis becomes inevitable in cases where individuals whose ability to walk effectively and safely are affected. The traditional gait cycle comprises of primarily eight periods or events (see Figure 4.1),

---

*Corresponding author: saikat.sc@gmail.com

A. Suresh, S. Vimal, Y. Harold Robinson, Dhinesh Kumar Ramaswami and R. Udendhran (eds.)
Bioinformatics and Medical Applications: Big Data Using Deep Learning Algorithms, (63–72)
© 2022 Scrivener Publishing LLC

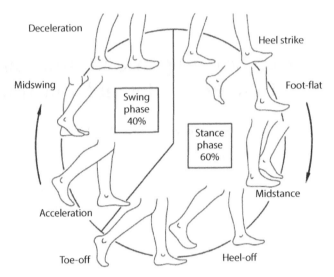

Figure 4.1 Cyclic nature of human gait (Vaughan *et al.* [9]).

i.e., three steps are a part of swing and five occur stance. The stance phase events, as described in the traditional nomenclature, are as follows:

    i.   The center of gravity is found to be at the lowermost position when the heel strike occurs. This marks the beginning of gait cycle.

    ii. When the ground is touched by the bottom of the foot, it is said to be in foot flat stage.

    iii. The moment when the highest position of the center of gravity is achieved and swinging foot and stance foot pass by simultaneously, the midstance is said to occur.

    iv. The moment the heel loses touch with the ground, the push-off stage begins via the triceps surae muscles and initiates heel off stage.

    v. Just when the foot contact is lost from the ground, toe off occurs and stance phase occurs.

The swing phase events are described as follows:

    i.   When the foot leaves the ground, it activates the hip flexor muscles which, in turn, accelerates the leg forward, thus acceleration occurs.

    ii. When the foot passes exactly below the body, and at this position, the other foot is at the same level, midstance is said to occur in the swing phase.

iii. At last, when leg slows down due to the muscle action, and this is followed by foot stabilization in order to start preparing for the next set of events in the subsequent gait cycle.

4.2 Background

4.2.1 LSTM

Long short-term memory (LSTM) units and its variants which combine in the form to layers are a mere improvement on RNNs. They deal effectively against vanishing gradient problem and are apt for dealing with time series data. The following are the variants of LSTM on which the gait data has been implemented.

4.2.1.1 Vanilla LSTM

LSTM is an improvised version of the traditional architecture used in artificial recurrent neural network (RNN). It is used extensively in the field of deep learning. LSTM includes feedback connections which are unlike basic MLP models which make use of forward propagation. An entire sequence of data (for example, speech or video) can be processed by making use of the architecture as its application is not constrained to single data points (such as images) only. A common LSTM unit (see Figure 4.2) is basically a cell which consists of an output gate, an input gate, an output gate, and forget gate. The gates manage the flow of information through all the cells. They remember what is to be retained and what is to be allowed to let go. The values are memorized over arbitrary time intervals. Time series data are well suited for LSTM networks because there can be random intervals of time with an arbitrary duration between fixed events and trials in a time series. LSTM was designed with an intent to tackle vanishing gradient problem which is a drawback in case of RNN, encountered while training it. The comparative insensitivity due to this undetermined gap length is a pro in case of LSTM networks over RNNs, hidden Markov models, etc., in similar use cases dealing with sequential data. The LSTM units can undergo training in supervised way on a set of given sequences using algorithms which aim at optimization, like gradient descent which is, in fact, combined with back propagation through time to calculate the values of gradients required for optimization. This is required so that we can alter the weights of the very same network in accordance to the derivative of

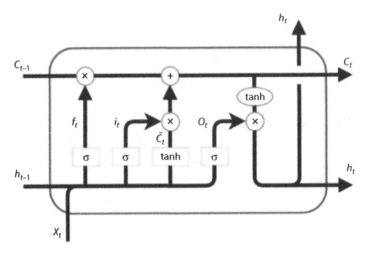

Figure 4.2 LSTM unit (Bouktif *et al.* [2]).

the error as computed in case of MLP with respect to the corresponding weights. However, we encounter a change in case of LSTM units, where in the error values are propagated in the backward direction from the output layer in LSTM units. Also, error persists in the unit cell of LSTM. This error carousel continually supplements the individual error values to every gate until they have learnt to get rid off that value.

4.2.1.2 Bidirectional LSTM

Bidirectional RNNs (BRNNs) (see Figure 4.3) maintain an architecture by connecting two otherwise normal LSTM layers which act as hidden layers in two distinct directions and result in the same output. Through this structure, the LSTM architecture becomes more capable of getting information from sequences already processed and from the ones that are about to be processed by the network. This modification to the existing LSTM network was made in order to mount more and more information regarding the input and at the same time, inputs need not be fixed. Also, one can reach their future states from the state they are currently in. BRNNs are generally useful when the importance of the context of the input is primary. In working, the two opposite states' outputs are not connected essentially to the inputs of the states which are at opposite directions.

An added advantage is that there is no requirement of the time for including future information. The training process in case of BRNNs is almost the

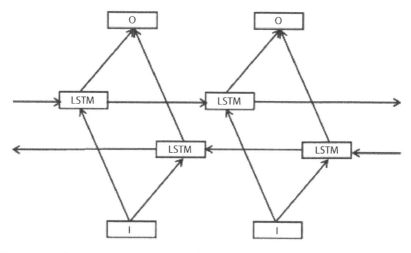

Figure 4.3 Bidirectional LSTM (Yulita *et al.* [10]).

same as that of RNNs. This is because of the absence of interactions in the directions of neurons. The process is described as follows:

- In forward pass, the states for the forward direction and backward subsequent states are sent for computation initially, and then, the output neurons are made to pass.
- In the backward pass, initially, the output neurons are let go and then the forward, next the backward state, all are passed one by one. Weights are updated once the forward and backward states are passed.

4.3 Related Works

Many studies [4, 8, 12] have justified that the problem caused due to cerebral palsy can now directly be dealt by machine learning and deep learning techniques. Modern-day machine learning techniques have now started complementing traditional statistical tools. LSTM performed satisfactorily in detection of gait abnormality [4, 6]. Other variations of LSTM like time-aware LSTM [1] and attention based time-aware LSTM [13] have also been explored that help overcome certain glitches that ultimately resulted in accuracy improvement for the data that they dealt with. Thus, clinical professionals have been assisted in the classification process with the deep learning techniques. Kamruzzaman *et al.* [5] investigated SVM kernels and found that stride length and cadence are efficient enough to detect abnormal gait in children with CP.

Utility of Bayesian classifier was harnessed by Zhang *et al.* [11] to diagnose CP gait. Wolf *et al.* [9] demonstrated a modular framework to assess gait features automatically. Rueangsirarak *et al.* [7] presented three new features based on lower extremities to detect abnormal gait. Cui *et al.* [3] presented a multi-modal architecture to detect gait abnormalities. These techniques act as an objective reference to them in Motion Analysis Labs. We have tried to put in practice the existing methods like SVM, LSTM, MLP, and compared the results.

4.4   Methods

4.4.1   Data Collection and Analysis

Data were collected using three Kinect v2 sensors by placing them linearly. In addition, 20 normal and 20 CP patients were recruited and explained the experimental protocol. Approval for the experiment was taken from the local ethical committee. Consent form was signed from each of the subjects. They were directed to walk for 10 m at self-determined speed. Velocity of seven joints (pelvis, hips, knees, and ankles of both limbs) was captured. The x, y, and z coordinates of seven joints at each time instant has been considered as a single data point. So, the number of features considered during classification is 21. The ratio for train and test set was fixed at 7:3. It was observed that the number of time instants vary from one gait cycle to another gait cycle. Hence, in order to maintain uniformity, necessary interpolation was carried out. The technique of cross validation used was "leave one out". For hyperparameter tuning, grid search was used.

Hyperparameters are extremely important because they directly have a control on the behavior of the training process and exhibit significant performance later. LSTM is a training intensive process and it took the longest time to sum up the entire training process. Once the best suited model was found, it was saved. For SVM (RBF), hyperparameters were regularization parameter and gamma. In addition to these, polynomial kernel has degree as a hyperparameters. For MLP, the architecture was chosen such that the input layer had 21 nodes and output layer had two nodes. In this case, the hyperparameters were number of nodes, epoch, and activation function. In case of vanilla LSTM, the architecture consisted of four layers, with each of them followed by dropout layers. There were 100 units each in the LSTM layers and 2 out of every 10 nodes were dropped in the network. This entire combination was followed by a dense layer consisting of 1 unit. Mean squared loss was used to find the losses incurred, and Adam optimizer was used. In this case, the hyperparameters were number of nodes, epoch, batch size, and activation function. Bidirectional LSTM is just the concatenation of vanilla LSTM layers, and they are connected in reverse. The architecture consists of two bidirectional layers followed by a dense layer. Binary cross entropy loss was computed in each step and an Adam optimizer was used in place.

4.4.2   Results and Discussion

The performance metrics that have been used to judge the methods are as follows: accuracy, sensitivity, specificity, and F1 score. All these values are computed from the generated confusion matrix values.

There are four kinds of labeling possible (see Table 4.1):

1. True Positive (TP): When an object belongs to positive class and is predicted as belongs to the positive class.
2. False Positive (FP): When an object belongs to negative class and is predicted as belongs to the positive class.

Table 4.1 Confusion matrix for binary classification.

	Class 1 predicted	**Class 2 predicted**
Class 1 actual	TP	FN
Class 2 actual	FP	TN

Source: Wikipedia.

3. True Negative (TN): When an object belongs to negative class and is predicted as belongs to the negative class.
4. False Negative (FN): When an object belongs to positive class and is predicted as belongs to the negative class.

The formula for various performance metrics is

$$Accuracy = \frac{TP + TN}{TP + FP + FN + TN} \tag{4.1}$$

$$Sensitivity = \frac{TP}{TP+FN} \tag{4.2}$$

$$Specificity = \frac{TN}{TN+FP} \tag{4.3}$$

$$F1\,Score = \frac{2 * sensitivity * Precision}{sensitivity + Precision} \tag{4.4}$$

Accuracy will determine how many abnormal gait patterns are correctly predicted as abnormal and how many normal gait patterns are correctly predicted as normal ones.

But in our case, we have to deal with a lot of cases where our data is affected by both false negatives and false positives. Hence, in order to handle them, it is inevitable to keep a track of the precision, recall, and F1 score. The precision value will tell what part of the results are important to the data, while recall refers to the chunk of total relevant results that have been classified correctly by the model designed. There always exists a trade-off because of which we cannot maximize them both. This is because, to maintain a high recall, results which are not accurate need to be generated which, in turn, reduces the precision. Thus to maintain a trade-off on their part, the F1 score comes into the picture. Thus, in addition to accuracy as a metric, we need to also keep a track of the other performance metrics as mentioned. Table 4.2 shows that Vanilla LSTM is competing in diagnosing CP gait.

Table 4.2 Performance analysis of different classifiers.

Classifiers	Accuracy (%)	Sensitivity (%)	Specificity (%)	F1 score (%)
SVM (RBF)	81.27	92.06	70.67	82.96
SVM (linear)	67.12	94.31	40.41	73.97
SVM (polynomial)	66.11	95.48	37.26	79.63
MLP	67.23	59.43	69.92	64.25
Vanilla LSTM	80.40	93.08	74.04	82.47
Bidirectional LSTM	73.65	71.79	75.67	72.92

Source: Experimentation Results.

4.5   Conclusion and Future Work

With the given data in hand, we have a piecewise non-deterministic signal to deal with. Through the classification methods that have been worked upon, the typical characteristics of data had been tried to be found out. We have proposed few models which can carry out the purpose of classification. These methods intend to detect abnormalities so that we can successfully chalk out the abnormal gait patterns from normal ones. Through the methods implemented, we have found numerous methods that overcome the shortcomings of its predecessor methods and hence slowly help alleviate the issues and in the end devise methods for efficient classification, and among all of them, it has been seen that SVM has shown the best results. In future we will work to generate a combined model to get better performance.

4.6   Acknowledgments

The authors would like to express thanks to Science and Engineering Research Board (SERB), DST, Govt. of India to partially support this research work (File No: ECR/2017/000408). We would also like to thank Indian Institute of Cerebral Palsy, Kolkata and REC School NIT Rourkela Campus for providing Cerebral Palsy patients and normal subjects, respectively.

References

1. Baytas, I.M., Xiao, C., Zhang, X., Wang, F., Jain, A.K., Zhou, J., Patient subtyping via time-aware LSTM networks. *Proceedings of the ACM SIGKDD International Conference on Knowledge Discovery and Data Mining, Part F1296*, pp. 65–74, 2017, https://doi.org/10.1145/3097983.3097997.
2. Bouktif, S., Fiaz, A., Ouni, A., Serhani, M.A., Single and multi-sequence deep learning models for short and medium term electric load forecasting. *Energies*, 12, 1, 249, 2019, https://doi.org/10.3390/en12010149.
3. Cui, C., Bian, G.B., Hou, Z.G., Zhao, J., Su, G., Zhou, H., Peng, L., Wang, W., Simultaneous Recognition and Assessment of Post-Stroke Hemiparetic Gait by Fusing Kinematic, Kinetic, and Electrophysiological Data. *IEEE Trans. Neural Syst. Rehabil. Eng.*, 26, 4, 856–864, 2018, https://doi.org/10.1109/TNSRE.2018.2811415.
4. De Laet, T., Papageorgiou, E., Nieuwenhuys, A., Desloovere, K., Does expert knowledge improve automatic probabilistic classification of gait joint motion

patterns in children with cerebral palsy? *PLoS ONE*, 12, 6, 1–18, 2017, https://doi.org/10.1371/journal.pone.0178378, Ferrari, A., Bergamini, L., Guerzoni, G., Calderara, S., Bicocchi, N., Vitetta, G., Borghi, C., Neviani, R., Ferrari, A., Gait-based diplegia classification using lsmt networks. *J. Healthcare Eng.*, 2019, 2019(i), https://doi.org/10.1155/2019/3796898.

5. Kamruzzaman, J. and Begg, R.K., Support vector machines and other pattern recognition approaches to the diagnosis of cerebral palsy gait. *IEEE Trans. Biomed. Eng.*, 53, 12, 2479–2490, 2006, https://doi.org/10.1109/TBME.2006.883697.

6. Khokhlova, M., Migniot, C., Morozov, A., Sushkova, O., Dipanda, A., Normal and pathological gait classification LSTM model. *Artif. Intell. Med.*, 94, November 2018, 54–66, 2019, https://doi.org/10.1016/j.artmed.2018.12.007.

7. Rueangsirarak, W., Zhang, J., Aslam, N., Ho, E.S.L., Shum, H.P.H., Automatic Musculoskeletal and Neurological Disorder Diagnosis with Relative Joint Displacement from Human Gait. *IEEE Trans. Neural Syst. Rehabil. Eng.*, 26, 12, 2387–2396, 2018, https://doi.org/10.1109/TNSRE.2018.2880871.

8. Van Gestel, L., De Laet, T., Di Lello, E., Bruyninckx, H., Molenaers, G., Van Campenhout, A., Aertbeliën, E., Schwartz, M., Wambacq, H., De Cock, P., Desloovere, K., Probabilistic gait classification in children with cerebral palsy: A Bayesian approach. *Res. Dev. Disabil.*, 32, 6, 2542–2552, 2011, https://doi.org/10.1016/j.ridd.2011.07.004.

9. Vaughan, C., Davis, B., O'Connor, J., Dynamics of Human Gait, 1992, Wolf, S., Loose, T., Schablowski, M., Döderlein, L., Rupp, R., Gerner, H.J., Bretthauer, G., Mikut, R., Automated feature assessment in instrumented gait analysis. *Gait Posture*, 23, 3, 331–338, 2006, https://doi.org/10.1016/j.gaitpost.2005.04.004.

10. Yulita, I.N., Fanany, M.I., Arymuthy, A.M., Bi-directional Long Short-Term Memory using Quantized data of Deep Belief Networks for Sleep Stage Classification. *Proc. Comput. Sci.*, 116, 530–538, https://doi.org/10.1016/j.procs.2017.10.042, 2017.

11. Zhang, B. l., Zhang, Y., Begg, R.K., Gait classification in children with cerebral palsy by Bayesian approach. *Pattern Recognit.*, 42, 4, 581–586, https://doi.org/10.1016/j.patcog.2008.09.025, 2009.

12. Zhang, Y. and Ma, Y., Application of supervised machine learning algorithms in the classification of sagittal gait patterns of cerebral palsy children with spastic diplegia. *Comput. Biol. Med.*, 106, August 2018, 33–39, https://doi.org/10.1016/j.comp-biomed.2019.01.009, 2019.

13. Zhang, Y., Yang, X., Ivy, J., Chi, M., Attain: Attention-based time-aware LSTM networks for disease progression modeling. *IJCAI International Joint Conference on Artificial Intelligence*, 2019-Augus, pp. 4369–4375, 2019, https://doi.org/10.24963/ijcai.2019/607.

5

Broad Applications of Network Embeddings in Computational Biology, Genomics, Medicine, and Health

Akanksha Jaiswar[1†], Devender Arora[2†], Manisha Malhotra[3], Abhimati Shukla[4] and Nivedita Rai[5*]

[1]Centre for Agricultural Bioinformatics (CABin), ICAR-Indian Agricultural Statistics Research Institute, New Delhi, India
[2]National Institute of Animal Science, Rural Development Administration, Jeonju, South Korea
[3]CSIR-Indian Institute of Petroleum, Dehradun, India
[4]Harcourt Butler Technical University, Kanpur, India
[5]School of Computational and Integrative Sciences, Jawaharlal Nehru University, New Delhi, India

Abstract

In this data-driven world, recent technologies are producing high-throughput genomics and biomedical data extensively. An enormous amount of relational data evolves that can interlink the genes, proteins, chemical compounds, drugs, and diseases. As biological networks are very complex and hard to interpret, a significant amount of progress is going on toward the graph or network embedding paradigm that can use for visualization, representation, interpretation, and their correlation. In this technique, diverse input data are systematically integrated to generate a unified vector representation. The current chapter mainly focuses on traditional and current development on the network or graph embedding and their applications in computational biology, genomics, and healthcare. Finally, to gain more biological insight, further quantification and evaluation of the network embedding technique and their key challenges are addressed here.

Keywords: Network embeddings, text mining, multi-omics data, drug-target interaction, protein-protein interaction

*Corresponding author: bioinfonivedta@gmail.com
†*Equal contribution as first author*

A. Suresh, S. Vimal, Y. Harold Robinson, Dhinesh Kumar Ramaswami and R. Udendhran (eds.) *Bioinformatics and Medical Applications: Big Data Using Deep Learning Algorithms*, (73–98) © 2022 Scrivener Publishing LLC

5.1   Introduction

Biological pathways are the epicenter to understand biological processes governed by group of genes that are functionally related [1, 2]. These pathways direct series of event and make biological network that ultimately involved in functional events and reflect the overall importance in building up the necessary process [3]. In this computational era, with ease of the internet and worldwide data availability, social and professional networking has been increased. Networking is a widely used method in various fields of biological sciences, the rapid growth of biomedical data raised concrete questions that we can undertake such as potential network consequences like disease mutations, diagnosis, and drug discovery that can help in treatment decisions. Overall, network biology is combining graph theory, systems biology, and statistical analyses for studying the holistic relationships between various biological components (Figure 5.1) [4].

Diseases mainly cause by combination of factors and biological processes involve a wide range of hierarchically layered intermolecular connections, such as protein-protein interactions (PPIs), protein-DNA interactions, functional gene regulatory modules, and signal transduction [5–7]. Decoding the pathway through which genetic factor affects is a difficult process and solving a complex disease is much more complicated since genetic factors in affected individuals might be different. In this regard, interdisciplinary approaches specifically network approach turn to be the most effective way to serve such diseases in much efficient and effective way [8]. We already have seen the shift in understanding of genetic variation in populations gained a new dimension, turning population genetics into population genomics approaches. These approaches provide scientists the way to quickly analyze genes and their products in no time [9, 10]. Still, these advances finding difficulties due to high rate of false positive results, and inefficient statistical approaches are some [11–13].

In the last 20 years, we have seen a transition phase to decode Human Genome Project, which depict how biological information is organized in a complex manner. Recent shift to "big data analysis in biology" is the key that can answer how these networks are controlling and maintaining the harmony of cell to cell and the whole system [14, 15]. To get answers from complex networks messed with small molecules, genes are always a tricky challenge where network genomics is emerging as a potential answer to decode all the mystery with efficient solution [16].

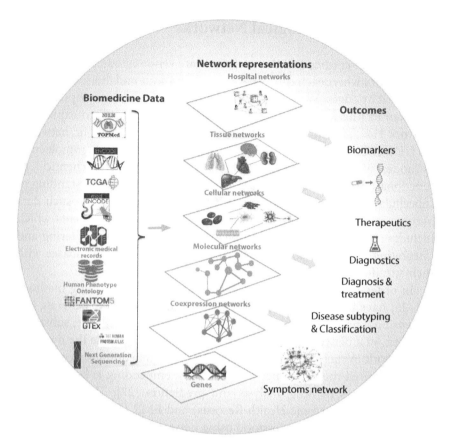

Figure 5.1 Network modeling approach that simplifies multi-omics data from the genome, transcriptome, proteome, and metablome allows the derivation of disease-associated information and outcomes like biomarkers, therapeutics targets, phenotype-specific genes and interactions, and disease subtypes. Source figure from ref [4].

In the last decade, genomics, proteomics, and metabolomics approaches already provided us the fundamental view of molecular aspect of cell in different conditions and these data have the potential to unlock mechanisms behind many complex diseases. Traditional network-based computational methods have given good results in analysis and prediction of drugs. These methods were very time consuming and required high computational and space cost. Network embedding compacts the nodes and edges of the networks but the structural information of the network is preserved.

5.2   Types of Biological Networks

The biological entities and their relations are represented by networks or graph theory where each entity represented by a node and their relationship are shown by edges. Various network approaches have been adopted ranging from PPI network [17], isoform-isoform network [18], co-expression network [19], genetic interaction network [20], and metabolic networks [21]. Describing via nodes and edges with sophisticated macromolecules as "nodes" and the large number of interactions (physical, biochemical, or functional) between them as "edges" offers a first-order understanding of subcellular systems at a global scale. Curation and analysis of such data become important after capturing data from various experiments which includes storage, retrieval, spreading around the world, and filtering and integrating the data. Table 5.1 describes the list of major databases with their specific contribution in network biology.

In order to analyze the graph, various network embedding methods [22–25] have been proposed, where their primary goal is to generate low dimensional network features corresponding to the node, edge, substructure, etc., in a network [26]. The basic principle is to encode the nodes in the network in such a way that the similarity of embedding space semantically captured the whole network. Network embedding is being widely used these days in drug analysis and prediction [27]. The representations of EHR (Electronic Health Records) and EMR (Electronic Medical Records) can be better understood using network embedding techniques. The GRAM model developed by Choi et al. provided better understanding of EHR representations by using hierarchical information inherent to medical ontologies [28].

This chapter is mainly introducing the network embedding as a paradigm in computational biology, genomics, medicine, and healthcare. We further described the latest state-of-the-art adopted in network embedding methods and their application in various fields of biology. Finally, we concluded the limitation and overall summary of network embedding.

5.3   Methodologies in Network Embedding

Network embedding aims to analyze the network problems more efficiently by converting the network into a low-dimensional vector space while maintaining the network structure [29–32]. Network embedding methods are involved in the optimization of the variation between the

Table 5.1 List of major biological network data resources.

Name	Description	Website	References
bioDBnet	bioDBnet is a comprehensive resource of most of the biological databases available from different sites like NCBI, Uniprot, EMBL, Ensembl, and Affymetrix.	https://biodbnet-abcc.ncifcrf.gov/db/db2db.php	[130]
BioGRID	Integrated protein-protein interaction data for all major model organisms.	http://thebiogrid.org	[131]
BioModels	BioModels is a repository of mathematical models of biological and biomedical systems.	https://www.ebi.ac.uk/biomodels/	[132]
Causal Biological Networks	CBN represent causal signaling pathways across a wide range of biological processes including cell fate, cell stress, cell proliferation, inflammation, tissue repair, and angiogenesis in the pulmonary and vascular systems.	http://causalbionet.com/	[133]
Easy Networks Database	esyN is a unique tool as it integrates tools for the creation of network models with an open repository that stores them.	http://www.esyn.org/	[134]

(Continued)

Table 5.1 List of major biological network data resources. (*Continued*)

Name	Description	Website	References
GO	The GO consists of three ontologies: molecular function (MF), biological process (BP), and cellular compartment (CC) each with hierarchically structured protein annotating terms.	geneontology.org	[135]
HPRD	Human protein-protein interaction data.	http://www.hprd.org	[136]
Interactome3D	Manually curated PPIs with known three-dimensional structure information.	http://interactome3d.irbbarcelona.org	[137]
IID	Predictions of human protein-protein interactions at the high resolution of transcript isoforms	http://syslab.nchu.edu.tw/IIIDB.	[138]
KEGG	Manually curated databases of pathways, chemical reactions and drugs based on literature mining, and biological networks based in interaction data.	www.kegg.jp/	[139]
KinomeNetworkX	Integrative kinase-substrate database.	https://bioinfo.uth.edu/kinomenetworkX/	[140]
MINT	Protein-protein interactions in refereed journals.	http://mint.bio.uniroma2.it/mint	[141]

(*Continued*)

Table 5.1 List of major biological network data resources. (*Continued*)

Name	Description	Website	References
Panther	The PANTHER (Protein ANalysis THrough Evolutionary Relationships) Classification System was designed to classify proteins (and their genes) in order to facilitate high-throughput analysis.	http://www.pantherdb.org/about.jsp	[142]
PathwayCommons	A database of biological concepts including biochemical reactions, GRNs, genetic interactions, transport and catalysis events, and physical interactions involving proteins, DNA, RNA, small molecules, and complexes	https://www.pathwaycommons.org/	[143]
PhosphositePlus	Database and tools for the study of protein post-translational modifications (PTMs) including phosphorylation, acetylation, and more.	https://www.phosphosite.org/homeAction.action	[144]
PhosphoNetworks	High-resolution phosphorylation network connecting the specific phosphorylation sites present in substrates with their upstream kinases.	http://www.phosphonetworks.org/	[145]

(*Continued*)

Table 5.1 List of major biological network data resources. (*Continued*)

Name	Description	Website	References
Reactome	Network of biological processes with GO-like hierarchical structure.	https://reactome.org/	[146]
String	Functional protein association networks database.	http://string-db.org	[147]
WikiPathways	WikiPedia-style community-curated and dynamically updated resource for models of biological pathways.	wikipathways.org	[148]

node similarity in the original network and under embedding. In this regard, various network embedding methods have been introduced, which include graph drawing algorithms, which are involved in visualization of graph in 2D space [33], spring-embedder model, a force-directed graph algorithm, designed for analysis and visualization of complex biological molecules [34–37], and Vicus matrix, a local neighboring version of Laplacian matrix, which maintains the original properties of Laplacian matrix and enhances the embedding quality by denoising the network. Viscus-based spectral methods found potential applications in stability of clusters, in network clustering of data from single-cell RNA-seq, and identification of genes involved in cancer [38].

Diffusion-based approaches initially establish a network neighborhood of every node in the network by focusing the nodes in low-dimensional vector spaces, and by taking it as an input, design an objective function to maintain the local and global network structures [24, 39, 40] . A potential method includes Mashup, which utilizes a dimensionality reduction step complementing the traditional random walks, resulting in reduction of noise in these diffusion computations [33]. Another potential network embedding algorithm based on random walks is node2vec [24]. A similar network embedding algorithm is DeepWalk [39], which can be potentially used to predict connection between miRNAs and diseases [41], drug target associations [42], and protein function [43].

Network embedding can be classified into non-attributed network embedding and attributed network embedding as shown in Figure 5.2.

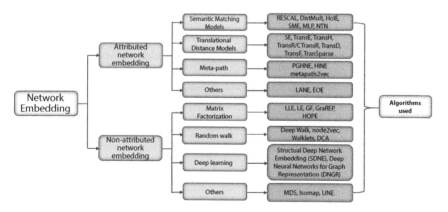

Figure 5.2 Classification of network embedding and algorithms used [17–47].

5.4 Attributed and Non-Attributed Network Embedding

The attributed networks are also termed as heterogeneous networks, of which all nodes and/or edges belong to multiple types. This network involves knowledge graphs, e.g., Freebase [44], DBpedia [45], YAGO [46], PharmGKB [47], DrugBank [48], and TTD [49]. For attributed network embedding, structural uniformity should be contemplated between various tasks. Various models used to tackle these issues involve semantic matching models and translational distance models Figure 5.3. A non-attributed network is also termed as homogeneous network, of which all nodes and edges belong to a single type and not multi type. Embeddings networks aims at maintaining local and global structural property Figure 5.3.

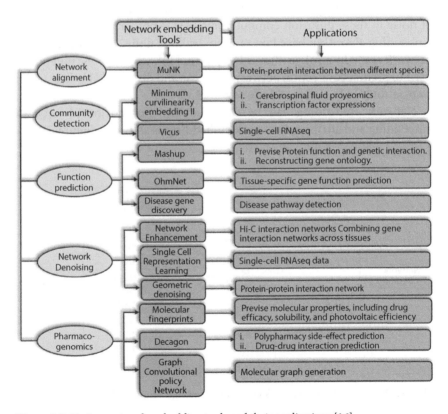

Figure 5.3 Various network embedding tools and their applications [16].

5.5   Applications of Network Embedding in Computational Biology

Network biology is a collective effort of statistics, graph theory methods, topology analysis, information theory, mathematical modeling, machine learning, and visualization tools to deepen our understanding of biological mechanisms [50, 51]. Applied application of these approaches is shown in Figure 5.3.

5.5.1   Understanding Genomic and Protein Interaction via Network Alignment

In computational biology, network alignment expedites in prevising the function of protein and measuring the correspondence between two proteins from different species, utilizing a global network alignment typically aligning PPI network of different species and by transfer of knowledge across these species [52–54]. Based on the similarities between the PPI network, phylogenetic trees can be constructed using network alignment, resulting in better understanding of evolutionary relationship between networks [55, 56]. Also, for carrying out the cellular processes, proteins interact with each other; these proteins are the products of genes and the interconnectivity between these genes can be ignored by genomic sequence alignment; hence, network alignment provides a potential application in understanding the interaction between the proteins leading to complex cellular events [57]. Various global network alignments used includes IsoRank algorithm [58], MAGNA [59], MAGNA++ [60], MuNK [61], WAVE [62], and L-GRAAL [63] and can be categorized as shown in Figure 5.4.

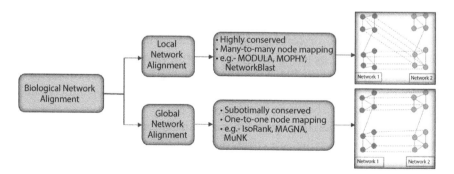

Figure 5.4 Taxonomy of biological network alignment.

5.5.2 Pharmacogenomics

Prevailing demand for therapeutics and their comparatively reduced production poses challenges to pharmaceutical sectors [64, 65]. To overcome such challenges and refine our knowledge about drugs, their side effects, and their interaction with target and other drugs, network embedding emerged as a potential method [66, 67].

5.5.2.1 Drug-Target Interaction Prediction

Downstream activities in a biological system are influenced by the interaction of the drug with its target protein [68]. Drug -target interaction (DTI) prediction can be formulated on a graph of drug and its target protein as a link prediction task [69–72], using network embedding methods such as node2vec [73], DeepWalk [74], and LINE [75], which helps in predicting the drugs having shared target protein or the proteins targeted by similar drugs by calculating the similarity between embeddings [76].

For known DTIs, a graph was obtained depending on the proximity matrix [77] which was then integrated with protein domains and drug side effects [78]. For unknown DTIs, proximity matrix was modified using interaction profiles of k-nearest neighbors for the addition of new drugs and targets [79]. Besides DTIs, heterogeneous frameworks are recently been used which include varied drug-related interactions. In a study, a heterogeneous biological knowledge graph was prepared where DTIs were amalgamated with GO, PPIs, gene-disease interactions, drug side effect, and disease phenotype [80]. A tripartite network composed of drug-target, drug-disease, and target-disease interactions was incorporated with DeepWalk [81].

5.5.2.2 Drug-Drug Interaction

Evaluation of drug-drug interaction is the effect on the activity of one drug when incorporated or consumed by the other drug that is highly significant for patients' health [82–84]. Drug-drug interaction at the cellular level [85, 86] can be predicted utilizing graph convolutional networks [87] where multi-view drug association graphs are embedded for understanding correspondence between two drugs [88, 89].

A different embedding approach can be used for developing new drug therapies and identifying Side effects of drug by constructing a multi-modal graph by combining drug-drug interaction with drug-protein interaction and protein-protein interaction [90].

5.5.2.3   Drug-Disease Interaction Prediction

Association between disease and drugs can be predicted by various network embedding approaches [91], by combining gene-gene, drug-gene, and disease-gene interaction network together and further developing a matrix factorization method [92].

5.5.2.4   Analysis of Adverse Drug Reaction

Any unwanted symptoms or effects of the drug other than the anticipated effects observed at the regular dosage are described as adverse drug reactions (ADRs) [93], which are a concern before any drug developed, and are up for the clinical applications. Figure 5.5 displays diverse network embedding methods that are utilized for the analysis of ADRs [91] including distance-based model similar to SE, TansE, and TransH, which recognize ADR indicated in social media by introducing drug knowledge graphs, DBpedia [94, 95].

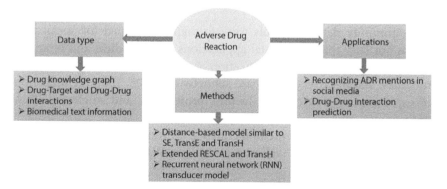

Figure 5.5 Illustration of data and methods used in analysis of Adverse Drug Reaction (ADR) [94, 96, 97].

5.5.3 Function Prediction

Network embedding provides potential applications in predicting the functions of protein and tissue-specific genes, in reconstructing gene ontology, in detection of disease pathways and prediction of genetic interactions [33]. The function of the protein can be predicted by direct counting the proteins with known functions in the neighboring network, an approach described as neighborhood counting [98, 99]. Tissue-specific protein function can be predicted by illustrating the features of protein similar to not only the proteins in the neighboring network but also with the active proteins in the similar tissues [100]. Various tools such as Mashup and OhmNet can be used for the prediction of protein function and tissue-specific protein function respectively. GeneMANIA, a web interface, can be used for predicting the gene function and works by performing label diffusion and functions efficiently on cellular compartment annotations. Mashup helps predicting the protein function utilizing support vector machines (SVMs), a traditional classification technique, and functions efficiently in biological process annotations [33].

5.5.4 Community Detection

Community detection is a potential computational technique for analyzing various networks and identifying the clusters or modules of similar nodes [101] and is useful in understanding the structural organization of network and the relationship between the structure and function [102].

Community detection tools were formally developed for social networks but later found potential applications in biomedical and bioinformatics field [103] such as identification of carriers of cancer [104], protein modules, and discovery of disease subnetworks [105, 106], identification of expression of transcription factors, proteomics, and single-cell RNA sequencing.

Community detection methods include Louvain [107], Infomap [108], label propagation [109], Walktrap [110] DeepWalk [111], and node2vec [112].

Community detections finds a potential application in an emerging field termed as single-cell RNA sequencing, a technique involved interpreting the heterogeneity of cell populations. The method involves clustering on established cell-to-cell networks [113].

5.5.5   Network Denoising

Networks are omnipresent in biology, encrypting connectivity patterns at various levels of organization, from molecular to biome. Constrains in evaluation technology and natural variations impede new network pattern location [114].

Examples include PPI network [114–117], in which intensity of physical interaction between proteins can be used to detect the function of protein [118], but due to technical and biological noises, accurate interpretation is hampered [119, 120]. Another example includes the histone ChIP-seq (chromatin immunoprecipitation followed by sequencing) experiments, which targets histone modifications and helps in profiling the genome-wide chromatin state in cell and tissue population [121]. However, various noises created by sequencing depth, library complexity, and specificity and efficiency of antibody hamper the quality of histone-ChIP experiment [122]. Other networks which are hampered by the noisy interactions include Hi-C netwok [123] and cell-cell interaction network [124].

To overcome these limitations, various computational methods have been introduced for denoising networks, which includes network enhancement (NE), a diffusion-based algorithm for denoising the network [114], diffusion maps [125], and tensor-based dynamical model [126]. For denoising PPI networks and obtaining accurate prediction of protein function, diffusion-state distance (DSD) can be utilized [127]. Network deconvolution (ND) can be used to overcome the issues of transitive edges in networks [128]. Embedding-based method can also be used for network denoising; example includes Mashup [129].

5.5.6   Analysis of Multi-Omics Data

Omics intents in understanding the structures, functions, and dynamics of molecules of the organisms both quantitatively and qualitatively, which can be obtained by implementing relational data analysis in omics and utilizing network embedding that also potentially expedite computational tasks in multi-omics including proteomics, genomics, and transcriptomics [92], as shown in Figure 5.6.

5.6   Limitations of Network Embedding in Biology

Genome-wide pathway analysis allows us to extract the information from the genomic data and allows us to evaluate even the effect of single variant

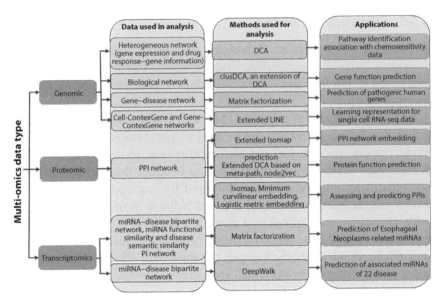

Figure 5.6 Illustration of data and methods used in multi-omics data analysis.

change in the whole genome that particularly later or deregulates the pathway. Data generated from the source have the most potential chances of some level of contamination and can affect these SNPs information accordingly. Dealing with false positive results is the major challenge followed by statistically rigorous approaches.

Among genomic scale network building, source of data and number of samples plays crucial role, and biological networks from single experiment or source remain biased in nature and offer incomplete picture underlying the complex network.

The network embedding technique, DeepWalk, relies on the rigid notion of network neighborhood. It also fails to analyze the closeness of different semantics. DeepWalk and node2vec techniques also fail to capture the similarity naturally observed in real-world networks.

The networks constructed using biomedical data are highly incomplete like the data extracted from EHRs are highly incomplete.

The training of time-sensitive models also is a big challenge in the field of network embedding, as the networks are growing in biomedicine, the results should also evolve following the network topology.

5.7 Conclusion and Outlook

As the field of biomedical research is advancing, the networks are also increasing which are high dimensional, noisy, sparse, and heterogeneous. So, early application of network embedding aids in understanding the topology and knowledge from complex networks. It also eases the projection of high-dimensional networks into low dimensions, thus reducing the space cost.

References

1. Maudsley, S. *et al.*, Bioinformatic approaches to metabolic pathways analysis. Signal Transduction Protocols. Humana Press. *Methods in Molecular Biology Totowa*, NJ. 756, 99–130, 2011.
2. Kumar, N. *et al.*, Integrative network biology framework elucidates molecular mechanisms of sars-cov-2 pathogenesis, *iScience,* 23, 9, 101526, 2020.
3. Alberts, B. *et al.*, Studying gene expression and function, in: *Molecular Biology of the Cell*, 4th edition, Garland Science, 2002.
4. Walhout, M., Vidal, M., Dekker, J. (Eds.), *Handbook of systems biology: concepts and insights*, Academic Press, 2012.
5. Mitra, K. *et al.*, Integrative approaches for finding modular structure in biological networks. *Nat. Rev. Genet.*, 14, 10, 719–732, 2013.
6. MacNeil, L.T. and Walhout, A.J.M., Gene regulatory networks and the role of robustness and stochasticity in the control of gene expression. *Genome Res.*, 21, 5, 645–657, 2011.
7. Abnizova, I., Subhankulova, T., Gilks, W.R., Recent computational approaches to understand gene regulation: mining gene regulation in silico. *Curr. Genomics*, 8, 2, 79–91, 2007.
8. Mulder, S. *et al.*, An integrative systems biology approach for precision medicine in diabetic kidney disease. *Diabetes Obes. Metab.*, 20, 6–13, 2018.
9. Wright, B. *et al.*, From reference genomes to population genomics: comparing three reference-aligned reduced-representation sequencing pipelines in two wildlife species. *BMC Genomics*, 20, 1, 1–10, 2019.
10. Jensen, E.L. *et al.*, Population genomics through time provides insights into the consequences of decline and rapid demographic recovery through head-starting in a Galapagos giant tortoise. *Evol. Appl.*, 11, 10, 1811–1821, 2018.
11. Zhang, B., Tian, Y., Zhang, Z., Network biology in medicine and beyond. *Circ.: Cardiovasc. Genet.*, 7, 4, 536–547, 2014.
12. Yambartsev, A. *et al.*, Unexpected links reflect the noise in networks. *Biol. Direct*, 11, 1, 1–12, 2016.

13. Zhuang, L. *et al.*, A network biology approach to discover the molecular bio-marker associated with hepatocellular carcinoma. *BioMed. Res. Int.*, 2014, 1–6, 2014.

14. Kanaya, S. *et al.*, Big data and network biology. *BioMed. Res. Int.*, 2014, 2, 2014.

15. Arora, D., Chaudhary, R., Singh, A., System biology approach to iden-tify potential receptor for targeting cancer and biomolecular interaction studies of indole [2, 1-a] isoquinoline derivative as anticancerous drug candidate against it. *Interdiscip. Sci.: Comput. Life Sci.*, 11, 1, 125–134, 2019.

16. Borry, P. *et al.*, The challenges of the expanded availability of genomic infor-mation: an agenda-setting paper. *J. Community Genet.*, 9, 2, 103–116, 2017.

17. Safari-Alighiarloo, N. *et al.*, Protein-protein interaction networks (PPI) and complex diseases. *Gastroenterol. Hepatol. Bed Bench*, 7, 1, 17, 2014.

18. Tseng, Y.-T. *et al.*, IIIDB: a database for isoform-isoform interactions and isoform network modules. *BMC Genomics*, 16, S2, BioMed Central, 2015.

19. Mishra, D.C. *et al.*, Weighted gene co-expression analysis for identification of key genes regulating heat stress in wheat. *Cereal Res. Commun.*, 56, 1–9, 2020.

20. Costanzo, M. *et al.*, A global genetic interaction network maps a wiring dia-gram of cellular function. *Science*, 56, 353, 6306, 2016.

21. Stitt, M., Sulpice, R., Keurentjes, J., Metabolic networks: how to identify key components in the regulation of metabolism and growth. *Plant Physiol.*, 152, 2, 428–444, 2010.

22. Perozzi, B., Al-Rfou, R., Skiena, S., Deepwalk: Online learning of social rep-resentations. *Proceedings of the 20th ACM SIGKDD international conference on Knowledge discovery and data mining*, 2014.

23. Tang, J. *et al.*, Line: Large-scale information network embedding. *Proceedings of the 24th international conference on world wide web*, 2015.

24. Grover, A. and Leskovec, J., node2vec: Scalable feature learning for networks. *Proceedings of the 22nd ACM SIGKDD international conference on Knowledge discovery and data mining*, 2016.

25. Ribeiro, L.F.R., Saverese, P.H.P., Figueiredo, D.R., struc2vec: Learning node representations from structural identity. *Proceedings of the 23rd ACM SIGKDD international conference on knowledge discovery and data mining*, 2017.

26. Cai, H., Zheng, V.W., Chang, K.C.-C., A comprehensive survey of graph embedding: Problems, techniques, and applications. *IEEE Trans. Knowl. Data Eng.*, 30, 9, 1616–1637, 2018.

27. Liu, Z. *et al.*, A Survey of Network Embedding for Drug Analysis and Prediction. *Curr. Protein Pept. Sci.*, 22, 3, 237–250, 2020.

28. Choi, E. *et al.*, GRAM: graph-based attention model for healthcare repre-sentation learning. *Proceedings of the 23rd ACM SIGKDD International Conference on Knowledge Discovery and Data Mining*, 2017.

29. Cai, H., Zheng, V.W., Chang, K.C.-C., A comprehensive survey of graph embedding: Problems, techniques, and applications. *IEEE Trans. Knowl. Data Eng.*, 30, 9, 1616–1637, 2018.

30. Wang, Q. *et al.*, Knowledge graph embedding: A survey of approaches and applications. *IEEE Trans. Knowl. Data Eng.*, 29, 12, 2724–2743, 2017.

31. Cui, P. *et al.*, A survey on network embedding. *IEEE Trans. Knowl. Data Eng.*, 31, 5, 833–852, 2018.

32. Goyal, P. *et al.*, Dynamicgem: A library for dynamic graph embedding methods. *J. Mach. Learn Res., arXiv preprint arXiv:1811.10734*, 2018.

33. Nelson, W. *et al.*, To embed or not: network embedding as a paradigm in computational biology. *Front. Genet.*, 10, 3815, 2019.

34. Eades, P., A heuristic for graph drawing. *Congressus numerantium*, vol. 42, pp. 149–160, 1984.

35. Tutte, W.T., How to draw a graph. *Proc. London Math. Soc.*, 3, 1, 743–767, 1963.

36. Fruchterman, T.M.J. and Reingold, E.M., Graph Drawing by Force-directed Placement Software-Practice and Experiences. 21, 11, 1129–1164, 1991.AU: Please provide journal title.

37. Baryshnikova, A., Spatial analysis of functional enrichment (SAFE) in large biological networks, in: *Computational Cell Biology*, pp. 249–268, Humana Press, New York, NY, 2018.

38. Wang, B. *et al.*, Vicus: Exploiting local structures to improve network-based analysis of biological data. *PLoS Comput. Biol.*, 13, 10, e1005621, 2017.

39. Perozzi, B., Al-Rfou, R., Skiena, S., Deepwalk: Online learning of social representations. *Proceedings of the 20th ACM SIGKDD international conference on Knowledge discovery and data mining*, 2014.

40. Tang, J. *et al.*, Line: Large-scale information network embedding. *Proceedings of the 24th international conference on world wide web*, 2015.

41. Li, G. *et al.*, Predicting MicroRNA-disease associations using network topological similarity based on deepwalk. *IEEE Access*, 5, 24032–2403955, 2017.

42. Zong, N. *et al.*, Deep mining heterogeneous networks of biomedical linked data to predict novel drug–target associations. *Bioinformatics*, 33, 15, 2337–2344, 2017.

43. Kulmanov, M., Khan, M.A., Hoehndorf, R., DeepGO: predicting protein functions from sequence and interactions using a deep ontology-aware classifier. *Bioinformatics*, 34, 4, 660–668, 2018.

44. Bollacker, K. *et al.*, Freebase: a collaboratively created graph database for structuring human knowledge. *Proceedings of the 2008 ACM SIGMOD international conference on Management of data*, 2008.

45. Lehmann, J. *et al.*, DBpedia–a large-scale, multilingual knowledge base extracted from Wikipedia. *Semant. Web*, 6, 2, 167–195, 2015.

46. Suchanek, F.M., Kasneci, G., Weikum, G., Yago: a core of semantic knowledge. *Proceedings of the 16th international conference on World Wide Web*, 2007.

47. Klein, T.E. *et al.*, Integrating genotype and phenotype information: an overview of the PharmGKB project. *Pharmacogenomics J.*, 1, 3, 167–170, 2001.

48. Wishart, D.S. *et al.*, DrugBank: a comprehensive resource for in silico drug discovery and exploration. *Nucleic Acids Res.*, 34, suppl_1, D668–D672, 2006.

49. Su, C. *et al.*, Network embedding in biomedical data science. *Briefings Bioinf.*, 21, 1, 182–197, 2020.

50. Zhang, P. and Itan, Y., Biological Network Approaches and Applications in Rare Disease Studies. *Genes*, 10, 10, 797, 2019.

51. Xia, K. and Wei, G.-W., A review of geometric, topological and graph theory apparatuses for the modeling and analysis of biomolecular data. *Biomolecules, arXiv preprint arXiv:1612.01735*, 2016.

52. Elmsallati, A., Clark, C., Kalita, J., Global alignment of protein-protein interaction networks: A survey. *IEEE/ACM Trans. Comput. Biol. Bioinf.*, 13, 4, 689–705, 2015.

53. Faisal, F.E., Zhao, H., Milenković, T., Global network alignment in the context of aging. *IEEE/ACM Trans. Comput. Biol. Bioinf.*, 12, 1, 40–52, 2014.

54. Guzzi, P.H. and Milenković, T., Survey of local and global biological network alignment: the need to reconcile the two sides of the same coin. *Briefings Bioinf.*, 19, 3, 472–481, 2018.

55. Kuchaiev, O. *et al.*, Topological network alignment uncovers biological function and phylogeny. *J. R. Soc. Interface*, 7, 50, 1341–1354, 2010.

56. Kuchaiev, O. and Pržulj, N., Integrative network alignment reveals large regions of global network similarity in yeast and human. *Bioinformatics*, 27, 10, 1390–1396, 2011.

57. Sharan, R. and Ideker, T., Modeling cellular machinery through biological network comparison. *Nat. Biotechnol.*, 24, 4, 427–433, 2006.

58. Singh, R., Xu, J., Berger, B., Global alignment of multiple protein interaction networks with application to functional orthology detection. *Proc. Natl. Acad. Sci.*, 105, 35, 12763–12768, 2008.

59. Saraph, V. and Milenković, T., MAGNA: maximizing accuracy in global network alignment. *Bioinformatics*, 30, 20, 2931–2940, 2014.

60. Vijayan, V., Saraph, V., Milenković, T., MAGNA++: Maximizing Accuracy in Global Network Alignment via both node and edge conservation. *Bioinformatics*, 31, 14, 2409–2411, 2015.

61. Leiserson, M.D., Fan, J., Cannistra, A., Fried, I., Lim, T., Schaffner, T., Crovella, M., Hescott, B., A multi-species functional embedding integrating sequence and network structure. preprint, bioRxiv. 229211, 2017.

62. Sun, Y., Crawford, J., Tang, J., Milenković, T., Simultaneous optimization of both node and edge conservation in network alignment via WAVE, in: *International Workshop on Algorithms in Bioinformatics*, 2015, September, Springer, Berlin, Heidelberg, pp. 16–39.

63. Malod-Dognin, N. and Pržulj, N., L-GRAAL: Lagrangian graphlet-based network aligner. *Bioinformatics*, 31, 13, 2182–2189, 2015.

64. Hodos, R.A., Kidd, B.A., Shameer, K., Readhead, B.P., Dudley, J.T., In silico methods for drug repurposing and pharmacology. *Wiley Interdiscip. Rev.: Syst. Biol. Med.*, 8, 3, 186–210, 2016.

65. Moffat, J.G., Vincent, F., Lee, J.A., Eder, J., Prunotto, M., Opportunities and challenges in phenotypic drug discovery: an industry perspective. *Nat. Rev. Drug Discovery*, 16, 8, 531–543, 2017.

66. Berger, S.I. and Iyengar, R., Network analyses in systems pharmacology. *Bioinformatics*, 25, 19, 2466–2472, 2009.

67. Hopkins, A.L., Network pharmacology: the next paradigm in drug discovery. *Nat. Chem. Biol.*, 4, 11, 682–690, 2008.

68. Imming, P., Sinning, C., Meyer, A., Drugs, their targets and the nature and number of drug targets. *Nat. Rev. Drug Discovery*, 5, 10, 821–834, 2006.

69. Chen, X., Liu, M.X., Yan, G.Y., Drug–target interaction prediction by random walk on the heterogeneous network. *Mol. Biosyst.*, 8, 7, 1970–1978, 2012.

70. Cheng, F., Liu, C., Jiang, J., Lu, W., Li, W., Liu, G., Zhou, W., Huang, J., Tang, Y., Prediction of drug-target interactions and drug repositioning via network-based inference. *PLoS Comput. Biol.*, 8, 5, e1002503, 2012.

71. Gönen, M., Predicting drug–target interactions from chemical and genomic kernels using Bayesian matrix factorization. *Bioinformatics*, 28, 18, 2304–2310, 2012.

72. Isik, Z., Baldow, C., Cannistraci, C.V., Schroeder, M., Drug target prioritization by perturbed gene expression and network information. *Sci. Rep.*, 5, 17417, 2015.

73. Grover, A. and Leskovec, J., node2vec: Scalable feature learning for networks, in: *Proceedings of the 22nd ACM SIGKDD international conference on Knowledge discovery and data mining*, 2016, August, pp. 855–864.

74. Perozzi, B., Al-Rfou, R., Skiena, S., Deepwalk: Online learning of social representations, in: *Proceedings of the 20th ACM SIGKDD international conference on Knowledge discovery and data mining*, 2014b, August, pp. 701–710.

75. Tang, J., Qu, M., Wang, M., Zhang, M., Yan, J., Mei, Q., Line: Large-scale information network embedding, in: *Proceedings of the 24th international conference on world wide web*, 2015, May, pp. 1067–1077.

76. Crichton, G., Guo, Y., Pyysalo, S., Korhonen, A., Neural networks for link prediction in realistic biomedical graphs: a multi-dimensional evaluation of graph embedding-based approaches. *BMC Bioinf.*, 19, 1, 176, 2018.

77. Yamanishi, Y., Araki, M., Gutteridge, A., Honda, W., Kanehisa, M., Prediction of drug–target interaction networks from the integration of chemical and genomic spaces. *Bioinformatics*, 24, 13, i232–i240, 2008.

78. Yamanishi, Y., Kotera, M., Moriya, Y., Sawada, R., Kanehisa, M., Goto, S., DINIES: drug–target interaction network inference engine based on supervised analysis. *Nucleic Acids Res.*, 42, W1, W39–W45, 2014.

79. Ezzat, A., Zhao, P., Wu, M., Li, X.L., Kwoh, C.K., Drug-target interaction prediction with graph regularized matrix factorization. *IEEE/ACM Trans. Comput. Biol. Bioinf.*, 14, 3, 646–656, 2016.

80. Alshahrani, M., Khan, M.A., Maddouri, O., Kinjo, A.R., Queralt-Rosinach, N., Hoehndorf, R., Neuro-symbolic representation learning on biological knowledge graphs. *Bioinformatics*, 33, 17, 2723–2730, 2017.

81. Zong, N., Kim, H., Ngo, V., Harismendy, O., Deep mining heterogeneous networks of biomedical linked data to predict novel drug–target associations. *Bioinformatics*, 33, 15, 2337–2344, 2017.

82. Chan, D.A. and Giaccia, A.J., Harnessing synthetic lethal interactions in anticancer drug discovery. *Nat. Rev. Drug Discovery*, 10, 5, 351–364, 2011.

83. Guthrie, B., Makubate, B., Hernandez-Santiago, V., Dreischulte, T., The rising tide of polypharmacy and drug-drug interactions: population database analysis 1995–2010. *BMC Med.*, 13, 1, 74, 2015.

84. Han, K., Jeng, E.E., Hess, G.T., Morgens, D.W., Li, A., Bassik, M.C., Synergistic drug combinations for cancer identified in a CRISPR screen for pairwise genetic interactions. *Nat. Biotechnol.*, 35, 5, 463, 2017.

85. Ryu, J.Y., Kim, H.U., Lee, S.Y., Deep learning improves prediction of drug-drug and drug–food interactions. *Proc. Natl. Acad. Sci.*, 115, 18, E4304–E4311, 2018.

86. Sridhar, D., Fakhraei, S., Getoor, L., A probabilistic approach for collective similarity-based drug–drug interaction prediction. *Bioinformatics*, 32, 20, 3175–3182, 2016.

87. Kipf, T.N. and Welling, M., Semi-supervised classification with graph convolutional networks. *Machine Learn.*, arXiv preprint arXiv:1609.02907, 2016.

88. Ma, T., Xiao, C., Zhou, J., Wang, F., Drug similarity integration through attentive multi-view graph auto-encoders. *Machine Learn.*, arXiv preprint arXiv:1804.10850, 2018.

89. Veličković, P., Cucurull, G., Casanova, A., Romero, A., Lio, P., Bengio, Y., Graph attention networks. *Machine Learn.*, arXiv preprint arXiv:1710.10903, 2017.

90. Zitnik, M., Agrawal, M., Leskovec, J., Modeling polypharmacy side effects with graph convolutional networks. *Bioinformatics*, 34, 13, i457–i466, 2018.

91. Su, C., Tong, J., Zhu, Y., Cui, P., Wang, F., Network embedding in biomedical data science. *Briefings Bioinf.*, 21, 1, 182–197, 2020.

92. Dai, W., Liu, X., Gao, Y., Chen, L., Song, J., Chen, D., Gao, K., Jiang, Y., Yang, Y., Chen, J., Lu, P., Matrix factorization-based prediction of novel drug indications by integrating genomic space. *Comput. Math. Methods Med.*, 9, 20152015.

93. James, I. and Henry, L., Adverse drug reactions. *Gen. Pract.*, 56, 193, 2007.

94. Stanovsky, G., Gruhl, D., Mendes, P., Recognizing mentions of adverse drug reaction in social media using knowledge-infused recurrent models, in: *Proceedings of the 15th Conference of the European Chapter of the Association*

for Computational Linguistics: Volume 1, Long Papers, 2017, April, pp. 142–151.

95. Lehmann, J., Isele, R., Jakob, M., Jentzsch, A., Kontokostas, D., Mendes, P.N., Hellmann, S., Morsey, M., Van Kleef, P., Auer, S., Bizer, C., DBpedia–a large-scale, multilingual knowledge base extracted from Wikipedia. *Semant. Web*, 6, 2, 167–195, 2015.

96. Zitnik, M. and Zupan, B., Collective pairwise classification for multi-way analysis of disease and drug data, in: *Biocomputing 2016: Proceedings of the Pacific Symposium*, pp. 81–92, 2016.

97. Graves, A., Sequence transduction with recurrent neural networks. *Neural and Evolutionary Comput.*, arXiv preprint arXiv:1211.3711, 2012.

98. Sharan, R., Ulitsky, I., Shamir, R., Network-based prediction of protein function. *Mol. Syst. Biol.*, 3, 1, 88, 2007.

99. Schwikowski, B., Uetz, P., Fields, S., A network of protein–protein interactions in yeast. *Nat. Biotechnol.*, 18, 12, 1257–1261, 2000.

100. Zitnik, M. and Leskovec, J., Predicting multicellular function through multilayer tissue networks. *Bioinformatics*, 33, 14, i190–i198, 2017.

101. Fortunato, S., Community detection in graphs. *Phys. Rep.*, 486, 3–5, 75–174, 2010.

102. Narayanan, T., *Community Detection in Biological Networks* (Doctoral dissertation), UC San Diego, Elsevier, 2013.

103. Barabási, A.L., Gulbahce, N., Loscalzo, J., Network medicine: a network-based approach to human disease. *Nat. Rev. Genet.*, 12, 1, 56–68, 2011.

104. Cantini, L., Medico, E., Fortunato, S., Caselle, M., Detection of gene communities in multi-networks reveals cancer drivers. *Sci. Rep.*, 5, 17386, 2015.

105. Ghiassian, S.D., Menche, J., Barabási, A.L., A DIseAse MOdule Detection (DIAMOnD) algorithm derived from a systematic analysis of connectivity patterns of disease proteins in the human interactome. *PLoS Comput. Biol.*, 11, 4, e1004120, 2015.

106. Menche, J., Sharma, A., Kitsak, M., Ghiassian, S.D., Vidal, M., Loscalzo, J., Barabási, A.L., Uncovering disease-disease relationships through the incomplete interactome. *Science*, 347, 6224, 2015.

107. Blondel, V.D., Guillaume, J.L., Lambiotte, R., Lefebvre, E., Fast unfolding of communities in large networks. *J. Stat. Mech.: Theory Exp.*, 2008, 10, P10008, 2008.

108. Rosvall, M. and Bergstrom, C.T., Multilevel compression of random walks on networks reveals hierarchical organization in large integrated systems. *PLoS One*, 6, 4, e18209, 2011.

109. Raghavan, U.N., Albert, R., Kumara, S., Near linear time algorithm to detect community structures in large-scale networks. *Phys. Rev. E*, 76, 3, 036106, 2007.

110. Pons, P. and Latapy, M., Computing communities in large networks using random walks, in: *International symposium on computer and information sciences*, 2005, October, Springer, Berlin, Heidelberg, pp. 284–293.

111. Perozzi, B., Al-Rfou, R., Skiena, S., Deepwalk: Online learning of social representations, in: *Proceedings of the 20th ACM SIGKDD international conference on Knowledge discovery and data mining*, 2014, August, pp. 701–710).

112. Grover, A. and Leskovec, J., node2vec: Scalable feature learning for networks, in: *Proceedings of the 22nd ACM SIGKDD international conference on Knowledge discovery and data mining*, 2016, August, pp. 855–864.

113. Wang, B., Huang, L., Zhu, Y., Kundaje, A., Batzoglou, S., Goldenberg, A., Vicus: Exploiting local structures to improve network-based analysis of biological data. *PLoS Comput. Biol.*, 13, 10, e1005621, 2017.

114. Wang, B., Pourshafeie, A., Zitnik, M., Zhu, J., Bustamante, C.D., Batzoglou, S., Leskovec, J., Network enhancement as a general method to denoise weighted biological networks. *Nat. Commun.*, 9, 1, 1–8, 2018.

115. Alanis-Lobato, G., Cannistraci, C.V., Ravasi, T., Exploitation of genetic interaction network topology for the prediction of epistatic behavior. *Genomics*, 102, 4, 202–208, 2013.

116. Cannistraci, C.V., Alanis-Lobato, G., Ravasi, T., Minimum curvilinearity to enhance topological prediction of protein interactions by network embedding. *Bioinformatics*, 29, 13, i199–i209, 2013.

117. Chua, H.N. and Wong, L., Increasing the reliability of protein interactomes. *Drug Discovery Today*, 13, 15–16, 652–658, 2008.

118. Zhong, Q., Pevzner, S.J., Hao, T., Wang, Y., Mosca, R., Menche, J., Taipale, M., Taşan, M., Fan, C., Yang, X., Haley, P., An inter-species protein–protein interaction network across vast evolutionary distance. *Mol. Syst. Biol.*, 12, 4, 865, 2016.

119. Rolland, T., Taşan, M., Charloteaux, B., Pevzner, S.J., Zhong, Q., Sahni, N., Yi, S., Lemmens, I., Fontanillo, C., Mosca, R., Kamburov, A., A proteome-scale map of the human interactome network. *Cell*, 159, 5, 1212–1226, 2014.

120. Costanzo, M., VanderSluis, B., Koch, E.N., Baryshnikova, A., Pons, C., Tan, G., Wang, W., Usaj, M., Hanchard, J., Lee, S.D., Pelechano, V., A global genetic interaction network maps a wiring diagram of cellular function. *Science*, 353, 6306, 2016.

121. Kundaje, A., Meuleman, W., Ernst, J., Bilenky, M., Yen, A., Heravi-Moussavi, A., Kheradpour, P., Zhang, Z., Wang, J., Ziller, M.J., Amin, V., Integrative analysis of 111 reference human epigenomes. *Nature*, 518, 7539, 317–330, 2015.

122. Jung, Y.L., Luquette, L.J., Ho, J.W., Ferrari, F., Tolstorukov, M., Minoda, A., Issner, R., Epstein, C.B., Karpen, G.H., Kuroda, M.I., Park, P.J., Impact of sequencing depth in ChIP-seq experiments. *Nucleic Acids Res.*, 42, 9, e74–e74, 2014.

123. Rao, S.S., Huntley, M.H., Durand, N.C., Stamenova, E.K., Bochkov, I.D., Robinson, J.T., Sanborn, A.L., Machol, I., Omer, A.D., Lander, E.S., Aiden, E.L., A 3D map of the human genome at kilobase resolution reveals principles of chromatin looping. *Cell*, 159, 7, 1665–1680, 2014.

124. Wang, B., Zhu, J., Pierson, E., Ramazzotti, D., Batzoglou, S., Visualization and analysis of single-cell RNA-seq data by kernel-based similarity learning. *Nat. Methods*, 14, 4, 414–416, 2017.

125. Coifman, R.R., Lafon, S., Lee, A.B., Maggioni, M., Nadler, B., Warner, F., Zucker, S.W., Geometric diffusions as a tool for harmonic analysis and structure definition of data: Diffusion maps. *Proc. Natl. Acad. Sci.*, 102, 21, 7426–7431, 2005.

126. Wang, B., Jiang, J., Wang, W., Zhou, Z., Tu, Z., Unsupervised metric fusion by cross diffusion, in: *2012 IEEE Conference on Computer Vision and Pattern Recognition*, pp. 2997–3004, 2012.

127. Cao, M., Zhang, H., Park, J., Daniels, N.M., Crovella, M.E., Cowen, L.J., Hescott, B., Going the distance for protein function prediction: a new distance metric for protein interaction networks. *PLoS One*, 8, 10, e76339, 2013.

128. Feizi, S., Marbach, D., Médard, M., Kellis, M., Network deconvolution as a general method to distinguish direct dependencies in networks. *Nat. Biotechnol.*, 31, 8, 726–733, 2013.

129. Cho, H., Berger, B., Peng, J., Compact integration of multi-network topology for functional analysis of genes. *Cell Syst.*, 3, 6, 540–548, 2016.

130. Mudunuri, U. *et al.*, bioDBnet: the biological database network. *Bioinformatics*, 25, 4, 555–556, 2009.

131. Oughtred, R. *et al.*, The BioGRID interaction database: 2019 update. *Nucleic Acids Res.*, 47, D1, D529–D541, 2019.

132. Li, C. *et al.*, BioModels Database: An enhanced, curated and annotated resource for published quantitative kinetic models. *BMC Syst. Biol.*, 4, 1, 1–14, 2010.

133. Boué, S. *et al.*, Causal biological network database: a comprehensive platform of causal biological network models focused on the pulmonary and vascular systems. *Database*, 2015, 2015.

134. Bean, D.M. *et al.*, esyN: network building, sharing and publishing. *PLoS One*, 9, 9, e106035, 2014.

135. Ashburner, M. *et al.*, Gene ontology: tool for the unification of biology. *Nat. Genet.*, 25, 1, 25–29, 2000.

136. Keshava Prasad, T.S. *et al.*, Human protein reference database—2009 update. *Nucleic Acids Res.*, 37, suppl_1, D767–D772, 2009.

137. Mosca, R., Céol, A., Aloy, P., Interactome3D: adding structural details to protein networks. *Nat. Methods*, 10, 1, 47, 2013.

138. Tseng, Y.-T. *et al.*, IIIDB: a database for isoform-isoform interactions and isoform network modules. *BMC Genomics*, 16, S2. BioMed Central, 2015.

139. Kanehisa, M. *et al.*, KEGG: new perspectives on genomes, pathways, diseases and drugs. *Nucleic Acids Res.*, 45, D1, D353–D361, 2017.

140. Cheng, F. *et al.*, Quantitative network mapping of the human kinome interactome reveals new clues for rational kinase inhibitor discovery and individualized cancer therapy. *Oncotarget*, 5, 11, 3697, 2014.

141. Licata, L. *et al.*, MINT, the molecular interaction database: 2012 update. *Nucleic Acids Res.*, 40, D1, D857–D861, 2012.

142. Thomas, P.D. *et al.*, PANTHER: a library of protein families and subfamilies indexed by function. *Genome Res.*, 13, 9, 2129–2141, 2003.

143. Cerami, E.G. *et al.*, Pathway Commons, a web resource for biological pathway data. *Nucleic Acids Res.*, 39, suppl_1, D685–D690, 2010.

144. Hornbeck, P.V. *et al.*, PhosphoSitePlus, 2014: mutations, PTMs and recalibrations. *Nucleic Acids Res.*, 43, D1, D512–D520, 2015.

145. Hu, J. *et al.*, PhosphoNetworks: a database for human phosphorylation networks. *Bioinformatics*, 30, 1, 141–142, 2014.

146. Fabregat, A. *et al.*, The reactome pathway knowledgebase. *Nucleic Acids Res.*, 46, D1, D649–D655, 2018.

147. Szklarczyk, D. *et al.*, The STRING database in 2017: quality-controlled protein–protein association networks, made broadly accessible. *Nucleic Acids Res.*, gkw937, 45, 2016.

148. Kutmon, M. *et al.*, WikiPathways: capturing the full diversity of pathway knowledge. *Nucleic Acids Res.*, 44, D1, D488–D494, 2016.

6

Heart Disease Classification Using Regional Wall Thickness by Ensemble Classifier

Prakash J.[1]*, Vinoth Kumar B.[2] and Sandhya R.[1]

[1]Department of Computer Science and Engineering, PSG College of Technology, Coimbatore, Tamil Nadu, India
[2]Department of Information and Technology, PSG College of Technology, Coimbatore, Tamil Nadu, India

Abstract

In recent years, heart disease is becoming a major problem in human beings. The diverse of syndromes that will infect the heart is known as the heart disease. Cardiac magnetic resonance images are formed using the radio waves and an influential magnetic field, which will produce pictures with a detailed structure of within and around the heart which can be used to identify the cardiac disease through various learning techniques that are used to evaluate the heart's anatomy and function in patients. In this chapter, ensemble classification model is used to classify the type of heart disease. Automated cardiac diagnosis challenge dataset is taken for prediction of heart disease that consists of 150 subjects which is evenly divided among all five classes. The dataset is initially pre-processed to eliminate the noise in image followed by the Region of Interest extraction and segmentation based on densely fully convolutional network, and the feature extraction to extract the values to calculate the ejection fraction value. Based on the Then, the heart disease is classified by using the ejection fraction value representing the regional wall thickness.

Keywords: Ensemble classifier, dense fully convolution network, K-fold cross-validation, confusion matrix, cardiac MRI images, heart regional wall thickness, heart diseases

*Corresponding author: jpk.cse@psgtech.ac.in

A. Suresh, S. Vimal, Y. Harold Robinson, Dhinesh Kumar Ramaswami and R. Udendhran (eds.) *Bioinformatics and Medical Applications: Big Data Using Deep Learning Algorithms*, (99–116) © 2022 Scrivener Publishing LLC

6.1   Introduction

The heart is a significant organ in a human body. The ventricle system is that one in the human body, which will pump the blood through the veins and the arteries. When the heart cannot pump out the blood to the body, then it cannot fulfil the requirements of the body which is called heart failure. The region of heart consists of four chambers which include right ventricle (RV), left ventricle (LV), right atrium (RA), and left atrium (LA). Each chamber can fail independently of the other side, leading to the heart condition of the right heart or the left heart. In India, over the past few years, various studies found that the people affected by heart disease and the death caused by those diseases are significantly increasing. Cardiac magnetic resonance imaging (MRI) permits the simultaneous visualization of both cardiac function and anatomy which is primarily used for diagnosis of Cardiovascular Diseases (CVDs). To compute the regional wall thickness the clinical parameters like ejection fraction, myocardial mass, stroke volume, and ventricular volumes are used, which are estimated by using the accurate method cardiac MRI (Sun *et al.* [1]). Cardiac diseases are a term covering any disorder of the heart. In cardiac MRI, the volumetric analysis of myocardium, RV, and LV is determined to identify cardiac contractile function.

The problem is based on the information about each individual to calculate whether they suffer from heart diseases like Dilated Cardio Myopathy (DCM), Abnormal Right Ventricle (ARV), Hypertrophic Cardio Myopathy (HCM), and Myocardial Infarction (MINF) or Normal (NOR). If the LV ejection fraction is lesser than 40% and abnormal contraction in myocardial, then it is MINF. If the ejection fraction is lower than 40% and the volume of end diastole is higher than 100 ml/m^2 in LV, then it is DCM. If ejection fraction value is normal but myocardial thickness during diastole is 15 mm, then it is called as HCM. If the ejection fraction value is lower than 40% in RV, then it is ARV. Literature reveals that many researchers have used many machine learning algorithms Vinoth *et al.* [10, 11]; Sandhya *et al.* [12] and evolutionary algorithms Vinoth *et al.* [13]; Hemanth *et al.* [14, 15]; Rajesh *et al.* [17] on medical data in order to predict or diagnose the disease Kim *et al.* [20]; Zriqat *et al.* [18]. The major objective of this work is to extract features from segmented image and passing the sequence to a separate classification model, which results in proper classification.

The organization of the paper is organized as follows. Section 6.2 will explain about the various related work, and Section 6.3 will illustrates the various methodology that contains the details about pre-processing, Region of Interest (ROI) extraction, segmentation of heart image, extraction of features, and ensemble classification. The implementation of heart disease classification and result analysis is explained in Section 6.4. In Section 6.5, the work is concluded.

6.2   Related Study

Sharon *et al.* [2] proposed neural networks model to detect in the detection and diagnosis of heart disease like dilated cardiomyopathy and hypertrophic cardiomyopathy. In this method, echocardiogram video is used, where the videos are processed into frames and individual frames are analyzed. Median filter, adaptive weighted median filter, and Fourier idea are used in the pre-processing stage, which will eliminate the noises that are present the frame. The FCM clustering is used to segment the LV. It uses the FCM threshold based on the intensity distribution which is computed using the histogram distribution. Statistical features like histogram, entropy, skewness, and mean are then extracted from the segmented images. By using the back-propagation neural network with Levenberg-Marquard classifier, it is being classified. The accuracy result of the proposed method is 90% in diagnosis of DCM and HCM.

Mahendra *et al.* [3] discuss about a memory efficient architecture based on fully convolution network (FCN) for the analysis of medical image. In this method, a fully convolutional multi-scale residual DenseNet is used in the automated cardiac segmentation (Tran *et al.* [16]). A memory efficient and highly parameter FCN-based architecture are used in segmenting the LV, RV, and myocardium from the short-axis cine magnetic resonance images. Three databases, namely, ACDC 2017 dataset, Kaggle Dataset, and LV11, were used in evaluation of this method. The initial NIfTI format of the dataset is been pre-processed to HDF5 format and followed by the ROI detection to localization of heart. Next, DFCN is used to segment which is efficient in feature mapping of LV, RV, and MYO followed by applying the classification model which uses both ensemble classifier and expert classifier (Bialy *et al.* [19]). This network requires the least number of trainable parameters when compared to other CNN approaches.

Wang *et al.* [4] suggested a segmentation method based on Fuzzy C-Means (FCM) and modified level set known as the automatic LV segmentation model. To decrease the cardiac images inhomogeneous intensity, the method of level set is used to define the estimated bias field and endocardium. Epicardium is segmented by using FCM followed by ROI extraction then the clustering technique of FCM is applied on the myocardium determination and the corrected image in the binary image. Finally, epicardium delineation is done based on the morphologic method. MICCAI 2009 dataset is used for evaluation. The results proved that this method is effective for both the epicardium and endocardium segmentation.

Jelmer *et al.* [5] proposed Convolutional Neural Network which is used to segment the images end systole (ES), myocardium in end diastole (ED), RV, and LV. Random Forest classifier is used to label the patients from the obtained features of segmentation as myocardial infarction, hypertrophic cardiomyopathy, dilated cardiomyopathy, right ventricular abnormality, suffering from heart failure, and no cardiac disease. Any errors during the segmentation shall influence the performance in the classification phase is being the major drawback of this approach. ACDC dataset is used for evaluation and used the ED and ES images. Fourfold stratified cross-validation was used for evaluation. The attained result of average dice score is 0.87 for myocardium, 0.88 for RV, and 0.94 for LV. The study suggested that cine MR cardiac scans have more accuracy in image-based diagnosis.

Nageswararao *et al.* [6] proposed a framework for automatic ventricular analysis using cardiac magnetic resonance images. In this framework, Bias Corrected FCM was used to correct the bias in the dataset. The segmentation was carried using sobel edge detector, and the statistical features like homogeneity, energy, correlation, and contrast are extracted from the main segments. Feedforward back-propagation network and Naïve Bayes classifier are used in disease classification based on the extracted features. The experimental results were verified on real CMR images.

Mahendra *et al.* [7] suggested a Random Forest classifier and a densely connected fully convolutional network (DFCN) for segmentation and heart disease diagnosis. Fourier-based techniques are used for ROI extraction which extracts temporal slices and harmonic images. DenseNet architecture is used for semantic segmentation, and DCM, HCM, ARV, MINF, and normal diseases are classified using Random Forest using 11 attributes. In this, the proposed architecture indicates that, with a very few trainable parameters, we shall achieve a higher performance, if the loss function and the network connectivity are considered appropriately. The proposed model attained a mean dice value of 0.87 for RV, 0.92 for LV, and 0.86 for myocardium.

6.3   Methodology

6.3.1   Pre-Processing

The cardiac MRI images of ACDC dataset are given as input for pre-processing to get the enhanced image. Then, the bilateral filter is applied on the input cardiac MRI images for edge preserving and noise-reducing later smoothing filter is applied on the images which will replace the intensity of each pixel with an average of nearby pixels. The heart metrics is estimated for every image and each input frame of the nifty format is pre-processed into HDF5 format (Prakash J. [8]). The patients are grouped according to their heart metrics. The overall architecture of the heart disease classification is shown in Figure 6.1.

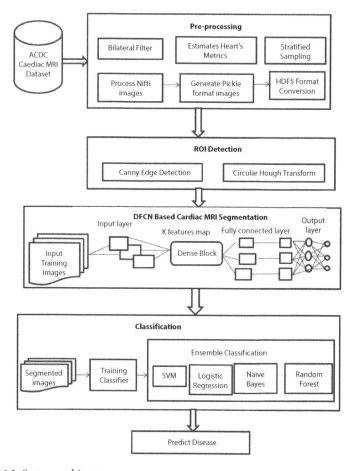

Figure 6.1 System architecture.

Pseudocode 6.1 Pre-processing of image
Input: *ACDC cardiac MRI dataset*
Output: *Pre-processed images*
   Read *Cardiac MRI images*
   Apply *Bilateral filter*
   Estimate *Heart metrics*
   for *each input frame*
            Process *NIfTI format and convert it into HDF5 format*
            Group *Patients based on heart metrics*
   End for

6.3.2   Region of Interest Extraction

Extracting the particular portion of an image to perform an operation is known as the ROI extraction. In this work, the ROI extraction is used to localize the heart from the pre-processed image which is used to define the structure of heart from neighboring tissues to find a nearby LV center and then extract a patch around it. Circular Hough Transform and canny edge detection are used for extraction. In Circular Hough Transform, the radius of the smallest and largest circles is estimated in millimeters from the training set, and then, it is converted to pixel count. By using it, the Hough circles are found and two radii are detected. For each radius, numbers of peaks are extracted, and most likely, ROI centers are selected. Then, the ROI radius is determined which returns the center and radius of ROI region. Canny edge detection is used to detect a wide range of edges in image. By using the canny edge detector, the contour voxels for each subgroup is identified. Figure 6.2 illustrates the ROI extraction of a normal person.

Pseudocode 6.2 ROI extraction
Input: *Processed dataset*
Output: *Localization of heart region in MRI*
   Determine *Radius of small and large circles from the dataset in millimeters.*
   Convert *into pixel counts*
   Find *Hough circle and detect two radii*
   For *each radius extract number of peaks*
   Select *most likely ROI*
   Determine *radius of ROI*
   Return *center and radii of ROI region*

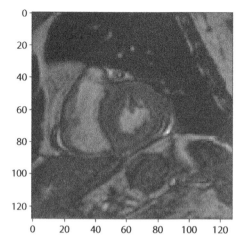

Figure 6.2 Localization of heart.

6.3.3   Segmentation

It is a technique that converts an image representation into simple form with more meaningful and easier to analyze. In this work, DFCN algorithm is used for segmentation which consists of modular blocks. The localized heart used as an input for the dense block initial layer which creates a k number of new feature maps. Then, the localized heart is given as input for the second layer with the new feature map. The same procedure is looped for thrice. The concatenation output of the three layers (i.e., 3 * k feature maps) is the outcome of the dense block. Here, the dense block is composition of batch normalization (i.e., standardized the input that reduces the number of epochs training), exponential linear unit (i.e., for negative values [a*(ez − 1)] where a is a positive value), convolution layer with 3 × 3 and dropout layer. In order to decrease feature maps spatial resolution, transition down is used as a network to increase the spatial resolution of feature map and then transition up is performed. Thus, the segmentation is performed and produces segmented images as output. Figure 6.3 represents the segmentation result.

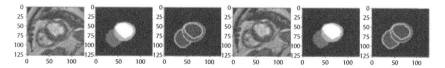

Figure 6.3 Outcome of segmentation.

Pseudocode 6.3 Segmentation of cardiac MRI
Input: Localized heart region
Output: Segmented images.
   Initial Layer *Create k number of new feature maps.*
   Inputted *localized heart is given to the second layer with new feature maps.*
   In next layer **loop** *the above procedure for three times*
   Concatenate *the output of the three layers.*
   Perform *transition down to decrease feature maps spatial resolution.*
   Perform *transition up to increase spatial resolution of feature map.*

6.3.4   Feature Extraction

The segmented images are given as input to extract the features. In this work, the feature extraction is used to extract the important features which are used to classify the disease later. The feature extraction is performed by using the Random Forest classifier which has 1,000 trees. The Random Forest classifier returns 20 features such as volume at ED and volume at ES. Then, by using these extracted features, the ejection fraction value is calculated as follows:

$$EF\,(\%) = \frac{SV}{EDV} * 100 \tag{6.1}$$

where SV (stroke volume) = EDV − ESV. The ejection fraction value represents the thickness of the region of the heart. Figure 6.4 illustrates the important features that are generated by the Random Forest classifier.

Pseudocode 6.4 Feature extraction
   Input: Segmented images
   Output: Calculated Ejection Fraction.
      Get *Segmented image.*
      Extract *Feature like end systole and diastole of both RV and LV.*
      Calculate *Ejection Fraction using Equation (6.1).*

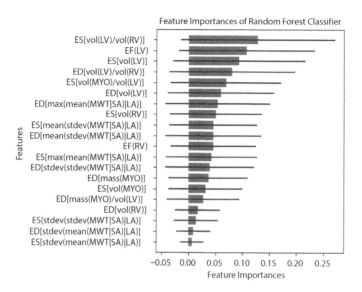

Figure 6.4 Feature extraction.

6.3.5   Disease Classification

The extracted features are being classified based on the disease. To classify the Heart MRI images into any one of the five classes. The ensemble classification is used to classify the disease where ensemble classifier is the combination of different classifier which produces the output based on the higher probability. Here, the classifier used under ensemble classifier is Random Forest classifier, Naïve Bayes classifier, XG Boost classifier, Support Vector Machine (SVM) classifier, MultiLayer Perceptron (MLP) classifier, K-Nearest Neighbor (KNN) classifier, and Logistic regression classifier. By using these classifier results, the ensemble classifier produces the best accuracy in disease classification.

Pseudocode 6.5 Disease classification
Input: *Calculated ejection fraction value.*
Output: *Disease Classification.*
    Create *Ensemble classifier comprising Support Vector Machine, Multilayer perceptron, Gaussian Naïve Bayes, Random Forest.*
    Train *the classifier independently.*
    Finalize *the predicted disease using voting classifier.*

6.4 Implementation and Result Analysis

6.4.1 Dataset Description

The ACDC 2017 (Automated Cardiac Diagnosis Challenge) dataset is used to evaluate this work (Bernard *et al.* [9]). This dataset is comprised of 150 subjects which are equally spread subcategories of four pathological and one healthy group. The names of the subgroups are HCM, DCM, ARV, MINF, and NOR. The dataset is provided with the height, weight, and systolic and diastolic phases for each patient. The 100 subject is taken for the training purpose, while the other 50 subjects are taken for the testing purpose. By the clinical experts, manual annotations of RV, LV, and MYO at diastolic and systolic phase are done.

6.4.2 Testbed

The methods were realized using Python in Google Colab IDE which is implemented on Intel Pentium Quad Core N4200 processor of 1.6 GHz, with 4 GB of RAM and 15-GB drive space. The deep learning environment was obtained using Google Colab which provided free Tesla K80 GPU. Some of the library packages used for the implementation include Numpy, TensorFlow, and Pandas.

6.4.3 Discussion

In this section, we discuss about the outcomes of various stages of disease classification. In the initial stage of pre-processing, the preparation of dataset is made by converting the image from NIfTI format to pickle format and then into HDF5 format. Then, the heart structure and appropriate region of heart LV is localized.

In medical image segmentation, it is found that architectures based on deep fully convolution neural network has revealed better results. With many number of parameters and insufficient training samples, it may lead to poor generalization and overfitting. So, a memory efficient fully convolution neural network and novel parameter-based architecture is used in this medical image analysis. In the segmentation, the features that are handcrafted and the parameters that are relevant clinically are extract; this will reflect on the diagnostic analysis that are used in training the ensemble system for classification.

The feature extraction is used to extract the important features that are useful in calculate the ejection fraction value. Myocardium (MYO), the volume of RV, and the volume of LV are extracted. The details of features extracted are shown in Table 6.1. The feature ejection fraction is also calculated by using the value of ED and ES.

The classification of disease was made by an ensemble classification system using two-stage classification. In this, multiple classifiers called as ensemble classifier are created and strategically combined. The ensemble classifier will make sure that the overall threat may be owing to poor selection of model and that can be reduced. The fivefold cross-validation scores are used in estimating the classifier accuracy. With the scores obtained from the cross-validation, the classifiers that are top performing are selected for joining into the ensemble system. During the initial phase of the ensemble, a voting classifier based on maximum vote is used to finalize the predicted disease. Then, ensemble classification on both ES and ED phase and five different cardiac diseases are predicted and final results are stored in text file with patient id. The accuracy of the classification model is evaluated for the given test set. K-fold cross-validation and confusion matrix are the evaluation metrics used to evaluate this work.

Table 6.1 Details of the extracted features.

Feature	Right Ventricle (RV)	Left Ventricle (LV)	Myocardium (MYO)
End Systole (ES) Volume	YES	YES	YES
End Diastole (ED) Volume	YES	YES	YES
Ejection Fraction (EF)	YES	YES	-
Ratio: End Systole [volume (Left Ventricle)| volume (Right Ventricle)]	YES	YES	-
Ratio: End Diastole [volume (Left Ventricle)| volume (Right Ventricle)]	YES	YES	-
Ratio: End Diastole [volume (Myocardium)| volume (Left Ventricle)]	-	YES	YES
Ratio: End Systole [volume (Myocardium)| volume (Left Ventricle)]	-	YES	YES

6.4.3.1   K-Fold Cross-Validation

This metric is one of the most powerful evaluation metrics which split the dataset into k different folds. In this work, the dataset is categorized to five different folds; hence, it is called as fivefold cross-validation. During the initial iteration, the first fold will be used in testing the model, while the other folds are used in training the model. At the next iteration, the second fold will be used in testing the model, while the other folds will be used in training the model. This will be iterated until all the five folds are been used as training set. The accuracy score for each classification model is illustrates in Table 6.2.

6.4.3.2   Confusion Matrix

This is one of the metrics, which will provide you with the summary of classification problem results. In this confusion matrix, the prediction values are summarized as count. This matrix will also depict about which model of classification is confused when it makes prediction. In neural network, confusion matrix basically gives an idea about how well the classifier has performed, with respect to performance on individual subgroups. So, typically, a confusion matrix is filled up based on the test set whose true labels are known. Figures 6.5 to 6.12 illustrate confusion matrix for ensemble classification, KNN classifier, SVM classifier, XG Boost classifier, Logistic regression classifier, MLP classifier, Random Forest classifier, and Naïve Bayes classifier, respectively. The ensemble classification confusion matrix is generated using MLP based on voting classifier which has highest accuracy score.

Table 6.2 Accuracy score of classification models.

Classification models	Ensemble classification
Logistic regression	0.88
Radom forest	0.84
Naïve Bayes	0.84
XG boost	0.82
MLP	0.82
KNN	0.80
SVM	0.88

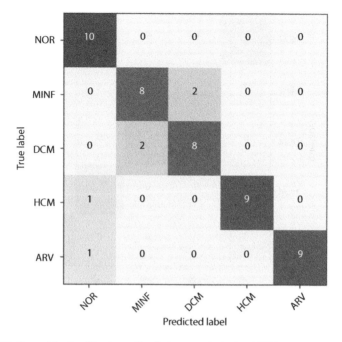

Figure 6.5 Ensemble classification—Confusion matrix (using MLP).

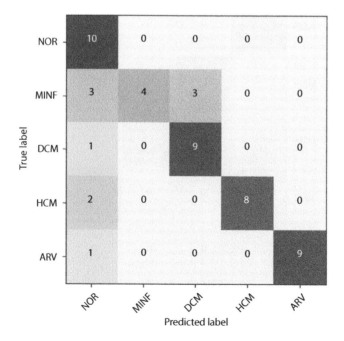

Figure 6.6 KNN classification—Confusion matrix.

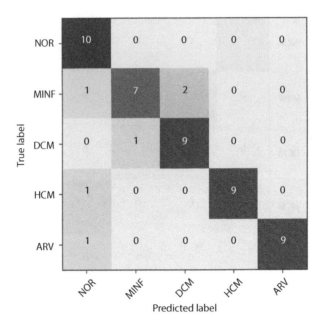

Figure 6.7 SVM classifier—Confusion matrix.

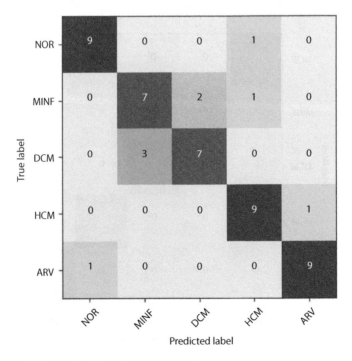

Figure 6.8 XG Boost classifier—Confusion matrix.

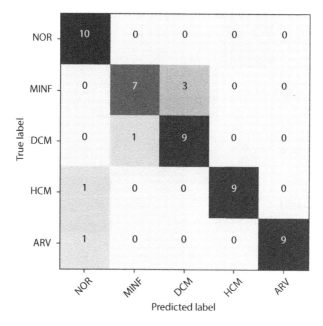

Figure 6.9 Logistic regression classifier—Confusion matrix.

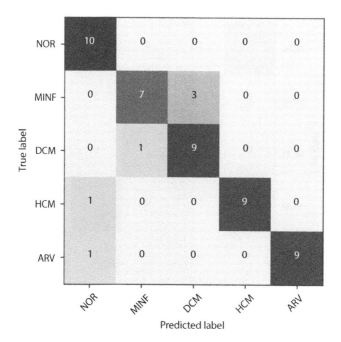

Figure 6.10 MLP classifier—Confusion matrix.

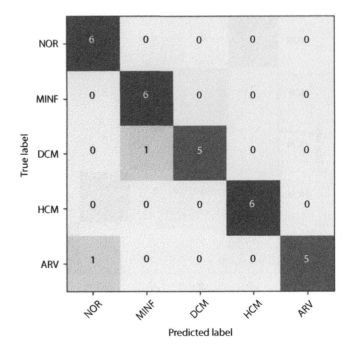

Figure 6.11 Random forest classifier—Confusion matrix.

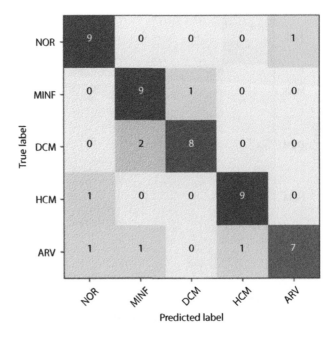

Figure 6.12 Naïve Bayes classifier—Confusion matrix.

6.5   Conclusion

In this chapter, the heart disease classification based on regional wall thickness was performed by considering the ACDC 2017 dataset. Initially, densely fully convolutional network was used in segmentation of myocardium, RV, LV, and in the image. After the segmentation, the important features are extracted from the segmented images by using the Random Forest classification. By using the extracted ejection fraction value, the thickness of the heart region is estimated. Then, the patients are classified according to their classes using ensemble classifier that uses voting classifier. The ensemble classifier used seven different classifiers, namely, SVM classifier, MLP classifier, Random Forest classifier, KNN classifier, Logistic regression classifier, Naïve Bayes classifier, and XG Boost classifier. The confusion matrix and fivefold cross-validation metrics were used for evaluating the classification. The results suggest that the ensemble classifier shows 88% accuracy in the disease classification.

References

1. Sun, H., Tobon-Gomez, C., Das, S.R., Huguet, M., Yushkevich, P.A., Frangi, A.F., Ventricularwall thickness analysis in acute myocardial infarction and hypertrophic cardiomyopathy. *2009 IEEE International Symposium on Biomedical Imaging: From Nano to Macro*, 2009.

2. Jenifa Sharon, J. and Jani Anbarasi, L., Diagnosis of DCM and HCM Heart Diseases Using Neural Network Function. *Int. J. Appl. Eng. Res.*, 13, 10, 8664–8668, 2018.

3. Khened, M., Kollerathu, V.A., Krishnamurthi, G., Fully convolutional multi-scale residual DenseNets for cardiac segmentation and automated cardiac diagnosis using ensemble of classifiers. *Med. Image Anal.*, 51, 21–45, 2019.

4. Wang, L., Ma, Y., Zhan, K., Ma, Y., Automatic left ventricle segmentation in cardiac MRI via level set and fuzzy C-means. *2015 2nd International Conference on Recent Advances in Engineering & Computational Sciences (RAECS)*, 2015.

5. Wolterink, J.M., Leiner, T., Viergever, M.A., Išgum, I., Automatic segmentation and disease classification using cardiac cine MR images. *Lect. Notes Comput. Sci.*, 10663, 101–110, 2018.

6. Nageswararao, A.V. and Srinivasan, S., A framework on automated ventricular analysis of CMR images. *2017 Trends in Industrial Measurement and Automation (TIMA)*, 2017.

7. Khened, M., Alex, V., Krishnamurthi, G., Densely connected fully convolutional network for short-axis cardiac cine MR image segmentation and heart diagnosis using random forest. *Lect. Notes Comput. Sci.*, 10663, 140–151, 2018.

8. Prakash, J., Enhanced Mass Vehicle Surveillance System. *J. Res.*, 4, 3, 5–9, 2018.

9. Bernard, O., Lalande, A., Zotti, C., Cervenansky, F., Yang, X., Heng, P.-A., Cetin, I. *et al.*, Deep learning techniques for automatic MRI cardiac multi-structures segmentation and diagnosis: Is the problem solved? *IEEE Trans. Med. Imaging*, 37, 11, 2514–2525, 2018.

10. Vinoth Kumar, B., Sabareeswaran, S., Madumitha, G., A decennary survey on artificial intelligence methods for image segmentation, in: *Advanced Engineering Optimization Through Intelligent Techniques*, pp. 291–311, 2019.

11. Sandhya, R. and Prakash, J., Comparative analysis of clustering techniques in anomaly detection wind turbine data. *J. Xi'an Univ. Archit. Technol.*, 12, 3, 5684–5694, 2020.

12. Vinoth Kumar, B., Karpagam, G.R., Devi, I., A survey of machine learning techniques. *Int. J. Comput. Syst. Eng.*, 3, 4, 203, 2017.

13. Vinoth Kumar, B., Karpagam, G.R., Zhao, Y., Evolutionary algorithm with memetic search capability for optic disc localization in retinal fundus images, in: *Intelligent Data Analysis for Biomedical Applications*, pp. 191–207, 2019.

14. Prakash, J., Vinoth Kumar, B., Shyam Ganesh, C.R., A comparative analysis of deep learning models to predict dermatological disorder. *J. Xi'an Univ. Archit. Technol.*, 12, 11, 630–639, 2020.

15. Hemanth, D.J., Kumar, B.V., Manavalan, G.R., An evolutionary memetic weighted associative classification algorithm for heart disease prediction, in: *Recent Advances on Memetic Algorithms and its Applications in Image Processing*, Springer Nature, Basingstoke, 2019.

16. Tran, P.V., A fully convolutional neural network for cardiac segmentation in short-axis MRI. *arXiv preprint arXiv:1604.00494*, 1–21, 2017.

17. Rajesh, R. and Mathivanan, B., Predicting flight delay using ANN with multi-core map reduce framework, in: *Communication and Power Engineering*, p. 280, Walter de Gruyter GmbH & Co KG, Berlin, 2017.

18. Zriqat, I.A., Altamimi, A.M., Azzeh, M., A comparative study for predicting heart diseases using data mining classification methods. *International Journal of Computer Science and Information Security (IJCSIS)*, 14, 12, 868–879. https://arxiv.org/abs/1704.02799, 2017.

19. El Bialy, R., Salama, M.A., Karam, O., An ensemble model for Heart disease data sets. *Proceedings of the 10th International Conference on Informatics and Systems - INFOS '16*, 2016.

20. Kim, H., Ishag, M., Piao, M., Kwon, T., Ryu, K., A Data Mining Approach for Cardiovascular Disease Diagnosis Using Heart Rate Variability and Images of Carotid Arteries. *Symmetry*, 8, 6, 47, 2016.

7

Deep Learning for Medical Informatics and Public Health

K. Aditya Shastry[1]*, Sanjay H. A.[2], Lakshmi M.[1] and Preetham N.[1]

[1]Department of Information Science and Engineering, Nitte Meenakshi Institute of Technology, Yelahanka, Bangalore, Karnataka, India
[2]M S Ramaiah Institute of Technology, Bengaluru, India

Abstract

The technology and healthcare intersect to constitute medical informatics (MI). MI enhances the outcomes of patients and healthcare through the skills of medical and computer sciences. The fusion of both these disciplines enables the related personnel to improve the patient care along with the research and clinical settings. Public health (PH) represents the science of safeguarding and improving community health. In this regard, deep learning (DL) represents an interesting area of research. DL application has been observed in several domains due to the fast growth of both data and computational power. In recent years, the application of DL in the domain of MI has increased due to the probable advantages of DL applications in healthcare. DL can aid medical experts in diagnosing several illnesses, detecting sites of cancer, determining the impacts of medicines on each patient, comprehending the association among phenotypes and genotypes, discovering novel phenotypes, and forecasting the outbreaks of contagious illnesses with higher precision. This chapter emphasizes on DL techniques applied in MI and PH, recent case studies related to the application of DL in MI and PH, and certain critical research questions.

Keywords: Deep learning, medical informatics, public health

*Corresponding author: adityashastry.k@nmit.ac.in

A. Suresh, S. Vimal, Y. Harold Robinson, Dhinesh Kumar Ramaswami and R. Udendhran (eds.)
Bioinformatics and Medical Applications: Big Data Using Deep Learning Algorithms, (117–146)
© 2022 Scrivener Publishing LLC

7.1 Introduction

For analysis of data layered algorithmic architecture such as DL or deep structured learning is employed. Hierarchical learning is another name given to DL which is a type of machine learning (ML). The models in DL filters data through numerous hidden layers. Each successive layer utilizes the output from previous layer to predict its results. Accuracy can be achieved by processing more data and refining the previous results that can lead to more correlations and connections. The idea for DL is roughly centered on the basic connection of biological neurons with one another in the brains of animals to process information. It is similar to how electrical signals travel across cells in living organisms. The nodes in the subsequent layer get activated when they receive a stimulus from their neighboring neurons [1].

Figure 7.1 demonstrates the fundamental design of a DL architecture.

As demonstrated in Figure 7.1, the network model comprises of many hidden layers with each layer containing several neurons. When each layer is allocated a portion of a transformation task, the layers process the data

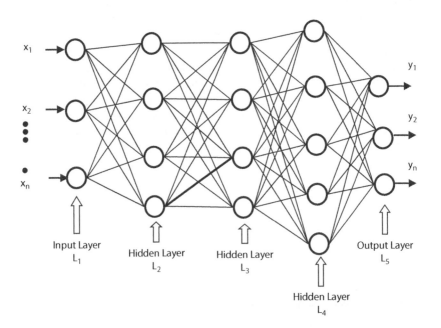

Figure 7.1 DL architecture [2].

multiple times to further refine and optimize the final output. Mathematical translation tasks are used by hidden layers to turn a raw input to a more significant output [2, 3].

Pre-processing of data is comparatively less in DL techniques. The filtering and normalization tasks in several other ML techniques need to be completed by a human programmer, whereas in DL, it is handled by the network only. As specified in article Nature, the conventional ML techniques have limited capacity for processing raw data.

For decades, substantial domain proficiency and cautious engineering was needed for creating an ML system for devising an attribute extractor capable of converting raw data (like values of image pixels) into an appropriate vector of attributes. This transformed data is given to the learning subsystem, usually a classifier, that could identify or classify patterns. DL networks have the capability to determine the patterns needed for automatic classification which reduces the need for supervision and which, in turn, helps speeding up the procedure of mining the essential understandings from datasets that have not been as extensively organized. DL models utilize advanced mathematical models for development of networks. Several variations of networks exist that control different sub-strategies within this field. The developing discipline of DL is very quickly powering the advanced computing capabilities in the world, bridging every industry and adding substantial value to user experiences and viable decision-making [1].

MI and systems which are related to supporting decisions form the basic components for DL in health informatics. The researchers train the models by feeding the data obtained from the clinical information provided by the clinicians by analyzing the patient condition. Data may include reading clinical images, outcome prediction, determining the relationships among genotypes and phenotypes or between the disease and phenotype, studying the response to the treatment, and tracking an abrasion/change in structure. Predicting results of a disease based on analysis of risks can be extended to develop a system that detects early symptoms of a disease. Recognizing correlations and patterns can be drawn-out to global pattern research and population healthcare, providing predictive treatment for the total population [2, 3].

DL in MI can be trained without a prior knowledge, which results in lack of labeled data and is a burden on clinicians. For instance, the target points that were overlapped and 3D/4D medical images dealt with complexity of data. Scientists delivered improved and understandable results by employing supervised/semi-supervised learning, transfer learning, and augmentation of information and architectures related to multi-modality [4–8]. Additionally, the research assisted the scientists in determining non-linear associations among variables which, in turn, assisted the medical experts in understanding the illness and its related solutions. Since decisions are based on data provided, no models or human interference can divide the category into subgroups according to their clinical data. Sequences of Ribonucleic Acid (RNA)/Deoxyribonucleic acid (DNA) in bioinformatics were researched to recognize alleles of genes along with ecological aspects that caused the illnesses. Secondly, it assisted in examining the interactions between proteins, comprehend processes at a higher level, devise therapies that were customized, determine resemblances among two phenotypes, etc. [9].

DL algorithms were applied to predict the interweaving movement of exons, the characteristics of the binding proteins of RNA/DNA, and DNA methylation [10–12]. Thirdly, it validates its effectiveness, particularly when predicting rapidly developing diseases such as acute renal failure. Instead of regular medical visits, research determined that it is adequate to employ novel phenotypes for forecasting in real time [13–21]. Fourth, it is anticipated to be extensively utilized for transferred patients, for first time inpatients, outpatients lacking the information of charts, and weak healthcare infrastructure patients [22, 23].

For instance, neuro signals such as EEG and PPG are utilized to forecast the freezing of Parkinson's illness. Also, information from accelerometer and mobile apps are employed for screening health status, arthritis, diabetes, heart-related illnesses, and chronic diseases for offering information related to health before the patients undergo hospitalization in emergency situations [24, 25]. Also, analysis of X-ray images captured by a mobile phone helped for treating marginalized communities and resource-poor people [26]. Clinical notes together with discharge notes summarization are intended to determine how summarization records express accurate, effective, and reliable information for comparing the information with medical records. Finally, social behavior, disease outbreaks, research related to medicines, and analysis of treatments have proven to avoid illnesses and lengthen life along with the monitoring of epidemics [2, 27–33].

Several hospitals are making use of the Electronic Health Record (EHR) systems. As per [34, 35], around 70% of clinicians and 90% of USA hospitals are utilizing EHR system for improving their competence levels and efficiency. Patient information can be recorded by employing technologies related to imaging, genomes, and sensors that are wearable. DL architectures with advanced computation power support GPUs have a major impact on the practical acceptance of DL. Hence, several experimental works have applied DL models for MI which is mostly being utilized by several clinical experts. Yet, the DL application to health informatics leaves us with a number of challenges that must be resolved, including lack of data (missing values, expensive labeling, and class imbalance), data interpretation (heterogeneity, high dimensionality, and multi-modality), reliability of information and integrity, reliability, and model interpretability (convergence issues and tracking along with overfitting), feasibility, scalability, and security [2].

The chapter remainder has four sections. The second section emphasizes the different DL methods in MI and PH. The third section demonstrates how DL can be applied in the field of MI and PH with different real-world case studies. The fourth section analyzes the various research issues related to DL in MI and PH that can be determined by various stakeholders in healthcare. The summary of the chapter is given at the end.

7.2 Deep Learning Techniques in Medical Informatics and Public Health

In this segment, we elaborate the operational functions of five DL models in which each model has various forms. When an input is given, an expected output is produced according to the fundamental principle of approximating a function. The diverse models are better suited to manage diverse challenges and diverse data types for performing the expected tasks [36].

The speech or time series classification model is comparatively different from that of image classification. The data dimensionality is reduced by applying a pre-processing phase in the models. Primarily, the model structure consists of several interconnected neurons to each other and hidden layer that links the input to the output. Consequently, an activation sequence is generated via the weighted connection from the neurons. This process is known as feedforward [37]. Comparison between DL and Artificial Neural Network (ANN) models puts forward the fact that DL model includes more of hidden layers than ANN. ANN model can be prepared only for supervised learning jobs whereas DL is used for training both unsupervised and supervised learning jobs. Output layer results are compared with the actual value at the end of the feedforward process. An error value is computed by calculating the difference in the values of predicted and actual targets. As the process of feedforward concludes, the weights of the ANN model are updated in order to reduce this error and make the predicted and actual values closer. This technique is known as backpropagation [38, 39].

7.2.1   Autoencoders

Autoencoder (AE) is intended for extraction of features by utilizing information driven learning. AE is subjected to unsupervised training since the training takes place for recreating the input vector instead of assigning the class label. Similar number of input and output neurons is present in AE with the neurons being fully connected (FC) with those of the next layers. The input neuron number is typically lesser than the hidden neuron number. The reason for this design is to code information in reduced feature space and to accomplish the mining of attributes. Whenever data dimensionality is high, several AEs are stacked together for the creation of a deep AE system. Several variants of AE have been devised over the previous decade for handling diverse patterns of data and for executing particular functions. For instance, Vincent *et al.* [40] proposed the denoising AE. Its purpose was to strengthen the traditional AE model. This technique reconstructs the input by inducing certain disturbances to the patterns, consequently compelling the design to grasp the input design.

Sparse AE represents another variant of the classic AE model. In this variant, sparse representation is utilized for making the data more separable [41]. Another variant of AE known as the convolutional AE [42] incorporates shared weights among nodes for processing 2D patterns and preserving spatial locality. Contractive AE is like denoising AE, yet as opposed to inducing noise to disrupt the training dataset, it alters the function to determine error by including analytical contractive cost [43, 44]. The learning procedure for AE is depicted as limiting a cost function C with the end goal that C (k, m(t(u))). t(u) is a capacity that maps u to h and the capacity k maps h to the output that is a reproduction of the input. r denotes the weight interfacing the layers. Figure 7.2 demonstrates the simple architecture of AE.

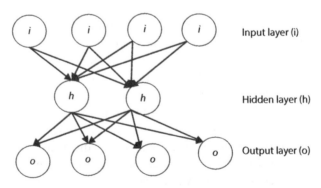

Figure 7.2 Autoencoders [36].

Figure 7.2 shows the design of a simple AE demonstrating the i, h, and o layers. The direction of the arrows depicts the interconnection between the neurons.

7.2.2   Recurrent Neural Network

Recurrent neural network (RNN) is a category of DL that comprises of associations with neurons in the "h" layer to create a series of directed graph. This component provides it a progressive unique mechanism. This is significant in situations where the output relies upon the past calculations, for example, the examination of texts, noises, Deoxyribonucleic acid (DNA) groupings, and persistent electrical body signs. The RNN training is done on information having dependencies for maintaining info about the preceding interval. Performance outcome at time "t – 1" impacts the selection at time t. It deliberates the preceding output (O) and the current input (I), and a number in the range of 0 to 1 are generated from the cell state M. Here, 1 denotes saving the value, while 0 signifies discarding the value.

Sigmoid layer (Gate layer) makes this choice. Hence, the RNN principle defines the recurring function with respect to time steps that are done utilizing the equation: $M = f(M \times W \times I \times W)$, where M signifies time state k, M denotes previous gate output, I represents input at time k, and W is the network weight parameters. The RNN can be regarded as a state that comprises of the feedback loop [45]. Feedforward RNN implementation is demonstrated in Figure 7.3.

The outcome of the output layer is looped back as input part to the input layer. The I_t and O_t denote the input and output at time t, and O_{t-1} represents

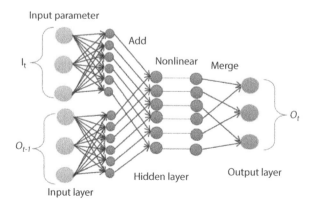

Figure 7.3 Feedforward RNN [36].

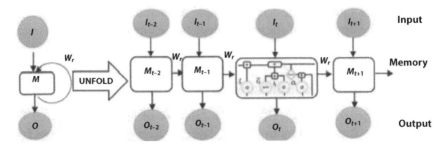

Figure 7.4 Long short-term memory (LSTM) [36].

the output for the preceding input at time t − 1. Apart from the structural difference, RNN utilizes similar weights across all layers, whereas other DLs employ diverse weights. This prominently reduces the total features that the system must study. In spite of the application of the effective model, the disappearing slope by extensive input order and detonating slope issues form the major hindrance as depicted in [46]. To deal with this constraint, LSTM was invented by [47]. In particular, LSTM shown in Figure 7.4 is mainly appropriate for applications possessing lengthy time lags having undefined sizes among vital events.

To accomplish this, LSTMs employ novel information sources for storing, writing, and reading to/from node at every step. At the training time, errors in classification are reduced by permitting either reading/writing [48]. One more form of RNN is the gated repetitive component, which denotes enhanced form of LSTM that performs comparable to LSTM [49].

7.2.3 Convolutional Neural Network (CNN)

Convolutional neural network (CNN) was motivated by natural procedures of the human cerebrum in which the connections of patterns are similar to the brain of humans [50, 51]. A classic CNN consists of input, several hidden layers, and an output layer. Following are the important elements of the hidden layers in CNN: layers of normalization, FC, pooling, and convolution. For instance, analyzing the imagery data represents a good example of CNN [52]. Figure 7.5 demonstrates a CNN architecture for recognizing a character from a 3 × 3 matrix image.

The model is intended to perceive X, O, and / characters. The filter is applied upon input image by convolution layer. Operation is done using two filters over the input image possessing similar weight. Hence, eight parameters are generated. For this example, the simplicity is preferred over bias. Frequently, an activation (nonlinear) layer called the rectified linear

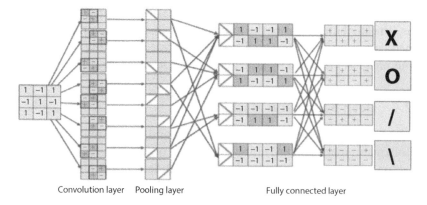

Convolution layer   Pooling layer   Fully connected layer

Figure 7.5 CNN architecture [36].

unit (ReLU) is included after the convolution layer. The function g(l) = max (0, l) is applied to all the values of the convolution layer by the activation layer. This process enhances the non-linear model properties and the network as a whole without impacting the convolution layer fields.

In this manner, the vanishing problem that occurs in the traditional ANNs is solved. The neuron cluster output present in the convolution layer is combined into a solitary neuron by the pooling layer [53]. The average, max, or sum pooling are used to achieve this [54].

In Figure 7.6, the general CNN model is introduced, that depict the layers of input, output, FC, and convolution+pooling.

The attribute mining is performed by conv+pool layers. In order to characterize the output, the FC layer plays the role of a classifier above the features and allots a likelihood score for the information image. In this layer, m × m × r image is the input (m -> image height, w -> image width, and r -> number of channels). The size of the filter (a privately associated structure) can be formed with the measurements of k having m − n + 1.

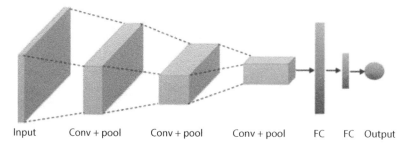

Input   Conv + pool   Conv + pool   Conv + pool   FC   FC   Output

Figure 7.6 Framework of CNN [36].

Each attribute map is applied with sigmoidal nonlinearity and additive bias. The attribute vector of the information which is a complex and combined data from the conv+pool layers is represented by the FC layer. The input image is predicted by utilizing the final feature vector [36].

7.2.4   Deep Boltzmann Machine

A system of evenly coupled stochastic visible and hidden units is known as a Boltzmann machine (BM) [55]. The design of BM is outlined in the first diagram of Figure 7.7. To assess the data dependent and independent prospects in a pair of connected binary features, BM algorithm needs Markov chains that are arbitrarily initialized to attain symmetric distributions [56]. Using this framework, learning strategy is extremely slow in real time [55]. Restricted BM (RBM) was devised to accomplish effective learning. RBM has no connections among hidden units [57].

A simple design of RBM with associations between neurons is as depicted in the second outline of Figure 7.7. An RBM feature which is valuable is the hidden unit distribution given the units that are visible. By directly increasing the probability, a cluster of marginal posterior distributions is obtained by considering the attribute representation of the RBM where the inferences are tractable. Besides, deep BM (DBM) and deep belief network (DBN) are the two fundamental DL systems in this class which have been introduced in literatures [58].

The DBM NN has more variables and layers that are hidden when compared to RBM. Inside all layers, DBM design has totally undirected associations between neurons [55]. In Figure 7.7, the image on RHS depicts the engineering of a basic DBM NN for one visible and hidden layer. Nevertheless, amid the neurons in a layer, it has connections that are undirected between all layers of the system. For DBM training,

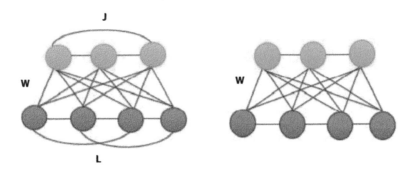

Figure 7.7 Structure of BM [36].

in order to boost the lower bound of the likelihood, a stochastic most extreme likelihood-based calculation is applied. This is on the grounds that computing the posterior hidden neurons distribution, given the neurons that are visible, cannot be accomplished by directly maximizing the probability due to the collaborations among the neurons that are hidden.

Also, in instances of semi-supervised learning, high level representation could be worked via restricted labeled information and huge contribution of untagged sources of input would then be able to be utilized to tweak the model for specific tasks. Feedback in top-down fashion can be incorporated to facilitate the propagation of uncertainty and therefore handle ambiguous inputs in a more robust fashion.

7.2.5   Deep Belief Network

DBN signifies another RBM variation in which several hidden layers learn by feeding one RBM output as input to another RBM layer [56, 57]. The connections among its two top most layers are undirected while the next layers are connected directly. The technique of training follows the greedy approach which is done during unsupervised training of the DBN. Based on the output, expected fine tuning of parameters is done.

The figure to the left of Figure 7.8 demonstrates the DBN design comprising of a three-layer configuration depicting the connections which are symmetric in nature. The design consists of numerous layers of hidden neurons that are trained utilizing BP algorithm [59, 60]. As demonstrated in Figure 7.8, the DBN design comprises of connection units among neurons present in different layers. Nevertheless, in contrast to RBM, intra-connections between neurons of a layer do not exist.

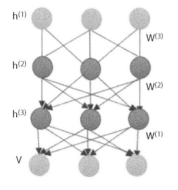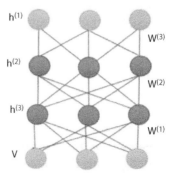

Figure 7.8 DBN architecture [36].

7.3   Applications of Deep Learning in Medical Informatics and Public Health

This section describes the different case studies of DL that is applied for doing MI and PH.

DL methods utilize data gathered in the records of EHR for addressing several issues related to healthcare such as reduction of the misdiagnosis rate and forecasting of the procedure results. ANNs are able to assist medical experts in analyzing vast data and identify numerous factors such as follows:

- Analysis of samples of blood
- Tracking of the levels of glucose in patients suffering from diabetes
- Identifying problems related to heart
- Detection of tumors by applying image analysis
- Cancer diagnosis by detecting cells that are cancerous
- Early diagnosis of osteoarthritis from a MRI scan

7.3.1   The Use of DL for Cancer Diagnosis

For many years, oncologists have been employing medical imaging approaches such as Computed Tomography (CT), MRI, and X-ray for diagnosing cancer. Though these methods are effective for detecting several cancer types, certain cancers still exist that are not diagnosable accurately. CNN shows a great potential for detecting such cancer types. ANNs are able to diagnose the cancer early with a reduced rate of misdiagnosis on similar medical images thus delivering improved results for the patients. Following are some studies in which scientists have effectively utilized DL models for diagnosing diverse cancer types with a higher accuracy:

- The rate of breast cancer misdiagnosis was reduced by around 85% by employing a DL model as per the Nvidia study.
- Hossam Haick designed a device to treat cancer motivated by the fact that his roommate was detected with leukemia. A team of scientists trained an ANN model based on his design. This model recognized 17 diverse cases based on the breath smell of patients with an accuracy of 86%.

- Effective lung cancer detection from CT images was demonstrated by a researcher's team at Enlitic. They were able to achieve a 50% higher rate of detection on test data when compared to a team of expert radiologists.
- Training of CNN model was done by Haenslle *et al.* for detecting skin cancer by assessing whether a skin lesion displayed in digital imaging can cause cancer with the same or higher accuracy of a skilled skin specialist.
- Google researchers have devised a CNN model for detecting cancer related to breast from images of pathology quicker with enhanced accuracy. The model called LYmph Node Assistant (LYNA) attained a very high success rate of around 99% in comparison to physicians who had an accuracy of only 38%.
- DL-based analysis of radiology images is being done in over 100 hospitals around the globe which has assisted radiologists in treating millions of patients [61–63].

7.3.2   DL in Disease Prediction and Treatment

The costs of hospitalization in US were in billions during 2006. All these hospitalizations could have been prevented. Majority of the patients who were hospitalized suffered from either heart-related ailments or diabetes. DL can be utilized for improving the rate of diagnosis and forecast more accurately which, in turn, can reduce the number of hospitalizations leading to reduced cost.

Some research teams have already applied their solutions to this problem. Researcher team from the University of Boston teamed up with hospitals in the Boston locality. They were able to achieve an accuracy of around 82% for predicting which patients suffering from heart ailments and diabetes would require hospitalization during the subsequent year. The EHR records were analyzed using DL model for forecasting heart failures for the subsequent 9 months before the medical experts could predict [61–63].

- Diabetic Retinopathy
  Diabetic retinopathy (DR) is a form of blindness caused due to poor control of diabetes. Around 415 million people in developing nations suffer from DR. DL has been found very effecting in preventing DR. For instance, the CNN technique analyzes the retinal image data for recognizing internal

bleedings in the eye, initial symptoms, and any characteristics indicating DR. The major cause of DR is due to the
extreme fluctuations in the levels of blood glucose. Regular
monitoring of the glucose levels of diabetic patients can be
a good way of controlling diabetes and hence preventing
DR. Hence, the DL model can be very effective in analyzing
the glucose level data for forecasting sharp surges or sharp
lows. This, in turn, can aid the patients in controlling their
diet. For instance, if low sugar occurs then they can eat sugar
related food or if high sugar occurs, they can inject insulin
[61–63].

- Human Immunodeficiency Virus
  It has been found that around 36 million people around the
  globe are affected by human immunodeficiency virus (HIV).
  Regular antiretroviral dosages are required by HIV affected
  patients. Since HIV can quickly mutate, the drugs given to
  the patients need to be periodically changed. A form of DL
  model called Reinforcement Learning (RL) can assist in this
  activity. For treating the HIV patients continuously, the RL
  technique can keep track of several indicators in the environment with each administration of the drug. This assists
  in providing the superlative action to modify the sequence
  of drugs for continuous treatment. Toronto University
  devised a CNN model called DeepBind which took genomic
  data and forecasted the DNA and RNA sequence binding
  proteins. It can detect changes in the DNA sequence that can
  lead to the development of improved tools for medical diagnosis and medications [61–63].
- Drug Discovery
  The discovery and development of drugs is significantly
  assisted by DL. The medical history of patient is analyzed
  for delivering the better treatment for them. Besides, DL is
  acquiring insights from the symptoms of patients and tests.
  The domain of drug discovery adds significant economic
  value to ML application developers and other stakeholders
  like physicians, CEOs, patients, nurses, and insurance companies, as it involves large incentives and profits. The pharmaceutical or drug companies are very lucrative industries
  that will become potential customers for the drug development process. IBM has started the concept of drug discovery from very early days. Nowadays, Google has also been

involved in the process of drug discovery using DL along with other major organizations [61–63].

- Medical Imaging

  Several dangerous illnesses like cancer, tumors related to brain, and diseases associated with heart can be diagnosed using medical imaging methods like scans of MRI, CT, and ECG. In this regard, DL assists medical experts for analysis of illness.

  The computer vision represents one of the noteworthy innovations that came up due to the ML and DL. It is being widely applied in medical informatics. For instance, an initiative called InnerEve from Microsoft that was found in 2010 is currently developing tools for image diagnostic. In this regard, they have published several videos describing their progress. DL plays a primary role in the application development related to diagnostic. This is very much possible as more data sources comprising of rich and diverse forms of medical imagery are being made available and accessible. Nevertheless, DL represents a "black box" in which their predictions cannot be explained even if they are accurate. This type of "black box" problem becomes even more challenging in medical related applications where it is a matter of life and death. This is because the medical experts require a clear understanding on how the DL application arrived at its outcome even if these forecasts were estimated to be precise earlier [61–63].

- Insurance fraud

  DL is effectively utilized to identify deceitful claims by analyzing medical insurance policies. Future occurrence of frauds can also be detected using the DL techniques. Additionally, DL assists the insurance companies in targeting potential customers/patients and sends them discounts to lure them [61–63].

- Alzheimer's Disease

  The early detection of this illness in humans has been a major challenge faced by the medical organizations. Currently, this illness can only be identified once it occurs in a person. Using traditional methods, early diagnosis of Alzheimer's disease is not possible. However, DL is being employed for identifying this illness during early stages [61–63].

- Genome

  DL methods are being employed to comprehend genomes and assist patients in understanding the illness that may impact them. The future of DL in the area of genomics and insurance industry is promising. For example, Entilic employs DL methods to assist doctors in making diagnosis faster and accurate. Cellscope utilizes DL strategies for assisting parents in monitoring their children's health via a smart device. This reduces the frequent visits to doctors. DL has the ability to deliver remarkable applications in public health and medical informatics that can aid doctors in providing improved medical treatments [61–63].

- Treatment Queries and Suggestions

  Disease diagnosis is a very difficult process and comprises of several varying factors that can vary from the person's color to what food he/she consumes. Currently, machines are not fully capable to match the diagnosis made by human doctors. Nevertheless, in future DL methods can assist the medical experts in the process of diagnosis and treatments, just by delivering an extension of medical knowledge. For example, the Department of Oncology of the Memorial Sloan Kettering (MSK) has a partnership with IBM Watson. The MSK possesses huge amount of medical data on cancer patients and the related treatments utilized over several years. Using this information, it can advise various treatment choices to physicians when they encounter future cancer cases by extracting useful information from the historic data. This tool is currently is in preliminary use [61–63].

- Scaled Up/Crowdsourced Medical Data Collection

  Nowadays, there is a lot of focus on collecting and analyzing live mobile data for medical informatics and public health. For instance, ResearchKit from Apple is focusing on the treatment of Parkinson's disease and Asperger's syndrome by permitting user access to interactive apps (such as ML application for recognition of faces). It is able to evaluate the conditions of the patient over a period of time. This app use allows data to be fed continuously creating a huge pool of data for experimentation and future predictions. Real-time health data related to insulin and diabetes is being collected by IBM in partnership with Medtronic for extracting useful diabetic knowledge. IBM also bought a Truven which is an analytics company related to healthcare for 2.6 billion dollars. Even though, tremendous medical data collection has taken place, the IT industry is still struggling to analyze this data and suggest treatments in real time. However, as the pooling of patient data is progressing, in future, researchers may come up with better innovations in handling diverse diseases [61–63].

- Robotic Surgery

  Recently, surgery performed by robots is gaining significance. In this domain, the da Vinci robot permits surgeons to make the limbs of robots nimbler that aids in precise surgeries with reduced tremors when compared to hands of humans. Although, all the surgical operations performed by robots do not employ DL, certain systems utilize computer vision which is assisted by DL in recognizing specific body parts (such as detecting follicles of hair during hair transplantation operation). Furthermore, DL can be employed to stabilize robotic motions when getting instructions from humans controlling the robot [61–63].

7.3.3 Future Applications

The list of DL applications in healthcare that are rapidly progressing are summarized as follows:

- Personalized Medicine (PM)

  It refers to the process of automatically prescribing drugs based on personalized recommendations. For instance, when a wisdom tooth is pulled from a child, usually a drug called Vicodin is given. Similarly, a person suffering infection of the urinary track usually gets a medicine named Bactrim. In the near future, it is expected that certain patients may get the same drug dose. Knowing the history and genetics of patients, certain patients may be prescribed with the same drugs. PM has the potential to make the medical recommendations and disease treatments of each person customized based on their genetics, levels of stress, past medical conditions, diet, etc. It is applicable to minor medical circumstances such as giving reduced Bactrim dosage for UTI as well as major medical conditions like deciding whether chemotherapy should be performed on a person based on his age, gender, genetics, etc. [61–63].

- Automatic Treatment or Recommendation

  The autonomous treatment refers to the process of treating patients automatically without disturbing his daily life. For instance, a machine may be developed that automatically adjusts the patient's drug dose of antibiotics by keeping track of their blood level, diet, levels of stress, and sleep. In such scenarios, humans need not remember how many medicines should be taken as an ML agent like Alexa may remind him about what pills to be taken, how much dose to be taken, what time to take or call a doctor if condition worsens. For instance, Hooman Hakami developed by Medtronic is able to autonomously monitor the levels of blood glucose and inject insulins as required without disturbing the daily activities of the patient. But there are several legal issues that need to be addressed before giving such power to machines especially in the medical domain since even small mistakes can cause loss of lives. So, lengthy trials need to be done before autonomous treatments can be introduced into real life [61–63].

- Enhancing Performance (Beyond Amelioration)

  Recently, IBM and Orreco have partnered for developing a software that could enhance the performance of athletes. A similar partnership exists between IBM and Armor. Although, the key objective of western medicine is on the treatment and cure of disease, greater focus must be given to prevention of diseases as well. In this regard, IoT devices are being employed. Apart from prevention of diseases and performance improvement of athletes, the DL-based healthcare apps can be employed to track performance of workers, reduce levels of job stress or seek optimistic enhancements in groups that are at a higher health risk. However, before these applications become feasible, lot of ethical issues need to be resolved [61–63].

- Autonomous Robotic Surgery

  Currently, robots mostly act as an extension to the human surgeon's abilities such as precision. For mastering surgeries, DL can be employed for integrating visual data and motor patterns within robots. In certain kinds of painting and visual art, machines have adapted the skill to go beyond the expertise of humans. For example, if a machine can simulate the creative ability of a Picaso, then with sufficient training, the machine can perform surgeries better than humans [61–63].

7.4 Open Issues Concerning DL in Medical Informatics and Public Health

Most of the modern statistical methods, DLs are offering novel prospects to put into operation the previously available and fast increasing data sources for the advantages of patients. In spite of progressive research being performed recently, particularly in imaging, the literature still lacks' transparency, lags in exploration for potential ethical worries, clarity in reporting to encourage duplicity, and does not effectively demonstrate. It may be beneficial for healthcare if interdisciplinary groups are combined to perform research and develop projects that involve DL which explicitly addresses a series of queries related to reproducibility, effectiveness, transparency, and ethics (TREE). The nine critical questions suggested here serve as a background for researchers to highlight the reporting, design, and conduct, for editors and peer reviewers for evaluating contributions toward literature; and critically review new findings by policy makers and clinicians for benefit of patients. Emphases on some of the critical questions are shown as follows:

Q.1) What is the safety concern for the value of the patient?
Majority of prediction models published are not practically applied by clinicians [65]. One of the factors is the nonexistence of a medical process for making decisions from which the model can learn meaningful information/optimize data. This has assisted in transitory invention from the previous years in DL for health [66]. Hence, it is strongly advised by researchers to see the context in a wider organizational perspective. Researchers need to be sensible during developing and implementing the parts of proposed research in healthcare data science. What is crucial is that this requirement is expressed up front, just like the principles on which research registration is based.

Q.2) What proofs exist to show that best clinical research practices and the design of epidemiological studies influenced the creation of the algorithm? Similar patterns to those of past problems with medical investigation have started to emerge in DL-based study, like utilizing the result attributes as

forecasters, not considering the underlying mechanisms, inadequate expla-
nations of the DL outputs, and recording precisely the type of patients that
were allowed in the research. The PECO design rules of epidemiology (i.e.,
identifying sample residents, contacts utilized, and medical results) play a
significant part in certain problems that emerged in medical science. These
rules constitute as effective guidelines for validity assessment and significance of research proof [67, 68].

Q.3) What is the Patient involvement in the gathering, review, delivery, and
utilization of data?
With the rising utilization of regularly gathered patient information, frequently having alternate lawful justification (i.e., valid interests) for specific
permission, it is now further significant that patient participation is viewed
as complimenting the healthcare investigation. Exempting researchers
from obtaining separate permission does not mean that they are excused
from involving the patients and the community completely. Consequently
(if applicable) healthcare DL plans must comprise of a clear strategy for
assessing the suitability of the devised technique and results for certain
data gathering entities, consumers (i.e., clinicians) and those affected (i.e.,
those who use the model to notify clinical management).

Several existing frameworks [69] explain how a research project could
include patients and the public. It is strongly recommended for the
researchers to decide the phases of their project, if any, which is appropriate for public and patient involvement (at the outset); for example, to define
the need for a predictive modeling approach, to support the improvement
of the algorithm, and to evaluate the algorithm's suitability.

Q.4) Do the data gathered answer the medical queries—i.e., are they het-
erogenous in nature as they exist in the real-world and is the quality of the
data sufficient?
The main problem here is to verify if the data available can address the
clinical query. For instance, a dataset that does not contain the (known)
appropriate or significant forecasters of a result is improbable to respond
reasonably to queries about it. Without sufficient data, no DL strategy can
produce accurate results. To assist in explaining certain possible problems
that are present in deciding if the information is of appropriate value.
Following are two key areas where researchers often find it difficult to
apply DL techniques to data relating to healthcare:

- Inherent sample features: When data are available but of low
  quality or are not appropriate, it is impossible to produce a

successful DL application. The correctness of data gathering approaches, participant sampling, eligibility requirements and missing information should be taken into consideration for evaluating the potential for the development of effective and generalizable DL strategies [70].

- Task significance: Because of the probability of failure while working beyond the training data range, techniques are frequently incapable of reaching the accuracy observed during training. For example, when you first encounter a cyclist at night, the DL system for identifying the image/driverless car may fail. The data including time scale and heterogeneity must therefore be consistent.

Q.5) Does the methodology for validation represent the practical restrictions and operating processes related with information gathering and storage?

DL work is gradually using regularly collected data, including healthcare data (e.g., genomic information and EHR), municipal organizational information (e.g., educational achievement and death records), and portable and wearable device data [71]. Despite the real-world limitations, DL algorithms are mostly tested on past data, providing definite results if the process of producing information does not alter. These conventions are frequently not followed in practice and results in DL techniques performing badly when installed as opposed to the performance observed in development [72].

This problem can be considered by researchers as two distinct but associated problems. The first concerns ensuring the development of a foolproof authentication system. For instance, approaches considering time and producing momentarily disorderly training and test data can be considered when collecting and processing the data [73, 74]. The issue number 2 is to avoid redundancy of a suitable result due to drift in institution data gathering, or methods of storage. However, developers and researchers can do little to prove their work in the future, apart from utilizing best reproducibility practices to decrease the volume of effort essential to reinstall the appropriate service.

Q.6) Which computational and technological resources are needed for the mission, and are the existing resources enough to deal with this issue?

Working with several factors is prevalent in predictive modeling associated with health like DL-based image and computational genetics [75]. It is therefore a normal routine to determine the data complication and the available resources for computation, since these resources form the restrictive feature (with conventional statistical models) that determine the analysis to be performed [76]. In certain instances, additional resources for computation might permit training of improved models. For instance, the utilization of prototypes centered on complicated ANNs can be absurdly tough without sufficient computer resources, particularly if these strategies need extra, complicated functions for preventing overfitting (e.g., regularization) [77]. Preferably, investigation should not be constrained by the amount of computation resources. However, scientists must appreciate the limitations that they work in, so that any study can be customized to the needs. Comparable issues may occur when utilizing protected computing scenarios, like reserves of data, wherever the applicable software systems might not be accessible and will therefore require implementation from scratch onward [78, 79]. Therefore, understanding the repercussions of using particular software's is also critical, as the underlying license may have comprehensive effects on the market prospective and additional traits of the future of the procedure [80].

Q.7) Are the metrics of performance stated applicable to the clinical context that the model should be used in?

Selecting metrics of performance is required for converting the good performance during training into good performance when the system is deployed in the real clinical environment. This disparity in the performance of the method may occur for many reasons; the most important of which is that assessment measures are not good alternatives for patients to demonstrate better results (e.g., mis-categorization error for unbalanced class screening application). Another common error is to select a success measure that is strongly connected to, nonetheless not demonstrative of better medical results for patients [81]. Nonetheless, published studies explaining WFO do not disclose performance indicators appropriate for statistics (e.g., calibration and discrimination) and clinical based (e.g., type of net benefit). Rather, they concentrate on consistency (true positive rate where physician offers the ground truth. To prevent these pitfalls, the following guidelines for researchers are presented: [82–84]

- Consult with all concerned stakeholders like patients, researchers, doctors, etc. to assess the suitable devising of the statistical objective, like forecasting an event's absolute risk, or determining a rank order or trend detection or classification.

- Choose the correct performance metrics. That target comprises of specific criteria and doing the statistical aim clear can assist scientists to decide what the appropriate prognostic success indicators are for every particular scenario. For instance, if forecasting is the objective, then standardization and discrimination form the basic reporting needs. In addition, the correct scoring rules (or at least side-byside histograms) should be used to compare two versions [85].
- Results to report. Even though outcomes of training may not be enough, to prove the model's usefulness, they provide valuable insights into the characteristics of samples and any out-of-sample outcomes that are also being produced. However, the most relevant to mention are reliable estimates (i.e., the ones that have been modified correctly for overfitting).

7.5   Conclusion

DL has achieved a significant position in recent years in the domain of MI and PH. ML is slowly impacting the manner in which treatment related to healthcare and nursing is being done. This is due to DL. In comparison with ML and feature engineering, DL can analyze big data in an effective manner. Several variants of DL methods have been developed across several domains such as processing of health records, images of biomedical, sensors and physiological processing of signals, and human motion and analysis of emotions. This chapter discusses the different DL techniques like RNN, DBN, AE, CNN, and DBM which are being used in MI and PH. Different case studies in real-world like diagnosis of cancer, prediction of DR, HIV, and its related treatment along with future applications have also been presented. Certain open research issues associated to the usage of DL in MI and PH are also discussed.

When compared to other domains, healthcare requires interactions between various disciplines, dedicated processes and information repositories. Hence, if large models are generated without completely comprehending the outcome, then it would be practically disastrous in healthcare. When compared to other domains in which researchers can work alone without much interaction, healthcare domain requires active collaboration between the medical experts, data scientists, and experts related to informatics. Comprehensive knowledge of present medical workflow is required so that the models can extract data from appropriate sources of data and apply them in real world. In conclusion, DL is being prominently utilized in the domain of MI and PH.

References

1. Lauzon, F.Q., An introduction to deep learning, in: *11th International Conference on Information Science, Signal Processing and their Applications (ISSPA)*, Montreal, QC, pp. 1438–1439, 2012.
2. Hyunjung Kwak, G. and Hui, P., *DeepHealth: Review and challenges of artificial intelligence in health informatics*, 42 pages, September 2019, (In press) arXiv:1909.00384.
3. Ravi, D., Wong, C., Deligianni, F., Berthelot, M., Andreu-Perez, J., Lo, B., Yang, G.-Z., Deep Learning for Health Informatics. *IEEE J. Biomed. Health Inf.*, 21, 1, 4–21, 2017.
4. Chang, H., Han, J., Zhong, C., Snijders, A.M., Mao., J.-H., Unsupervised transfer learning via multi-scale convolutional sparse coding for biomedical applications. *IEEE Trans. Pattern Anal. Mach. Intell.*, 40, 5, 1182–1194, 2017.
5. Nie, D., Zhang, H., Adeli, E., Liu, L., Shen, D., 3D deep learning for multi-modal imaging guided survival time prediction of brain tumour patients, in: *International Conference on Medical Image Computing and Computer-Assisted Intervention*, Springer, pp. 212–220, 2016.
6. Samala, R.K., Chan, H.-P., Hadjiiski, L., Helvie, M.A., Wei, J., Cha, K., Mass detection in digital breast tomosynthesis: Deep convolutional neural network with transfer learning from mammography. *Med. Phys.*, 43, 12, 6654–6666, 2016.
7. Xu, T., Zhang, H., Huang, X., Zhang, S., Metaxas, D.N., Multimodal deep learning for cervical dysplasia diagnosis, in: *International Conference on Medical Image Computing and Computer-Assisted Intervention*, pp. 115–123, Springer, Athens, Greece, 2016.
8. Yan, Z., Zhan, Y., Peng, Z., Liao, S., Shinagawa, Y., Zhang, S., Metaxas, D.N., Zhou, X.S., Multi-instance deep learning: Discover discriminative local anatomies for bodypart recognition. *IEEE Trans. Med. Imaging.*, 35, 5, 1332–1343, 2016.
9. Cho, K., Van Merriënboer, B., Gulcehre, C., Bahdanau, D., Bougares, F., Schwenk, H., Bengio, Y., Learning phrase representations using RNN encoder-decoder for statistical machine translation, in: *Proceedings of the 2014 Conference on Empirical Methods in Natural Language Processing (EMNLP)*, Doha, Qatar, pp. 1724–1734, 2014.
10. Alipanahi, B., Delong, A., Weirauch, M.T., Frey, B.J., Predicting the sequence specificities of DNA-and RNA-binding proteins by deep learning. *Nat. Biotechnol.*, 33, 8, 831–838, 2015.
11. Angermueller, C., Lee, H.J., Reik, W., Stegle, O., Accurate prediction of single-cell DNA methylation states using deep learning. *Genome Biol.*, 18, 1, 1–13, 2016.

12. Xiong, H.Y., Alipanahi, B., Lee, L.J., Bretschneider, H., Merico, D., Yuen, R.K., Hua, Y., Gueroussov, S., Najafabadi, H.S., Hughes, T.R., Morris, Q., Barash, Y., Krainer, A.R., Jojic, N., Scherer, S.W., Blencowe, B.J., Frey, B.J., The human splicing code reveals new insights into the genetic determinants of disease. *Science*, 347, 6218, 1–20, 2015.

13. Bamgbola, O., Review of vancomycin-induced renal toxicity: an update. *Ther. Adv. Endocrinol. Metab.*, 7, 3, 136–147, 2016.

14. Davis, S.E., Lasko, T.A., Chen, G., Siew, E.D., Matheny, M.E., Calibration drift in regression and machine learning models for acute kidney injury. *J. Am. Med. Inf. Assoc.*, 24, 6, 1052–1061, 2017.

15. Goldstein, S.L., Nephrotoxicities. *F1000Research*, 6, 55, 2017.

16. Hoste, E.A.J., Kashani, K., Gibney, N., Perry Wilson, F., Ronco, C., Goldstein, S.L., Kellum, J.A., Bagshaw, S.M., Impact of electronic alerting of acute kidney injury: workgroup statements from the 15th ADQI Consensus Conference. *Can. J. Kidney Health Dis.*, 3, 1, 1–9, 2016.

17. Knaus, W.A. and Marks, R.D., New Phenotypes for Sepsis. *JAMA*, 321, 20, 1981–1982, 2019.

18. Prendecki, M., Blacker, E., Sadeghi-Alavijeh, O., Edwards, R., Montgomery, H., Gillis, S., Harber, M., Improving outcomes in patients with Acute Kidney Injury: the impact of hospital based automated AKI alerts. *Postgrad. Med. J.*, 92, 1083, 9–13, 2016.

19. Seymour, C.W., Kennedy, J.N., Wang, S., Chang, C.-C.H., Elliott, C.F., Xu, Z., Berry, S., Clermont, G., Cooper, G., Gomez, H., Huang, D.T., Kellum, J.A., Mi, Q., Opal, S.M., Talisa, V., van der Poll, T., Visweswaran, S., Vodovotz, Y., Weiss, J.C., Yealy, D.M., Yende, S., Angus, D.C., Derivation, Validation, and Potential Treatment Implications of Novel Clinical Phenotypes for Sepsis. *JAMA*, 321, 20, 2003–2017, 2019.

20. Tomašev, N., Glorot, X., Rae, J.W., Zielinski, M., Askham, H., Saraiva, A., Mottram, A., Meyer, C., Ravuri, S., Protsyuk, I., Connell, A., Hughes, C.O., Karthikesalingam, A., Cornebise, J., Montgomery, H., Rees, G., Laing, C., Baker, C.R., Peterson, K., Reeves, R., Hassabis, D., King, D., Suleyman, M., Back, T., Nielson, C., Ledsam, J.R., Mohamed, S., A clinically applicable approach to continuous prediction of future acute kidney injury. *Nature*, 572, 116–119, 2019.

21. Wang, L., Zhang, W., He, X., Zha, H., Supervised reinforcement learning with recurrent neural network for dynamic treatment recommendation, in: *Proceedings of the 24th ACM SIGKDD International Conference on Knowledge Discovery & Data Mining*, ACM, pp. 2447–2456, 2018.

22. Barth, J., Klucken, J., Kugler, P., Kammerer, T., Steidl, R., Winkler, J., Hornegger, J., Eskofier, B., Biometric and mobile gait analysis for early diagnosis and therapy monitoring in Parkinson's disease, in: *Annual International Conference of the IEEE Engineering in Medicine and Biology Society*, IEEE, pp. 868–871, 2011.

23. Wilson, S., Ruscoe, W., Chapman, M., Miller, R., General practitioner-hospital communications: A review of discharge summaries. *J. Qual. Clin. Pract.*, 21, 104–108, 2002.

24. Jindal, V., Birjandtalab, J., Baran Pouyan, M., Mehdad Nourani. An adaptive deep learning approach for PPG-based identification, in: *38th Annual international conference of the IEEE engineering in medicine and biology society (EMBC)*, IEEE, pp. 6401–6404, 2016.

25. Nurse, E., Mashford, B.S., Yepes, A.J., Kiral-Kornek, I., Harrer, S., Freestone, D.R., Decoding EEG and LFP signals using deep learning: heading TrueNorth, in: *Proceedings of the ACM International Conference on Computing Frontiers*, ACM, pp. 259–266, 2016.

26. Cao, Y., Liu, C., Liu, B., Brunette, M.J., Zhang, N., Sun, T., Zhang, P., Peinado, J., Garavito, E.S., Garcia, L.L. *et al.*, Improving tuberculosis diagnostics using deep learning and mobile health technologies among resource-poor and marginalized communities, in: *IEEE First International Conference on Connected Health: Applications, Systems and Engineering Technologies (CHASE)*, IEEE, pp. 274–281, 2016.

27. Alimova, I., Tutubalina, E., Alferova, J., Gafiyatullina, G., A Machine Learning Approach to Classification of Drug Reviews in Russian, in: *Ivannikov ISPRAS Open Conference (ISPRAS)*, IEEE, Moscow, pp. 64–69, 2017.

28. Bodnar, T., Barclay, V.C., Ram, N., Tucker, C.S., Salathé, M., On the ground validation of online diagnosis with Twitter and medical records, in: *Proceedings of the 23rd International Conference on World Wide Web*, ACM, pp. 651–656, 2014.

29. Chae, S., Kwon, S., Lee, D., Predicting infectious disease using deep learning and big data. *Int. J. Environ. Res. Public Health*, 15, 8, 1–20, 2018.

30. de Quincey, E., Kyriacou, T., Pantin, T., # hayfever; A Longitudinal Study into Hay Fever Related Tweets in the UK, in: *Proceedings of the 6th international conference on digital health conference*, ACM, pp. 85–89, 2016.

31. Garimella, V.R.K., Alfayad, A., Weber, I., Social media image analysis for public health, in: *Proceedings of the CHI Conference on Human Factors in Computing Systems*, ACM, pp. 5543–5547, 2016.

32. Phan, N.H., Dou, D., Piniewski, B., Kil, D., Social restricted Boltzmann machine: Human behavior prediction in health social networks, in: *Proceedings of the 2015 IEEE/ACM International Conference on Advances in Social Networks Analysis and Mining*, ACM, pp. 424–431, 2015.

33. Tuarob, S., Tucker, C.S., Salathe, M., Ram, N., An ensemble heterogeneous classification methodology for discovering health-related knowledge in social media messages. *J. Biomed. Inf.*, 49, 255–268, 2014.

34. Birkhead, G.S., Klompas, M., Shah, N.R., Uses of electronic health records for public health surveillance to advance public health. *Annu. Rev. Public Health*, 36, 345–359, 2015.

35. Henry, J., Pylypchuk, Y., Searcy, T., Patel, V., Adoption of electronic health record systems among US non-federal acute care hospitals: 2008–2015. *ONC Data Brief*, 35, 1–9, 2016.

36. Tobore, I., Li, J., Yuhang, L., Al-Handarish, Y., Kandwal, A., Nie, Z., Wang, L., Deep Learning Intervention for Healthcare Challenges: Some Biomedical Domain Considerations. *JMIR Mhealth Uhealth*, 7, 8, 1–58, 2019.

37. Schmidhuber, J., Deep learning in neural networks: an overview. *Neural Netw.*, 61, 85–117, 2015.

38. Yousoff, S.N., Baharin, A., Abdullah, A., A Review on Optimization Algorithm for Deep Learning Method in Bioinformatics Field, in: *Proceedings of the Conference on Biomedical Engineering and Sciences*, IEEE, Kuala Lumpur, Malaysia, pp. 707–711, 2016.

39. LeCun, Y., Bengio, Y., Hinton, G., Deep learning. *Nature*, 521, 7553, 436–444, 2015.

40. Vincent, P., Larochelle, H., Bengio, Y., Manzagol, P.A., Extracting and Composing Robust Features with Denoising Autoencoders. *Proceedings of the 25th International Conference on Machine learning; ICML'08*, Helsinki, Finland, July 5–9, 2008, pp. 1096–103, 2008.

41. Ranzato, M.A., Poultney, C., Chopra, S., LeCun, Y., Efficient Learning of Sparse Representations With an Energy-Based Model. *Proceedings of the 19th International Conference on Neural Information Processing Systems; NIPS'06*, Vancouver, British Columbia, Canada, December 4–7, 2006, pp. 1137–44, 2006.

42. Masci, J., Meier, U., Cirean, D., Schmidhuber, J., Stacked Convolutional Auto-Encoders for Hierarchical Feature Extraction. *Proceedings of the Artificial Neural Networks and Machine Learning; ICANN'11*, Espoo, Finland, June 14–17, 2011, pp. 52–9, 2011.

43. Ororbia, L.A., Kifer, D., Giles, C.L., Unifying adversarial training algorithms with data gradient regularization. *Neural Comput.*, 29, 4, 867–87, 2017.

44. Rifai, S., Vincent, P., Muller, X., Glorot, X., Bengio, Y., Contractive Auto-Encoders: Explicit Invariance During Feature Extraction. *Proceedings of the 28th International Conference on Machine Learning; ICML'11*, Bellevue, Washington, USA, June 28-July 2, 2011, pp. 833–40, 2011.

45. Tobore I, Li J, Yuhang L, Al-Handarish Y, Kandwal A, Nie Z, Wang L. Deep Learning Intervention for Healthcare Challenges: Some Biomedical Domain Considerations. JMIR Mhealth Uhealth. 2019 Aug 2;7(8):e11966. PMID: 31376272; PMCID: PMC6696854.

46. Bengio, Y., Simard, P., Frasconi, P., Learning long-term dependencies with gradient descent is difficult. *IEEE Trans. Neural Netw.*, 5, 2, 157–66, 1994.

47. Hochreiter, S. and Schmidhuber, J., Long short-term memory. *Neural Comput.*, 9, 8, 1735–80, 1997 Nov 15.

48. Krizhevsky, A., Sutskever, I., Hinton, G.E., ImageNet classification with deep convolutional neural networks. *Commun. ACM*, 60, 6, 84–90, 2017.

49. Cho, K., van Merriënboer, B., Gulcehre, C., Bahdanau, D., Bougares, F., Schwenk, H., Bengio, Y., Learning Phrase Representations Using RNN Encoder-Decoder for Statistical Machine Translation. *Proceedings of the Conference on Empirical Methods in Natural Language Processing; EMNLP'14*, Doha, Qatar, October 25–29, 2014, pp. 1724–34, 2014.

50. Matsugu, M., Mori, K., Mitari, Y., Kaneda, Y., Subject independent facial expression recognition with robust face detection using a convolutional neural network. *Neural Netw.*, 16, 5–6, 555–9, 2003.

51. Hubel, D.H. and Wiesel, T.N., Receptive fields, binocular interaction and functional architecture in the cat's visual cortex. *J. Physiol.*, 160, 1, 106–54, 1962.

52. Lecun, Y., Bottou, L., Bengio, Y., Haffner, P., Gradient-based learning applied to document recognition. *Proc. IEEE*, 86, 11, 2278–324, 1998.

53. Krizhevsky, A., Sutskever, I., Hinton, G.E., ImageNet classification with deep convolutional neural networks. *Commun. ACM*, 60, 6, 84–90, 2017 May 24.

54. Cirean, D., Meier, U., Schmidhuber, J., Multi-Column Deep Neural Networks for Image Classification. *Proceedings of the Conference on Computer Vision and Pattern Recognition; IEEE'12*, Providence, RI, USA, June 16–21, 2012, pp. 3642–9, 2012.

55. Salakhutdinov, R. and Larochelle, H., Efficient Learning of Deep Boltzmann Machines. *Proceedings of the Thirteenth International Conference on Artificial Intelligence and Statistics; AISTATS'10*, Sardinia, Italy, May 13–15, 2010, pp. 693–700, 2010.

56. Hinton, G.E., Osindero, S., Teh, Y.W., A fast learning algorithm for deep belief nets. *Neural Comput.*, 18, 7, 1527–54, 2006 Jul.

57. Hinton, G.E. and Salakhutdinov, R.R., Reducing the dimensionality of data with neural networks. *Science*, 313, 5786, 504–7, 2006 Jul 28.

58. Ravi, D., Wong, C., Deligianni, F., Berthelot, M., Andreu-Perez, J., Lo, B., Yang, G.Z., Deep learning for health informatics. *IEEE J. Biomed. Health Inform.*, 21, 1, 4–21, 2017.

59. Ryu, S., Noh, J., Kim, H., Deep neural network-based demand side short term load forecasting. *Energies*, 10, 1, 3, 2016.

60. Goodfellow, I., Bengio, Y., Courville, A., *Deep Learning (Adaptive Computation and Machine Learning Series)*, MIT Press, Cambridge, Massachusetts, 2016.

61. Esteva, A., Robicquet, A., Ramsundar, B., Kuleshov, V., DePristo, M., Chou, K., Cui, C., Corrado, G., Thrun, S., Dean, J., A guide to deep learning in healthcare. *Nat. Med.*, 25, 24–29, 2019, https://doi.org/10.1038/s41591-018-0316-z.

62. https://www.allerin.com/blog/top-5-applications-of-deep-learning-in-healthcare.

63. https://emerj.com/ai-sector-overviews/machine-learning-healthcare-applications/.

64. Vollmer, S., Mateen, B.A., Bohner, G., Király, F.J., Ghani, R., Jonsson, P., Cumbers, S., Jonas, A., McAllister, K.S.L., Myles, P., Granger, D., Birse, M., Branson, R., Moons, K.G.M., Collins, G.S., Ioannidis, J.P.A., Holmes, C.,

Hemingway, H., Machine learning and artificial intelligence research for patient benefit: 20 critical questions on transparency, replicability, ethics, and effectiveness. *BMJ*, 368, l6927, 2020 Mar 20.

65. Steyerberg, E.W., Moons, K.G., van der Windt, D.A. *et al.*, PROGRESS Group. Prognosis Research Strategy (PROGRESS) 3: prognostic model research. *PLoS Med.*, 10, e1001381, 2013.

66. Snooks, H., Bailey-Jones, K., Burge-Jones, D. *et al.*, Effects and costs of implementing predictive risk stratification in primary care: a randomised stepped wedge trial. *BMJ Qual. Saf.*, 28, 697–705, 2019.

67. Avati, A., Jung, K., Harman, S., Downing, L., Ng, A., Shah, N.H., Improving palliative care with deep learning. *BMC Med. Inform. Decis. Mak.*, 18, Suppl 4, 122, 2018.

68. Avati, A., Jung, K., Harman, S., Downing, L., Ng, A., Shah, N.H., Improving palliative care with deep learning. *BMC Med. Inform. Decis. Mak.*, 18, Suppl 4, 122, 2018.

69. *UK Standards for Public Involvement in Research. Homepage*, 2018, NIHR Centre for Engagement and Dissemination, UK, https://sites.google.com/nihr.ac.uk/pi-standards/home.

70. Cortes, C., Jackel, L.D., Chiang, W.P., Limits on learning machine accuracy imposed by data quality, in: *Advances in neural information processing systems*, pp. 239–46, 1995.

71. Willetts, M., Hollowell, S., Aslett, L., Holmes, C., Doherty, A., Statistical machine learning of sleep and physical activity phenotypes from sensor data in 96,220 UK Biobank participants. *Sci. Rep.*, 8, 7961, 2018.

72. Siontis, G.C., Tzoulaki, I., Castaldi, P.J., Ioannidis, J.P., External validation of new risk prediction models is infrequent and reveals worse prognostic discrimination. *J. Clin. Epidemiol.*, 68, 25–34, 2015.

73. Hyndman, R.J. and Athanasopoulos, G., *Forecasting: principles and practice*, OTexts, Melbourne, Australia, 8 May 2018, https://otexts.com/fpp2/.

74. Lyddon, S., Walker, S., Holmes, C.C., Nonparametric learning from Bayesian models with randomized objective functions, in: *Advances in neural information processing systems*, pp. 2072–82, 2018.

75. Simonyan, K. and Zisserman, A., Very deep convolutional networks for large-scale image recognition, 3rd International Conference on Learning Representations, ICLR 2015, San Diego, CA, USA, May 7-9, 2015

76. Inouye, M., Abraham, G., Nelson, C.P., UK Biobank CardioMetabolic Consortium CHD Working Group *et al.*, Genomic risk prediction of coronary artery disease in 480,000 adults: implications for primary prevention. *J. Am. Coll. Cardiol.*, 72, 1883–93, 2018.

77. Chitra Dhawale, Kritika Dhawale, Rajesh Dubey. A Review on Deep Learning Applications. In book: Deep Learning Techniques and Optimization Strategies in Big Data Analytics, pp. 21–31, 2020.

78. Zaamout K., Zhang J.Z. , Improving Neural Networks Classification through Chaining. In: *Artificial Neural Networks and Machine Learning – ICANN 2012*,

Villa A.E.P., Duch W., Érdi P., Masulli F., Palm G. (eds.), ICANN 2012, Lecture Notes in Computer Science, vol. 7553. Springer, Berlin, Heidelberg, 2012, https://doi.org/10.1007/978-3-642-33266-1_36

79. Collins, G.S. and Moons, K.G.M., Comparing risk prediction models. *BMJ*, 344, e3186, 2012.

80. Morin, A., Urban, J., Sliz, P., A quick guide to software licensing for the scientist-programmer. *PLoS Comput. Biol.*, 8, e1002598, 2012.

81. Epstein, A.S., Zauderer, M.G., Gucalp, A. *et al.*, Next steps for IBM Watson Oncology: scalability to additional malignancies. *J. Clin. Oncol.*, 32, Suppl, 6618, 2014.

82. Suwanvecho, S., Suwanrusme, H., Sangtian, M., Norden, A., Urman, A., Hicks, A. *et al.*, Concordance assessment of a cognitive computing system in Thailand. *J. Clin. Oncol.*, 35, 15_suppl, 6589, 2017.

83. Somashekhar, S., Kumarc, R., Rauthan, A., Arun, K., Patil, P., Ramya, Y., Double blinded validation study to assess performance of IBM artificial intelligence platform, Watson for oncology in comparison with Manipal multidisciplinary tumour board – First study of 638 breast cancer cases. *Cancer Res.*, 77, 4 suppl, S6–07, 2017.

84. Baek, J., Ahn, S., Urman, A. *et al.*, Use of a cognitive computing system for treatment of colon and gastric cancer in South Korea. *J. Clin. Oncol.*, 35, 15_suppl, e18204, 2017.

85. Moons, K.G.M., Altman, D.G., Reitsma, J.B. *et al.*, Transparent Reporting of a multivariable prediction model for Individual Prognosis or Diagnosis (TRIPOD): explanation and elaboration. *Ann. Intern. Med.*, 162, W1–73, 2015.

An Insight Into Human Pose Estimation and Its Applications

Shambhavi Mishra[1]*, Janamejaya Channegowda[2] and Kasina Jyothi Swaroop[3]

[1]CBP Government Engineering College, Delhi, India
[2]Ramaiah Institute of Technology, Bengaluru, India
[3]Indian Institute of Technology (Indian School of Mines), Dhanbad, India

Abstract

Human pose estimation has been an active research area in computer vision and has received great attention till date. Motion tracking and activity recognition are some of the applications that utilize pose estimation. We define human pose estimation as localization of human joints (these joints are called key points—elbows, wrists, etc.) as well as labeling them in our data comprising either images or videos. In this chapter, we will describe fundamentals of human pose estimation and study different research approaches available in literature.

We will discuss different categories within pose estimation and mention key differences between them. The chapter will begin by reporting classical methods of pose estimation such as human pose recognition using motion segmentation and as well as deep learning–based methods explored in recent years. The chapter will also touch upon drawbacks of classical models and the evolution of Convolutional Neural Networks developed to overcome these shortcomings.

Keywords: Action recognition, pose estimation, pose detection, human activity recognition, human pose estimation, 2D pose estimation, 3D pose estimation, body joints localization

8.1 Foundations of Human Pose Estimation

Human pose estimation has been one of the most sought after fields in the domain of computer vision, thus receiving great attention from researchers.

---

*Corresponding author: shambhavimishra26@gmail.com

A. Suresh, S. Vimal, Y. Harold Robinson, Dhinesh Kumar Ramaswami and R. Udendhran (eds.)
Bioinformatics and Medical Applications: Big Data Using Deep Learning Algorithms, (147–170)
© 2022 Scrivener Publishing LLC

It can be described as the task of localization of body joints. The key positions, such as elbows, wrists, and knee joints, are body joints. Alternatively, we can characterize the estimation of the human pose as a problem statement where we predict a desired pose from a space of potential poses.

Human pose can be defined as spatial arrangement of key points or body joints. Analyzing human pose is of great interest and importance as it enables us to understand and retrieve important data regarding human activity. While text annotations describing movement in images or video can help us analyze the activity being performed, the prediction of the same becomes a challenging task.

In Figure 8.1, it is illustrated how the key points and thus the pose can be estimated in various different activities such as sports related (cricket, tennis, and swimming) as well as in a general conversational setting.

Video understanding is enhanced to a good effect with human pose estimation where we not only can label an image retrieved from a video with key points but also can also track movement of those key points in the subsequent frames.

There are multiple challenges associated with the task of HPE, and thus, there have been efforts to deal with them as well. In this chapter, we will explore challenges such as motion blur, indistinct background, occlusion, and lighting condition for the BBC Dataset [7] which introduced these difficulties for a more robust estimation model.

HPE can be approached in two ways, (a) *Top to Down Method* approaches the problem by first performing object detection and subsequently

Figure 8.1 Different poses are illustrated in the figure with the detected key points. Pose estimation in different scenarios can be understood from this figure [1].

generating bounding boxes which leads to pose estimation, while (b) *Bottom to Up Method* labels all the body parts and key points first and later grouping them by fitting a human body model.

Apart from the methodologies based on how to approach the problem, HPE can also be classified on the basis of a regression-based model or a detection-based model. We can understand the regression-based approach as a mapping technique between the key points of body models to the frame containing the object. The detection model is a goal-based technique, in which each body part is viewed as a target and depicted as an image patch or a heat map of the body joints.

Another classification can be dimension based where we consider human pose estimation in 2D and 3D. In the following sections, we will go through each one in depth.

It is also important to understand the human body models that we referenced in detection-based approach to HPE.

Human Body Models: Using a human body model as a guide to estimate the pose is an important part of our task. We can formulate human body models in majorly three types of representations: (a) skeleton-based models, (b) contour-based models, and (c) volume-based models.

As illustrated in Figure 8.2a, the *skeleton-based model* is a graphical topology where vertices are the body joint or key points. This model is extremely simple and thus is widely used in human pose estimation. However, it lacks important information about the general body make-up. *Contour-based model* as illustrated in Figure 8.2b calculates estimates of the shape of body parts. Such models have been exploited during the initial attempts at HPE such as cardboard models (Ju *et al.*) [3] and Active Shape Models (ASMs) (Cootes *et al.*) [4]. *Volume-based models* consist of 3D human body shapes described with the help of geometric shapes or meshes. While conic sections can be used to model the limbs, meshes are more flexible and thus proven to be a better representation for the human body.

8.2   Challenges to Human Pose Estimation

Tracing the origins of our HPE, the proposed methods by Hogg *et al.* [5] and O'Rourke *et al.* [6] in the 1980s garnered great attention. Although the introduction of Deep Learning for the task has facilitated the progress of research, we still face all the difficulties of a natural environment such

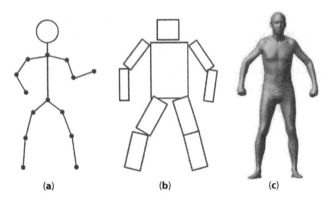

(a)   (b)   (c)

Figure 8.2 Image illustrating different body models [2].

as presence of multiple objects in the frame to be considered, occlusion, illumination, and variation in textural information.

8.2.1   Motion Blur

As illustrated in Figure 8.3a, the hands of the TV anchor are motion blurred and have no solid region for inferences; thus, motion blur poses a challenge to pose estimation and gesture recognition for BBC Dataset [7]. BBC TV Signing Dataset is a part of VGG human pose estimation datasets and contains 20 video sequences with a length of 30 to 90 minutes each. The dataset was created with the help of a sign language interpreter.

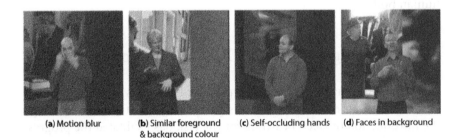

(a) Motion blur   (b) Similar foreground   (c) Self-occluding hands   (d) Faces in background
                       & background colour

Figure 8.3 Challenges to human pose estimation [7].

Sometimes, when the motion is too quick or fast and we are unable to capture it at our selected frames per second (fps) rate, we end up facing motion blur. It can also take place due to a longer exposure.

Tracking the object and thus the key points becomes difficult and motion blur during these rapid movements result in loss of data for pose estimation.

8.2.2   Indistinct Background

Color information is less helpful when the foreground and background colors are identical. From Figure 8.3b, we can understand that the color scheme of the anchor complements the background, thus making it a challenging task to segment the body and locate the key points.

As illustrated in the fourth image, the presence of more than one face also makes it difficult to analyze the pose and motion of the primary object. Recent advances, on the other hand, have allowed us to estimate the pose of multiple objects or people in a single frame. We shall study these approaches as we move ahead in the chapter.

8.2.3   Occlusion or Self-Occlusion

Occlusion is defined as the state of complete obstruction of the object in focus, thus making pose estimation a challenge. Self-occlusion is the state when an object occludes itself. For example, one hand overlapping another or face being occluded by hands, it can also be seen in Figure 8.3c, where anchor's hands are occluded and thus we are unable to track her pose.

In real-time human pose estimation, occlusion or self-occlusion is one of the most common problems. Occlusion often occurs when more than one person is present in a frame.

8.2.4   Lighting Conditions

Images can be taken at any time, in any location leading to different lighting conditions. For example, due to the existence of the shadows, the overall brightness of the same scene may be different. Moreover, cameras tend to automatically adjust exposure for the environmental lighting that may lead to over-exposed or under-exposed problems. As in a video sequence, the lighting conditions are prone to constant changes, and thus, it is a challenge to track the key points. Natural scenes also offer a great deal of variance of brightness, and thus, this problem needs attention from researchers in the domain of human pose estimation.

Other physical factors like difference in color and texture of clothing make segmentation of primary objects a challenge. Also, presence of multiple objects such as in Figure 8.3d faces in the background also makes it difficult for the correct pose to be estimated for a given primary object. However, this difficulty was overcome by models suitable for multi-person human pose estimation. We also have to consider that articulated objects like human bodies can take on a large variety of possible body poses, and in an unconstrained situation, pose estimation can be quite challenging.

8.3   Analyzing the Dimensions

Human pose estimation can be done with either two-dimensional or three-dimensional coordinates from an RGB image. We will talk about them, as well as the improvement in 2D and 3D human pose estimation, in this section.

8.3.1   2D Human Pose Estimation

In the case of 2D HPE, 2D pose (x, y) coordinates from monocular images or videos are considered for each key point. The extraction of fabricated features was a part of the standard approach to human pose estimation. Single-person pose estimation and multi-person pose estimation are two forms of modern 2D human pose estimation based on Deep Learning. In the following subsections, let us research these approaches in detail. A methodology to extract a two-dimensional human pose from an image and subsequently estimate a three-dimensional pose has been illustrated below in Figure 8.4.

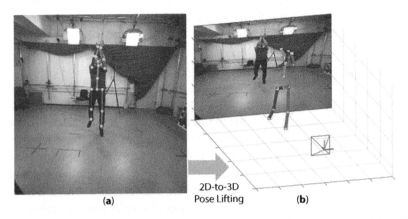

Figure 8.4 The figure illustrates 2D pose estimation extracted from an image and then the subsequent estimated 3D pose [8].

8.3.1.1   Single-Person Pose Estimation

The traditional method for estimating the articulated human pose involves inferring a series of data collected on body parts and their spatial interconnections. With the introduction of "DeepPose" by Toshev *et al.* [10], the research on human pose estimation saw a dynamic shift from traditional approaches to deep networks. Since their conception, Convolution Neural Networks (CNNs) have significantly expanded the scope of study in order to achieve local observations of body parts. Tompson *et al.* [11] developed a deep architecture that generates heat maps by passing an image through multiple resolution banks using a graphical model. Furthermore, Pfister *et al.* [12] used CNNs to indirectly capture global spatial dependencies by building networks with wide receptive fields. Later, Carreira *et al.* [13] introduced a concept in which a self-correcting model was used instead of directly predicting the outcomes in one go, and this process is known as Iterative Error Feedback. Iterative Error Feedback progressively enhances an initial solution by feeding back predictions of error. This was followed by stellar methods like Stacked Hourglass Networks for human pose estimation [14]. We shall discuss more about these methods later in the chapter.

8.3.1.2   Multi-Person Pose Estimation

Multi-person pose estimation overcomes the limitations of occlusion by more than one person in a frame being considered for pose estimation. It involves estimating poses of all present people in the video sequence or image frame. A top-down technique has previously been used for multi-person pose estimation. The top-down approach initially executes detection, and the pose is calculated on each detected region uniquely for each individual after identifying individuals in the frame being considered. In contrast to this approach, Cao *et al.* [9] introduced OpenPose, which introduced the first bottom-up representation using Part Affinity Fields (PAFs) of association scores, a set of 2D vector fields that represent the position and orientation of limbs across the image's domain. OpenPose was followed by HRNet (High-Resolution Network) by Sun *et al.* [15] which outperforms all the prior methodologies utilizing key point detection and pose estimation. Further in the chapter, we will study all the important propositions and methodologies. In Figure 8.5, we can observe pose estimation for multiple people in a given frame.

8.3.2   3D Human Pose Estimation

We attempt to detect the (x, y, z) coordinates for each joint (key point) on the human body from a picture containing an individual in the case of 3D

Figure 8.5 The image illustrates multi-person pose estimation for different numbers of people in the frames.

human pose estimation. We can deduce that recovering 3D pose from 2D RGB images is more difficult than 2D pose estimation due to the larger 3D pose space and other related ambiguities.

We can approach 3D pose estimation through two different ideologies: first one involves a model capable of inferring 3D key points from image under analysis and the other approach first considers 2D key points and then transforms them into 3D. Based on the first approach, EpipolarPose is a model that has been learned to estimate both 2D and 3D key points simultaneously. It overcomes the problem of a lack of high-quality 3D pose annotations by creating a self-supervised 3D ground truth by applying epipolar geometry to 2D predictions.

Multiple models such as PoseNet and HRNet utilise the second approach for 3D HPE.

Alternatively, we can also consider a multi-view visual data based approach where we capture the object from different possible angles. This approach facilitates a depth-based detection and also overcomes challenges such as occlusion.

8.4   Standard Datasets for Human Pose Estimation

Datasets are central to developments in deep learning. They are not only an important parameter for comparing different approaches, but they also allow robust techniques to be formulated to address challenges and complexities in the real world. In this section of the chapter, we will look at some common datasets for the human pose estimation task. Table 8.1 lists all of the related datasets that were used for benchmarking and evaluation.

Table 8.1 The table contains a list of datasets in 2D and 3D human pose estimation and their features [16].

Dataset	2D or 3D	Features	Content/Frames/Images
Pascal VOC 2009	2D	Actions included such as riding a horse, running and walking, etc.	7054 images
KTH Multi-View Football Dataset I	2D	Football players' annotated joints to utilize for multi-view reconstruction.	771 images
MPII Human Pose Dataset	2D	Actions included rope skipping, batting, rock climbing, etc.	25,000 frames
BBC Pose	2D	Sign Language based Dataset	20 Videos
COCO 16 COCO 17	2D	Various body poses from Google, Bing, etc.	200,000 images, 250,000 labeled instances
Joint annotated human motion database (J-HMDB)	2D	Large body movements dataset with 21 actions in total.	31,838 annotated frames
KTH Multi-View Football Dataset II	3D	Professional footballers with their joints labelled and the ground truth available in both 2D and 3D	800 time frames with 14 annotated joints
Human 3.6M	3D	11 subjects and 17 actions	3.6 Million 3D Human Poses
DensePose	3D	Extension on 50K images on COCO	50K Humans
AMASS Dataset	3D	Unifies 15 different optical marker-based human motion capture datasets. Each body joint has 3 rotational Degrees of Freedom	40 hours of motion data, 300 subjects, more than 11K motions

8.4.1 Pascal VOC (Visual Object Classes) Dataset

Figure 8.6 Object annotated images from Pascal VOC Dataset.

The Pascal VOC Dataset is a series of object detection datasets obtained as part of the PASCAL VOC project [17]. Figure 8.6 demonstrates a few annotated images with their bounding boxes from the Pascal VOC Dataset. From 2005 to 2012, the project ran competitions to evaluate results on object class recognition. The generally accepted benchmark is to use the 2012 training and evaluation sets, as well as the 2007 validation test set.

8.4.2 KTH Multi-View Football Dataset I

Figure 8.7 These images are from KTH Multi-view Football Dataset [18].

This dataset [18] is composed primarily of pictures from three different cameras of three professional footballers during the Allsvenskan League match as illustrated in Figure 8.7. A total of 771 photos of football players are included in the dataset, which contains pictures taken with 14 annotated body joints from three views at 257 time instances.

8.4.3 KTH Multi-View Football Dataset II

This is a KTH Multi-View Football Dataset I 3D extension and includes multi-view pictures of professional football players with a 3D pose of ground reality. There are 800 time frames in the dataset, captured from three views (2,400 images). The views are calibrated and synchronized with the images. For each frame, we also have a 3D ground truth pose and orthographic camera matrix. The dataset consists of two distinct players with 14 annotated joints and two sequences per player.

8.4.4   MPII Human Pose Dataset

Figure 8.8 MPII Human Pose Dataset with annotated body joints.

The MPII Dataset [19] is a state-of-the-art benchmark for estimating articulated human pose comprising 25,000 images with annotated body joints for more than 40,000 individuals as shown in Figure 8.8. In addition, 410 human movements that were derived from a YouTube video comprise the dataset.

8.4.5   BBC Pose

Figure 8.9 BBC Pose Dataset with overlaid sign language interpreter.

BBC Pose [7] is part of the VGG human pose estimation datasets, which are a series of massive video datasets annotated with human upper-body pose as shown in Figure 8.9. BBC Pose has 20 videos filmed with an overlaid sign language interpreter from the BBC with a period of 0.5 to 1.5 hours each.

We have already explored challenges that this dataset proposes when we analyzed the challenges to human pose estimation. The dataset is created with 9 signers with different background and illumination conditions.

8.4.6   COCO Dataset

Figure 8.10 COCO Dataset with the object classes.

Another benchmark for assessment is Microsoft Common Objects in Context (COCO) Dataset [20]. COCO is a large-scale dataset originally suggested for natural environments for everyday object detection and segmentation. More than 200,000 images were gathered from Google, Bing, and Flickr image searches. A few samples from the COCO dataset are illustrated above in Figure 8.10. In addition, suitable cases for HPE were chosen from this dataset, resulting in two more datasets for public key point detection problems, COCO key points 2016, and COCO key points 2017.

8.4.7   J-HMDB Dataset

Joint-annotated Human Motion Database (J-HMDB) [21] is derived from the HMDB51 dataset, a dataset for action recognition. Out of 51 actions from HMDB51, 21 actions were chosen due to their large body movements such as jump, throw, wave, and kick. A total of 31,838 annotated frames from 928 clips were selected.

8.4.8   Human3.6M Dataset

Figure 8.11 Human3.6M Dataset.

The Human3.6M Dataset [22] includes 3.6 million 3D human poses performed by 11 professional actors (six men and five women) from four different perspectives. A total of 17 scenarios were considered while creating the dataset which include discussion, smoking, and taking photographs as illustrated in Figure 8.11.

8.4.9   DensePose

Facebook researchers suggested "DensePose: Dense Human Pose Estimation in the Wild" [23] to establish dense correspondences (as in the Figure 8.12) from a 2D RGB image to a 3D surface of the human body. The COCO-DensePose Dataset for dense real-life image correspondence comprises over 5 million manually annotated translations from 2D images to 3D surfaces, with over 50,000 human annotations.

Figure 8.12 Image correspondence with DensePose.

8.4.10   AMASS Dataset

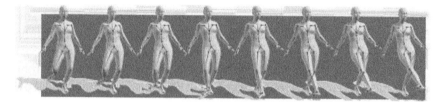

Figure 8.13 AMASS Dataset.

AMASS [24] is a broad human motion dataset that includes a recently introduced method, MoSh++, which converts data from MoCap to 3D human meshes as illustrated in Figure 8.13. MoCap, or Motion Capture character animation, is the process of capturing and applying the action of an actor to a 3D character. There are more than 40 hours of motion data in the dataset, covering more than 300 topics, more than 11,000 movements, and is available for study.

8.5   Deep Learning Revolutionizing Pose Estimation

In this part, we will look at some of the most important models in the field of human pose estimation.

8.5.1   Approaches in 2D Human Pose Estimation

The first significant paper developing a Deep Learning–based approach to HPE was DeepPose by Toshev *et al.* [10]. As a DNN-based regression task considering key points, it formulates the task of pose estimation. Utilizing a cascade of multiple DNN regressors resulted in an estimation of poses with high precision. The inspiration behind exploring DNN came from the impressive findings on both classification and localization tasks.

Figure 8.14 Left: pose regression; Right: pose refinement.

The model approaches the task through refinement of pose estimates using cascaded regressors as illustrated in Figure 8.14. The input frame is refined by a DNN-based refiner to obtain a good approximation, and images are then cropped to correspond to the intended joint and transferred to the next stage as input. As a result, the regressors learn features from the higher resolution images, resulting in improved precision.

DeepPose outperformed other state-of-the-art models by a wide margin on the metric Percentage of Correct Parts (PCP) on Leeds Sports Dataset (LSP) and Frames Labeled In Cinema (FLIC) Dataset.

Efficient Object Localization Using Convolutional Networks by Tompson *et al.* [11]

Convolutional Neural Networks (CNNs) provide layers of pooling and subsampling that decrease computational requirements, add invariance, and escape over-training. Pooling, however, comes along with the expense of decreased accuracy of localization.

The emphasis of this approach was on an effective method of object localization using ConvNets. It suggested a novel architecture with an effective model of "position refinement" trained to estimate the joint location in a limited image area. This method reuses convolution functions to decrease the number of trainable parameters, unlike a traditional cascade of models. Generation of heat maps by processing an image multiple times through resolution banks as illustrated in Figure 8.15. Helps in capturing the features. A heatmap predicts the likelihood of the joint occurring at each pixel.

Convolutional Pose Machines by Wei *et al.* [25] utilizes a pose machine. Pose machines consist of two sequential modules, the first one computes features from an image while the second one is a prediction module. For the task of pose estimation for learning image features and image-dependent spatial models, this method combines convolution networks with the pose machine paradigm. The model aims to achieve long range spatial relationships using larger receptive fields. The Figure 8.16 details the output from such a model.

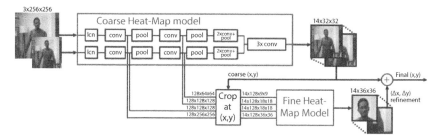

Figure 8.15 Overview of the cascaded architecture.

Figure 8.16 Results from a convolutional pose machine.

Human Pose Estimation With Iterative Error Feedback by Carriera *et al.* [12] proposes a self-correcting model that feeds back error predictions to progressively modify an initial solution as illustrated in Figure 8.17. IEF outperforms the state-of-the-art in the challenging MPII and LSP benchmarks for articulated pose estimation, matching the state-of-the-art without requiring ground truth scale annotation.

Stacked Hourglass Networks for Human Pose Estimation [14] was a landmark paper that reformed the following approaches for human pose estimation. The name "Stacked Hourglass" is inspired by its construction, consisting of measures of pooling and upsampling layers that look like a

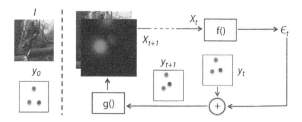

Figure 8.17 Iterative Error Feedback (IEF) mechanism for 2D human pose estimation.

stacked hourglass which can also be observed from the Figure 8.18 below. Although local evidence is necessary for characteristics such as face and hands to be established, global context is needed for a final pose estimate. The hourglass helps to collect data on all scales, thus fully capturing global and local information.

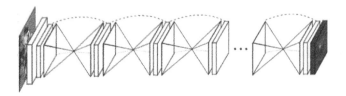

Figure 8.18 Stacked hourglass module.

The latest state-of-the-art High Resolution Net (HRNet) model [15] has outperformed all the previous models on the COCO dataset for key point recognition, multi-person pose estimation, and pose estimation tasks. Unlike previous models focused on restoring high-resolution representations, during the entire process, HRNet follows a high-resolution representation.

The HRNet (High-Resolution Network) model outperformed all current techniques on the COCO dataset for key point Identification, multi-person pose estimation, and pose estimation tasks. A very basic concept is pursued by HRNet. Most of the previous papers were portrayed in a high, low, high-resolution rendering. Throughout the entire process, HRNet retains a high-resolution representation, and this functions very well.

As illustrated in Figure 8.19, in its first phase, the architecture consists of a high-resolution subnetwork that is connected to the multi-resolution

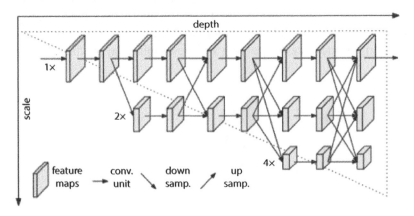

Figure 8.19 Architecture for HRNet.

subnetworks in parallel by successively adding high to low-resolution sub-networks. Such parallel multi-resolution networks thus conduct multi-scale fusions.

8.5.2   Approaches in 3D Human Pose Estimation

3D Human Pose Estimation = 2D Pose Estimation + Matching by Chen *et al.* [26], by intermediate 2D pose predictions, approaches the challenge of 3D pose estimation which is also detailed in Figure 8.20.

A single RGB image is taken into account by the model and a probabilistic formulation is used over the variables: image I, 3D pose X and 2D pose x, and the joint likelihood is computed as follows:

$$p(X, x, I) = p(X|x, I) \cdot p(x|I) \cdot p(I)$$

The first term, p(X, x, I), is a Nearest Neighbor Model, while the second term, p(X, x, I), is a CNN that returns "n" 2D heat maps (n: no. of joints). The third term is modeled using a Nearest Neighbor Model, which returns 1-Nearest Neighbor (1NN) 3D depth.

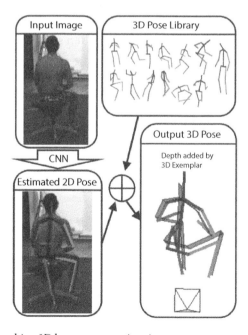

Figure 8.20 Approaching 3D human pose estimation.

DensePose by Guler *et al.* [23]: The aim is to establish dense correspondences between an RGB image and a surface-based representation of a human body, a role we call "density human pose estimation". Some results from DensePose are illustrated in the Figure 8.21.

DensePose-RCNN Results   DensePose COCO Dataset

Figure 8.21 Left: Results from DensePose-RCNN; Middle: DensePose COCO Dataset annotations; Right: Partitioning and UV parametrization of the body surface.

The COCO-DensePose dataset introduced includes annotations of more than 5 million correspondences for 50,000 humans.

As shown in Figure 8.22, the model architecture consists of a completely convolutional network (FC) that performs both classification and regression tasks. In order to approximate surface coordinates coarsely, we first identify an individual pixel as either a part of the context or one of the many area components. The exact coordinates of the pixel inside the portion of the region are then shown using a regression model.

Region-based DensePose Regression was also addressed in the paper where a cascade of proposed regions of interest (ROI) was discovered and area-adapted characteristics were extracted through ROI pooling which were then fed into region specific branches of the model.

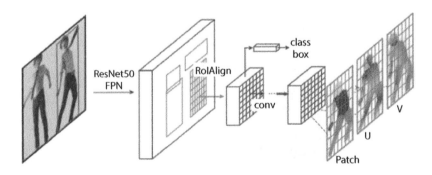

Figure 8.22 DensePose-R CNN model.

8.6   Application of Human Pose Estimation in Medical Domains

Human pose estimation in the medical field is heavily used for a wide range of surgical tests. The applications range from gait analysis to the detection of a particular pattern of room use for the same type of procedure and the distinction of different types of operations. HPE in bed or patients in rest has also been researched upon.

In this section, we study "Human Pose Estimation under Blanket Occlusion" for patients in bed. Human pose estimation was majorly considered as a classification task to classify the physical status of a patient [26, 27]. Li *et al.* [27] retrieve the patient location using a Kinect sensor and calculate the related status for an exposed patient body.

A method to track breathing patterns and various sleeping positions by extracting torso and head locations was suggested by Yu *et al.* [28]. Shotton *et al.* [29] and Girshick *et al.* [30] train Random Forests on a large, non-public virtual dataset of depth frames in attempt to achieve a wide range of human forms and poses.

With advances in Deep Learning, Belagiannis *et al.* [31] propose the use of a CNN to locate 2D key points in RGB images. Furthermore, Fragkiadaki *et al.* [32] attempted to utilize an RNN to improve the results of a CNN for predicting pose from an RGB video.

Felix Achilles *et al.* [33] proposed a novel dataset "*Patient MoCap Dataset*" and a new methodology to approach the pose detection under blanket occlusion. A few results on this dataset are illustrated below in the Figure 8.23.

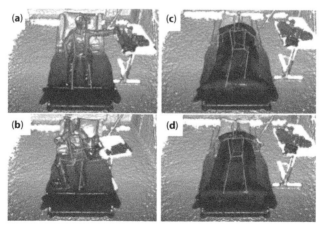

Figure 8.23 Left: pose estimation without blanket; Right: pose estimation with occlusion from a blanket.

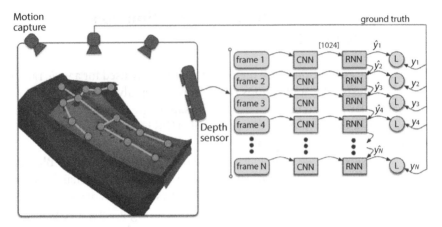

Figure 8.24 Combined CNN-RNN model.

A collection of sequences is included in the Patient MoCap Dataset: (a) simpler sequences with no occlusion and restricted movement, and (b) another harder series with high occlusion and a high degree of movement. A total of 10 subjects (5 female and 5 male) were requested to repeat 10 sequences at 30 fps. Fourteen body joints or key points were annotated for 180,000 frames comprising the dataset.

The end-to-end learning feature for the integrated CNN-RNN model, illustrated in Figure 8.24, was suggested by the model proposed by Felix Achilles at al., which enables it to effectively respond to the low contrast of the occluded limbs, making it a useful tool in realistic environments for activity recognition.

S. Liu *et al.* [34] suggested a novel vision-based method inspired by physics that solves the difficult problems associated with in-bed pose estimation, including tracking a fully clothed person in total darkness. Simultaneously collected multimodal Lying Pose (SLP), a fully annotated in-bed pose dataset comparable to existing large-scale human pose datasets (such as MPII), was also published to aid in the training and evaluation of complex models.

8.7   Conclusion

Since the invention of CNNs, we may infer that human pose estimation has advanced significantly. The advancement is no longer limited to 2D HPE and now includes 3D HPE as well.

We went through all the potential classifications in great detail, as well as the benchmarking datasets. Recent and important Deep Learning–based models were also examined.

References

1. Figure 8.1 https://nanonets.com/blog/human-pose-estimation-2d-guide/
2. Figure 8.2 Human Body Models: https://www.mdpi.com/1424-8220/16/12/1966/htm
3. Ju, S.X., Black, M., Yacoob, Y., Cardboard people: A parameterized model of articulated image motion. *Proceedings of the Second International Conference on Automatic Face and Gesture Recognition.* IEEE, 38–44, 1996.
4. Hill, A., Cootes, T., Taylor, C., Active Shape Models and the Shape Approximation Problem. *Image Vision Comput.*, 14, 601–607, 1996, 10.1016/0262-8856(96)01097-9.
5. Hogg, D., Model-based vision: a program to see a walking person. *Image Vision Comput.*, 1, 1, 5–20, 1983.
6. O'Rourke, J. and Badler, N.I., Model-based image analysis of human motion using constraint propagation. *Pattern Anal. Mach. Intell., IEEE Trans.*, 6, 522–536 1980.
7. Charles, J., Pfister, T., Magee, D., Hogg, D., Zisserman, A., Domain Adaptation for Upper Body Pose Tracking in Signed TV Broadcasts. *BMVC 2013 - Electronic Proceedings of the British Machine Vision Conference 2013*, pp. 47.1–47.11, 2013, 10.5244/C.27.47.
8. Figure 8.4: https://www.groundai.com/project/absposelifter-absolute-3d-human-pose-lifting-network-from-a-single-noisy-2d-human-pose/1
9. Cao, Z., Hidalgo, G., Simon, T., Wei, S.-E., Sheikh, Y., OpenPose: Realtime Multi-Person 2D Pose Estimation using Part Affinity Fields, arXiv:1812.08008, IEEE transactions on pattern analysis and machine intelligence, 43, 172–186, 2019.
10. Toshev, A. and Szegedy, C., DeepPose: Human Pose Estimation via Deep Neural Networks. *2014 IEEE Conference on Computer Vision and Pattern Recognition*, Columbus, OH, pp. 1653–1660, 2014.
11. Tompson, J.J., Jain, A., LeCun, Y., Bregler, C., Joint training of a convolutional network and a graphical model for human pose estimation, in: *NIPS*, 1325–1339, 2014.
12. Pfister, T., Charles, J., Zisserman, A., Flowing convnets for human pose estimation in videos, in: *ICCV*, 2015.
13. Carreira, J., Agrawal, P., Fragkiadaki, K., Malik, J., Human Pose Estimation with Iterative Error Feedback, IEEE conference on computer vision and pattern recognition, 4733–4742, 2015.

14. Newell, A., Yang, K., Deng, J., *Stacked Hourglass Networks for Human Pose Estimation*, IEEE conference on computer vision and pattern recognition, vol. 9912, Springer, pp. 483–499, 2016, 10.1007/978-3-319-46484-8_29.

15. Sun, Xiao, B., Liu, D., Wang, J., Deep High-Resolution Representation Learning for Human Pose Estimation. *Proceedings of the IEEE/CVF Conference on Computer Vision and Pattern Recognition*, 5686–5696, 2019.

16. Figure 8.5 Multi Person Pose Estimation http://pages.iai.uni-bonn.de/iqbal_umar/multiperson-pose/

17. Everingham, M., Gool, L.V., Williams, C., Winn, J., Zisserman, A., The PASCAL Visual Object Classes Challenge 2009 (VOC2009). http://www.pascal-network. org/challenges/VOC/voc2007/workshop/index. html

18. Kazemi, V. and Sullivan, J., Using Richer Models for Articulated Pose Estimation of Footballers. *BMVC 2012 - Electronic Proceedings of the British Machine Vision Conference 2012*, 2012, 10.5244/C.26.6.

19. Andriluka, M., Pishchulin, L., Gehler, P., Schiele, B., 2D Human Pose Estimation: New Benchmark and State of the Art Analysis, 2014 IEEE Conference on Computer Vision and Pattern Recognition, 3686–3693, 2014, 10.1109/CVPR.2014.471.

20. Lin, T.-Y., Maire, M., Belongie, S., Bourdev, L., Girshick, R., Hays, J., Perona, P., Ramanan, D., Zitnick, C.L., Dollár, P., Microsoft COCO: Common Objects in Context, in: *Computer Vision – ECCV 2014. 13th European Conference, Proceedings, Part V*, vol. 8693 Springer, Cham, pp. 740–755, 2014.

21. Jhuang, H., Gall, J., Zuffi, S., Schmid, C., Black, M., Towards Understanding Action Recognition. *Proceedings of the IEEE International Conference on Computer Vision*, pp. 3192–3199, 2013, 10.1109/ICCV.2013.396.

22. Ionescu, C., Papava, D., Olaru, V., Sminchisescu, C., Human3.6M: Large Scale Datasets and Predictive Methods for 3D Human Sensing in Natural Environments. *IEEE Trans. Pattern Anal. Mach. Intell.*, 36, 1325–1339, 2013, 10.1109/TPAMI.2013.248.

23. Guler, R., Neverova, N., Kokkinos, I., *DensePose: Dense Human Pose Estimation in the Wild*, IEEE conference on computer vision and pattern recognition, pp. 7297–7306, 2018, 10.1109/CVPR.2018.00762.

24. Mahmood, N., Ghorbani, N., Troje, N., Pons-Moll, G., Black, M., AMASS: Archive of Motion Capture As Surface Shapes. Proceedings of the IEEE/CVF International Conference on Computer Vision, 5441–5450, 2019.

25. Wei, S.-E., Ramakrishna, V., Kanade, T., Sheikh, Y., Convolutional Pose Machines, IEEE conference on Computer Vision and Pattern Recognition, 4724–4732, 2016.

26. Chen, C.-H. and Ramanan, D., 3D Human Pose Estimation = 2D Pose Estimation + Matching. *Proceedings of the IEEE Conference on Computer Vision and Pattern Recognition*, 5759–5767, 2017.

27. Li, Y., Berkowitz, L., Noskin, G., Mehrotra, S., Detection of Patient's Bed Statuses in 3D Using a Microsoft Kinect, in: *EMBC 2014*, 2014 36th Annual

International Conference of the IEEE Engineering in Medicine and Biology Society, IEEE, 2014.

28. Yu, M.C., Wu, H., Liou, J.L., Lee, M.S., Hung, Y.P., Multiparameter Sleep Monitoring Using a Depth Camera, in: *Biomedical Engineering Systems and Technologies*, Springer, Berlin, Heidelberg, 2012.

29. Shotton, J., Sharp, T., Kipman, A., Fitzgibbon, A., Finocchio, M., Blake, A., Cook, M., Moore, R., Real-Time Human Pose Recognition in Parts from Single Depth Images. *Commun. ACM*, 56, 1, 116–124, 2013.

30. Girshick, R., Shotton, J., Kohli, P., Criminisi, A., Fitzgibbon, A., Efficient Regression of General-Activity Human Poses from Depth Images, in: *ICCV 2011*, IEEE, 2011.

31. Belagiannis, V., Rupprecht, C., Carneiro, G., Navab, N., Robust Optimization for Deep Regression, in: *ICCV 2015*, IEEE, 2015.

32. Fragkiadaki, K., Levine, S., Felsen, P., Malik, J., Recurrent Network Models for Human Dynamics, in: *ICCV 2015*, IEEE, 2015.

33. Achilles, F., Ichim, A.-E., Coskun, H., Tombari, F., Noachtar, S., Navab, N., Patient MoCap: Human Pose Estimation Under Blanket Occlusion for Hospital Monitoring Applications. International conference on medical image computing and computer-assisted intervention. Springer, Cham, 491–499, 2016.

34. Liu, S., Huang, X., Fu, N., Li, C., Su, Z., Ostadabbas, S., Simultaneously-Collected Multimodal Lying Pose Dataset: Towards In-Bed Human Pose Monitoring under Adverse Vision Conditions, *arXiv preprint arXiv:2008.08735*, 2020.

Brain Tumor Analysis Using Deep Learning: Sensor and IoT-Based Approach for Futuristic Healthcare

Rohit Rastogi[1]*, D.K. Chaturvedi[2], Sheelu Sagar[3], Neeti Tandon[4]
and Akshit Rajan Rastogi[1]

[1]Department of CSE, ABES Engineering College Ghaziabad, U.P., India
[2]Department of Electrical Engineering, Dayalbagh Educational Institute, Agra, India
[3]Amity International Business School, Amity University, Noida, U.P., India
[4]Vikram University, Ujjain, M.P., India

Abstract

One of the biggest problems in the quantitative evaluation of brain tumor treatment is finding the tumor type. The ambiguous magnetic resonance imaging (MRI) imaging strategy is currently the best classroom analysis tool for radiation-free brain tumors. Studies have shown that attractive imaging (MRI) features of different brain tumors can be used recently to make correction decisions. The manual part of a brain tumor to identify malignant growth is a tedious, tedious, and tedious task of teaching MRI clinical images. Recently, programming sections that use deep learning strategies are imaginative projects. These techniques yield the best results in the classroom and are easier to perform than other access methods. The ultimate goal of this investment is to use MRI images of the framed brain to create deep neural system models that can be isolated between different types of heart tumors. CNN is an iterative architecture that uses circular filters to perform complex operations in recent years. Precision is used as the basis for system performance. Trained neural networks show about 98% accuracy. There are too many connections for the Rain Collection and the 95% Credit Collection. We plan to improve accuracy and eliminate excesses.

*Corresponding author: rohit.rastogi@abes.ac.in

A. Suresh, S. Vimal, Y. Harold Robinson, Dhinesh Kumar Ramaswami and R. Udendhran (eds.)
Bioinformatics and Medical Applications: Big Data Using Deep Learning Algorithms, (171–190)
© 2022 Scrivener Publishing LLC

Keywords: Big data analytics in healthcare, artificial intelligence for health informatics, sensors for the Internet of Things, deep neural network, multimodal data fusion for healthcare, brain tumors, confusion matrix

9.1 Introduction

9.1.1 Brain Tumor

The human brain is naturally at the apex and very complicated body part and can function in billions of cells. Brain tumors occur when ill and spurious cells replicate and grow in an uncontrolled manner. This dangerously increasing population of cells is capable of destroying healthy cells and also, affecting the normal functioning of the brain. Brain tumors are classified into categories: first one is "benign or low-grade" and the second one is "malignant or high-grade".

Because a benign tumor is non-progressive (non-cancerous), it is less vascular and grows and exhibits more slowly in the brain. Also, other parts of the body are not affected by this tumor. But, on the other hand, the malignant tumor is cancerous or destructive and grows rapidly at unknown boundaries [1, 3].

9.1.2 Big Data Analytics in Health Informatics

Live computer programming element is the main difference between big data health and traditional health analysis. When we look toward traditional systems, for analyzing big data, the healthcare industry is totally dependent on other industries. Due to the significant impact of information technology, many healthcare professionals rely on it because the operating systems are functional and capable of processing data in standard formats [5, 7].

Presently, the rapid development of large amounts of healthcare data is becoming a major challenge for the healthcare industry. With the expanding and ingesting field of big data analytics, useful insights into healthcare systems can be provided. As mentioned above, most of the data generated by this system are stored and printed as there may be a requirement to be digitized [7, 8].

9.1.3   Machine Learning in Healthcare

Data mining uses the concept of scanning two pieces of data which helps in identifying scanning patterns. This concept of data mining is quite similar to machine learning. Machine learning does not use data extraction programs such as data mining programs which are based on human understanding to extract data but it uses these data in order to enhance the understanding of program. Also, machine learning helps in recognizing data patterns and modifying performance of programs accordingly [9].

9.1.4   Sensors for Internet of Things

A brand new model that facilitates our lives by connecting electronic devices and sensors through internal networks is termed as the Internet of Things (IoT). The IoT uses smart devices and the Internet to provide innovative solutions to a variety of challenges and problems related to various commercial, public, and public and private industries around the world. IoT has become an important aspect of our lives that we can feel around us. In general, the IoT is an innovation that integrates various intelligent systems, frameworks, and smart devices and sensors. Also, it uses quantum and nanotechnology in terms of unimaginable memory, measurement, and processing speed. This can be seen as a prerequisite for creating an innovative business plan with security, reliability, and collaboration in mind [11–13].

Here are 9 most popular IoT sensors:

1. Temperature
2. Moisture
3. Pressure
4. Adjacent
5. Surface
6. Accelerometer
7. Gyroscope
8. Gas
9. Infrared [11]

Let us look at some statistics to see the progress of IoT in healthcare.

Business Insider forecasts more than 161 million healthcare IoT devices by 2020 (Figure 9.1).

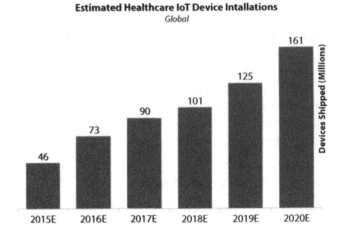

Figure 9.1 Estimated healthcare IoT device installation [14].

9.1.5   Challenges and Critical Issues of IoT in Healthcare

Data security and privacy are the most important challenges of IoT. Smart phones or other smart devices like smart TVs, smart speakers, toys, and wearable are equipped with real-time IoT recording data, but most of them are not compliant with data protocols and standards. There are many ambiguities in data ownership and organization. As a result, the data stored on IoT devices are at risk of data theft, and this data can be exposed to cyber-crime and penetrate the system, compromising personal health information. Fake IDs for health fraud and drug trafficking claims are some of the examples where misuse of IoT data can be seen [14].

- Integration: Multiple devices and protocols
- Data overload and accuracy
- Cost [14, 15]

9.1.6   Machine Learning and Artificial Intelligence for Health Informatics

In 1970s, artificial intelligence (AI) appeared in healthcare. The first AI system is essentially a knowledge-based decision support system, and the first machine learning method is used to approximate the classification rules of a label set. These first systems are working well. However, it is not commonly used in real patients. One of the reasons is that these systems are independent and have nothing to do with the patient's electronic medical records. Another reason is that the proficiency indicated in the knowledge field of these specialist systems expresses the non-acceptance of developed systems and that most systems are medically more academic practice [16].

After winning several championships, drug abuse has been transformed into a new mode of learning devices, by improving an intensive artificial neural network, focusing on complex intensive learning. In May 2019, a team from New York University and Google reported that the accuracy can be improved by using deep learning models which are used in diagnose lung cancer, and the study quickly covered magazines headlines and many newspapers [16, 17].

9.1.7   Health Sensor Data Management

Wide impact have been made on people's day-to-day lives by the latest technologies such as wearable sensor devices, cloud computing, and big data. These technologies have great future in the ecosystem based on Internet. It provides personal consumption and sharing and information about the development of the health and welfare sector. Many new ways to collect information manually and automatically are provided by these tools. Numerous modern smart phones have multiple internal sensors, such as a microphone, camera, gyroscope, accelerometer, compass, proximity sensor, GPS, and ambient light [18].

It can easily connect a new generation of new wearable medical sensors to smart phones and send measurement results directly. It will be a more effective and convenient set of personal health information such as blood oxygen saturation, blood pressure, pulse rate, blood sugar, electroencephalogram (EEG), electrocardiogram (ECG), and electrocardiogram (EKG) with all sensors and devices. In future, the process of collecting and interpreting health and activity data is not so far. The number of mobile phone sensor analysis and data collection is expanding rapidly. This graph of massive growth has created the ability to manage both data and challenge collaboration [18].

9.1.8   Multimodal Data Fusion for Healthcare

Healthcare is one of the areas of continuous improvement because of the proliferation of IoT technologies which are used to support the central functions of healthcare organizations. Thus, traditional hospitals have become the next generation of intelligent digital environments that use widely interconnected sensor systems and large-scale data acquisition and processing technologies. With the help of this entire scenario, smart health can be supported as a complex ecosystem of smart spaces such as ambulances, hospital wards, and pharmacies and backed by strong framework stacks such as sensor networks and edge devices, using innovative business models and rules industries [19].

9.1.9   Heterogeneous Data Fusion and Context-Aware Systems a Context-Aware Data Fusion Approach for Health-IoT

Advances in low-cost sensor equipment and communications technologies are rapidly accelerating the evolution of smart homes and environments. The health industry is growing rapidly with the development of human body networks, big data technologies, and cloud computing. While using IoT, several challenges can be faced by an individual, such as text recognition, heterogeneous data mixing, reliability, complex query processing, and accuracy [10].

For more reliable, accurate, and complete results, personal data from your sensor source are collected. In addition to the wearable sensor, an additional background sensor has been added to create the background. The IoT Health Program uses the potential benefits of combining knowledge data in this area. Background information can be used to tailor the behavior of the app to a specific situation [20].

9.1.10   Role of Technology in Addressing the Problem of Integration of Healthcare System

Information and communication technology offers the opportunity to revolutionize healthcare. Technology-based healthcare coordination and care systems, including web, mobile, measurement, computing, and bioinformatics technologies, offer great potential to enable a whole new model of healthcare both at home and abroad. They provide a formal care system and have the opportunity to have a major impact on public health. Increasingly, decision support tools are being built to help people better understand, access, and make decisions about treatment [21, 24].

The integration of behavioral healthcare into a care center that largely manages physical health has great expectations for improving care coordination, quality, and impact, but it also creates scenarios that physicians must now overcome. The limits may not feel the expertise, time, or resources that affect the client's behavioral health needs (e.g., substance use and mental health). In this way, technology reduces the quiet and dedicated care of illnesses and provides countless opportunities for tailors to monitor the behavior and provide intervention to each individual in response to therapeutic behavior that changes over time [21].

9.2 Literature Survey

Various strategies for segmenting, locating, and identifying images of brain tumors have been proposed from the late request to group MRI images.

Parveen and Amritpal Singh proposed a method for data extraction. The grouping method is done in three stages: preprocessing, extraction, and highlight grouping. The main tissues improve speed and accuracy by improving and eradicating the skull. Fluffy C Fluffy Pan (FCM) uses a portion of the grid in the dimension of the Dim dimension (GLRLM) to extract highlights in brain images. Sorting brain MRI images using the SVM method gives accurate accuracy and results [1, 23].

There are more than 120 types of brain tumors of different origin, location, size, and tissue characteristics, as per the reports of the World Health Organization. Articles on three types of malignancies are as follows:

Glioblastoma: An early malignant brain tumor consisting of astrocytes, called astrocytes, which support nerve cells and are classified as tetraploids. It usually starts in the brain.

Sarcoma: The degree varies from 1 to 4 degrees and occurs in connective tissues such as blood vessels.

Metastatic bronchial cancer: A secondary malignant brain tumor that has spread from a lung tumor to a bronchial cancer [1].

According to Maoguo Gong [2], Fuzzy Algorithm C (FCM) provides improved fuzzy image segmentation by introducing weight-lifting fuzzy factors and core metrics. The fuzzy weight factor in the exchange depends on the distance in the space of all adjacent pixels and the difference between their gray surfaces simultaneously. The new algorithm uses fast bandwidth selection rules to determine core parameters based on the distribution of distances from all points in the dataset. Also, both the business-based fuzzy weight factor and the core distance measurement are parameter-free. Results of experiments on artificial and real images manifest that the new algorithm is successful and systematic and is relatively independent of this type of noise [2].

The paper titled "Emerging applications of artificial intelligence in neuro-oncology" is written by Rudie, J. D. *et al.* [4]. They showed that AI methods were developed to enhance the accuracy of medical and therapeutic diagnosis by increasing the computational algorithms. The field of radiology in neuroscience is now and perhaps at the forefront of this revolution. Advanced neuro-MRI data and the types of AI techniques used in conventional tumors and permeability margins for glioma diffusion determine true progression assumptions and are used in routine clinics. Recurrence and survival are more predictable than what happens.

According to him, the radio genomics also facilitate understanding of cancer biology and enable high-resolution non-invasive sampling of the molecular environment, and providers understand the level of systems of heterogeneous cellular and molecular processes by making spatial and molecular heterogeneous markers in the body; these radiographs and radiographs are based on AI and classify patients using more accurate diagnostic and treatment methods. It also can better monitor dynamic therapy. Although the basic challenges remain, radiology is changing dramatically given the ever-increasing development and validation of AI technologies for clinical use.

They revealed the purpose of this study that was to improve outcomes in patients with central nervous system neoplasms through advances in diagnostics and therapeutics. Tools of AI that help in combining clinical, radiological, and genomic information with predictive models promise critical guidance and guidance on personal care. However, there are many challenges and many things need to be done to keep promises.

Nevertheless, the use of AI technology will dramatically change the progress of radiology, improving the accuracy and efficiency of radiologists. As these powerful tools will be integrated into daily practice in the coming years, radiologists should need to know and use these powerful tools [4].

According to Amin J. and his team, diagnosing brain tumors is an active area for brain imaging research. This study proposes a methodology for presenting and classifying brain tumors using magnetic resonance imaging (MRI). In order to segment the tumor, an architecture-based deep neural network (DNN) is used [5, 22].

The proposed model that consists of seven layers—including three concealers, three ReLUs, and a softmax layer—will be used for classification. The DNN determines the label based on the center pixel and performs the division. They described extensive experiments using eight large standard datasets including BRATS 2012 (image and artificial datasets), visual and artificial datasets, and ISLES (cerebral infarction ischemic stroke).

According to Amin J., the results are proved with accuracy (ACC), attribute (SP), sensitivity (SE), accuracy, alopecia similarity coefficient (DSC), false-positive coefficient (FPR), true positive rate (TPR), and Jacquard similarity index (JSI) [5].

Gopal S. Tandel and his team member pointed out in a February 2018 World Health Organization (WHO) report that the death rate from the central nervous system (CNS) or brain cancer is the highest in Asia. Early diagnosis of cancer is critical, as it can save many lives. Cancer grading is a necessary feature of targeted therapy [6].

According to him, the diagnosis of cancer is very aggressive, expensive, and time-consuming. There is an urgent need to describe and evaluate non-invasive, cost-effective, and effective brain cancer tools.

In this article, they tried to briefly describe the patho-physiology of brain cancer, a cancer treatment method, and an automatic computer method for describing brain cancer and deep learning of brain cancer patterns and equipment. It also aims to investigate issues with existing engineering methods and design future models. Besides, they emphasized the association of brain tumors with stroke, brain diseases (such as Alzheimer's, Parkinson's, and Wilson's), leukemia, and neurological diseases in other machine learning and deep learning paradigms. His main research areas are cancer pathway physiology, imaging technology, WHO's tumor classification guidelines, early detection methods, and existing computer algorithms that use deep equipment to classify brain cancer.

Finally, they contrasted brain tumors with other brain diseases. They made a conclusion that the ability to automatically extract DL-based methods is once again more common than traditional medical image classification methods. If cancer is evaluated and treated quickly and cost-effectively, then many lives can be saved. Therefore, there is a need for a rapid, non-invasive, and cost-effective diagnostic method. The DL method can play an important role here. According to him, the use of DL technology and its full potential to evaluate automatic tumors has been completed, but the work is still very little and no research has been carried out [6].

9.3 System Design and Methodology

9.3.1 System Design

The analysis has been done on the benchmark dataset provided by the Appolo Cancer Hospital, NCR, India, and they have been tested and visualized in the study.

A block diagram shows the working of our project in a step-by-step manner (as per Figure 9.2).

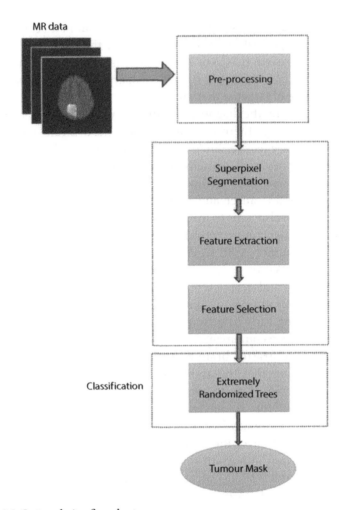

Figure 9.2 System design flow chart.

9.3.2   CNN Architecture

An evolutionary neural system (CNN or ConvNet) is a profound neural system class, the most utilized in a visual examination. CNNs are multilayer perceptron regularization renditions. Multilayer perceptron for the most part allude to completely associated systems, which implies that each neuron in one layer is associated with the following layer, everything being equal.

The CNNs, however, embrace another way to deal with regularization: they utilize the various leveled design in the information and utilize littler

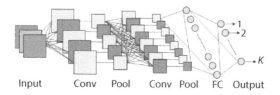

Figure 9.3 CNN architecture.

and increasingly basic examples to collect complex examples. Therefore, CNNs are on the lower extraordinary on the size of the association and multifaceted nature.

Natural procedures motivated progressive systems by the way that the example of the network between neurons resembles the creature's visual cortex association. The open fields of the different neurons mostly are covered, covering the whole field of vision.

Contrasted with other picture characterization calculations, CNNs utilize moderately little pre-handling. This implies the system discovers that channels are produced by delivering customary calculations. This autonomy from past information and human exertion in the plan of highlights is a significant advantage.

Figure 9.3 is a representation of the CNN architecture and various layers.

9.3.3   Block Diagram

Figure 9.4 represents the entire functioning of the project and how the CNN architecture is used to classify the type of tumor.

9.3.4   Algorithm(s)

Gradient Descent is a calculation of streamlining used to limit certain functionalities, moving to a lofty plummet toward the path characterized by the slope negative. We use the slope plunge in AI to refresh our model parameters. Parameters allude to straight relapse coefficients and neural system loads. According to our cost capacity, we can govern two parameters: m (weight) and b (inclination). We should consider fractional subsidiaries the impact everyone has on the last expectation. Concerning every parameter, the outcomes are stored in an inclination after we ascertain the halfway subordinates of the cost capacity.

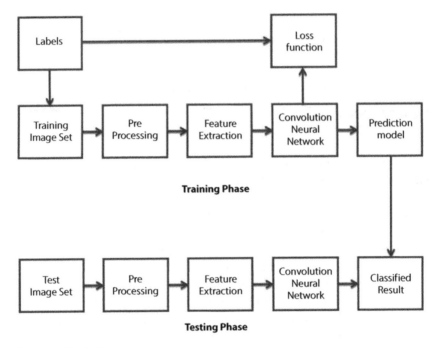

Figure 9.4 Block diagram.

The cost function is given as follows:

$$f(m,b) = \frac{1}{N} \sum_{i=1}^{n} (y_i - (mx_i + b))^2$$

The gradient can be calculated as follows:

$$f'(m,b) = \begin{bmatrix} \dfrac{df}{dm} \\[2mm] \dfrac{df}{db} \end{bmatrix} = \begin{cases} \dfrac{1}{N} \sum -2x_i(y_i - (mx_i + b)) \\[2mm] \dfrac{1}{N} \sum -2(y_i - (mx_i + b)) \end{cases}$$

To solve the gradient, we use our new m and b values to iterate through our data points and to calculate partial derivatives. This latest gradient expresses the slope of our cost function (current parameter values) to our current position and the direction to which we are to update our parameters. The learning rate controls the size of our update.

9.3.5   Our Experimental Results, Interpretation, and Discussion

Experimental Setup
  Hardware requirements

- 4GB RAM
- Intel Core i3 or higher processor
- GPU(recommended)
- 2GB available disk space

Software requirements

- Python 3
- Spyder IDE
- TensorFlow and Keras
- Scikit-Learn
- Numpy and Pandas
- Linux or Windows OS

Constraints

- Data limitation
- Hardware limitation
- Accuracy limitation

9.3.6   Implementation Details

Deep learning expanded the structure of traditional neural networks (NNs) between input and output layers to add hidden layers to the network architecture, creating a more complex and non-causal relationship. In recent years, the Reflection Neural Network (CNN) is a popular architecture that allows you to carry out complex operations using concealer filters. A set of feed forward layers that implement loop filters and pool layers makes the typical CNN architecture. After the last layer, some fully connected layers are enhanced by CNN. Manipulate one-dimensional vectors for classification work with CNN. Get the results you need in four major steps. Data collection and preparation is the first step. We are going to collect labeled MRI images of tumor brains and prepare them so we can use them for training.

9.3.7   Snapshots of Interfaces

Figure 9.5 shows the various classes of tumors that our model can classify.

Code Snippet: Figure 9.6 is the screenshot of the codes that we have used to train our CNN model.

Welcome page: Figure 9.7 is the snapshot of the welcome page. This is the first page that user will come across.

```
-----------------------------------------------------------------
Data source     | Tumor type        | No.of Images
-----------------------------------------------------------------
REMBRANDT       | Astrocytoma       |        21307
                | Glioblastoma      |        17983
                | Oligodendroglioma |        12460
                | Unidentified      |        13677
-----------------------------------------------------------------
MIRIAD          | Healthy brain     |        30688
-----------------------------------------------------------------
BRAINS          |                   |          556
-----------------------------------------------------------------
Total           |                   |        96115
-----------------------------------------------------------------
```

Figure 9.5 Various classes of tumors.

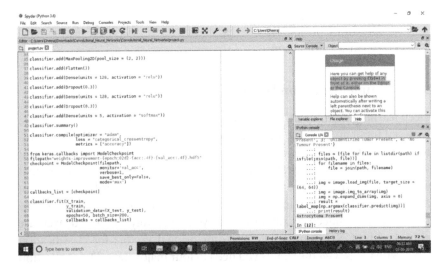

Figure 9.6 Codes used to train our CNN model.

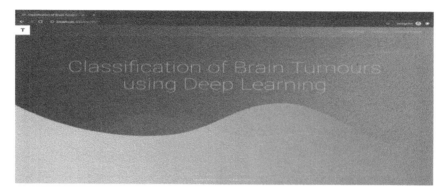

Figure 9.7 Loading page.

MRI selection: Figure 9.8 is the snapshot of the page where the user can select and upload the MRI image.

The result displayed: Figure 9.9 is the snapshot where the prediction result of the model is displayed.

About Section: Figure 9.10 is the page of the about section where information about this project is displayed.

Figure 9.8 Result displayed.

Figure 9.9 Result displayed.

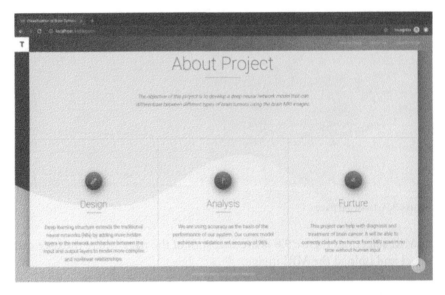

Figure 9.10 About section.

9.3.8   Performance Evaluation

We are using accuracy as the basis of the performance of our system. Our current model achieves a validation set accuracy of 96.95% in the training set and 96.03% in the validation set.

Figure 9.11 displays the accuracy score of the validation set.

We also have made a webpage with options to upload the MRI and get results online. It has an upload button to choose an image from the system to check against the project.

9.3.9   Comparison with Other Algorithms

Comparison chart: Figure 9.12 shows the performance of our model in comparison to other conventional models.

9.4   Novelty in Our Work

The DNN-based architecture and method will be the best method for most brain tumor classification contests. Many researchers are adding layers to CNNs to improve accuracy. This is a major aspect of scientist knowledge. Researchers and groups that work well with accurate learning methods and

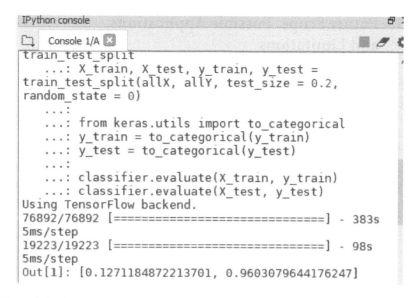

```
IPython console

Console 1/A

train_test_split
   ...: X_train, X_test, y_train, y_test =
train_test_split(allX, allY, test_size = 0.2,
random_state = 0)
   ...:
   ...: from keras.utils import to_categorical
   ...: y_train = to_categorical(y_train)
   ...: y_test = to_categorical(y_test)
   ...:
   ...: classifier.evaluate(X_train, y_train)
   ...: classifier.evaluate(X_test, y_test)
Using TensorFlow backend.
76892/76892 [==============================] - 383s
5ms/step
19223/19223 [==============================] - 98s
5ms/step
Out[1]: [0.1271184872213701, 0.9603079644176247]
```

Figure 9.11 Accuracy score.

Algorithm	Classification rate
DNN	96.97%
KNN K = 1	95.45%
KNN K = 3	86.36%
LDA	95.45%
aSMO	93.94%

Figure 9.12 Comparison chart.

algorithms were able to do this using tools outside the grid, such as adding new data or implementing preprocessing techniques.

By adding a step before the normalization process, we improved the generalization capability of the network without changing the CNN architecture. We also tested the gradient descent algorithm for cost over-optimization, but these methods have not yet been implemented in the field of brain tumor classification.

9.5   Future Scope, Possible Applications, and Limitations

I have too much fat now, the statement given by any patient could be improved by expanding the dataset and updating it to identify new types of tumors. Implementing deep learning techniques and algorithms for classifying brain tumor data poses a myriad of challenges.

The lack of large training datasets is a challenging barrier to deep learning techniques. The Health Label Structure Report is expected to facilitate future analysis, especially in the analysis of brain tumors. Especially in the area of brain tumor analysis, the use of non-textual and structural reports for network training is expected to grow rapidly in the future.

Deep learning techniques, which effectively learn from a limited number of classified data, are another major limitation of deep learning algorithms. However, it is not useful if the input field for image data from the entire network is small.

9.6   Recommendations and Consideration

Classification implementation in brain tumor analysis is a complex and rewarding task. This can be widely classified, processed, and post-processed. The above methods have many challenges and complicate the problem. So far, there are no ideal computer tools for adaptation, tumor grade, or aggression.

Therefore, rapid, non-invasive, and cost-effective diagnostic techniques are essential. DL techniques can play a big part here. To understand us, much less work has been done to classify automatic tumors using Max DL techniques and the likes. It is possible but not yet studied.

9.7   Conclusions

The main focus of data classification is brain cancer physiology, imaging techniques, tumor classification guidelines by World Health Organization, early detection procedures, and existing computer algorithms for classifying brain cancer using devices. The visualizations are clear to prove that the brain tumor can be more or less accurately detectable by the process defined above; however, accuracy can be increased with more refined dataset and improvised blend of algorithm.

References

1. Parveen, and Singh, A., Detection of Brain Tumor in MRI Images, Using Fuzzy C-Means Segmented Images and Artificial Neural Network, from book. *Proceedings of the International Conference on Recent Cognizance in Wireless Communication & Image Processing: ICRCWIP-2014*, pp. 123–131, 2016, 10.1007/978-81-322-2638-3_14.

2. Gong, M. *et al.*, Fuzzy C-Means Clustering With Local Information and Kernel Metric for Image Segmentation. *IEEE Trans. Image Process.*, 22, 2, 573–584, 2013.

3. Heba Mohsen El-Sayed, A. *et al.*, Classification using deep learning neural networks for brain tumors. *Future Comput. Inf. J.*, 3, 1, June 2018, 68–71, 2017, Received 26 October 2017, Accepted 5 December 2017, Available online 24 December 2017. https://doi.org/10.1016/j.fcij.2017.12.001.

4. Rudie, J.D. *et al.*, Emerging Applications of Artificial Intelligence in Neuro-Oncology. *Radiology*, 290, 3, 607–618, 2019, https://doi.org/10.1148/radiol.2018181928.

5. Javeria, A. *et al.*, Big data analysis for brain tumor detection: Deep convolutional neural networks. *Future Gener. Comput. Syst.*, 87, 290–297, 2018, 10.1016/j.future.2018.04.065.

6. Tandel, G.S., Biswas, M., Kakde, O.G., Tiwari, A., Suri, H.S., Turk, M., Laird, J.R., Asare, C.K., Ankrah, A.A., Khanna, N.N., Madhusudhan, B.K., Saba, L., Suri, J.S., A Review on a Deep Learning Perspective in Brain Cancer Classification. *Cancers*, 11, 1, 111, https://doi.org/10.3390/cancers11010111, 2019.

7. Herland, M., Khoshgoftaar, T.M., Wald, R., A review of data mining using big data in health informatics. *J. Big Data*, 1, 1, 2, 2014.

8. Sun, and Reddy, C.K., Big data analytics for healthcare, in: *Proc. 19th ACM SIGKDD International Conference on Knowledge Discovery and Data Mining*, 2013, pp. 1525–1525, 2013.

9. Mike, Hoover, W., Strome, T., Kanwal, S., Transforming healthcare through big data strategies for leveraging big data in the healthcare industry, *Health IT Outcomes*, 1, 1, 2013, http://ihealthtran.com/iHT2 BigData 2013.pdf.

10. Kumar, S. and Maninder, S., Big data analytics for the healthcare industry: impact, applications, and tools. *Big Data Min. Anal.*, 2, 48–57, 10.26599/BDMA.2018.9020031, 2019.

11. Wang, H., Choi, H.-S., Agoulmine, N., Deen, M.J., Hong, J.W.-K., Information-based sensor tasking wireless body area networks in U-health systems. *Proceedings of the 2010 International Conference on Network and Service Management*, Niagara Falls, ON, Canada, 25–29 October 2010, pp. 517–522.

12. Zanella, A., Bui, N., Castellani, A., Vangelista, L., Zorzi, M., Internet of things for smart cities. *IEEE Internet Things J.*, 1, 1, 22–32, 2014.

13. Bauer, H., Patel, M., Veira, J., *The Internet of Things: sizing up the opportunity*, McKinsey& Company, New York (NY), 2016, Available from: https://www.mckinsey.com/industries/semiconductors/our-insights/the-internet-of-things-sizing-up-the-opportunity.

14. Amyra, *Internet of Things in healthcare: Challenges and applications*, TECHNOLOGY AND APPS, USA, https://www.valuecoders.com/blog/technology-and-apps/iot-in-healthcare-benefits-challenges-and-applications/, 2019.

15. Devendran, T., D.A. *et al.*, Challenges and Issues of healthcare in the Internet of Things. *Int. J. Latest Trends Eng. Technol.*, 2, Special Issue April-2018.

16. Singh, Y. and Chauhan, A.S., Neural Networks in Data Mining. *J. Theor. Appl. Inf. Technol.*, 5, 6, 37–42, 2005, 14.

17. Dey, A., Machine Learning Algorithms: A Review. *(IJCSIT) Int. J. Comput. Sci. Inf. Technol.*, 7, 3, 1174–1179, 2016.

18. Li, Y., Wu, C., Guo, L., Lee, C.-H., Guo, Y., Wiki-Health: A Big Data Platform for Health Sensor Data Management, In *Cloud Computing Applications for Quality Healthcare Delivery*, A. Moumtzoglou, & A. Kastania (Ed.), IGI Global, pp. 59–77, 2014, 10.4018/978-1-4666-6118-9.ch004.

19. Haghighat, M., Abdel-Mottaleb, M., Alhalabi, W., Discriminant correlation analysis: real-time feature level fusion for multimodal biometric recognition. *IEEE Trans. Inf. Forensics Secur.*, 11, 9, 1984–96, 2016.

20. Baloch, Z., Shaikh, F., Unar, M., A context-aware data fusion approach for health-IoT. *Technol., Int. J. Inf. Tecnol.*, 10, 241–245, 2018, 10. 10.1007/s41870-018-0116-1.

21. Lisa, A. and Gustafson, D.H., The Role of Technology in Healthcare Innovation: A Commentary. *J. Dual Diagn.* Author manuscript; available PMC 2014 Jan 1, 2013, 9, 1, 101–103, 2013, J Dual Diagn.Published online 2012 Nov 27.

22. Rastogi, R. *et al.*, Intelligent Personality Analysis on Indicators in IoT-MMBD Enabled Environment, in: *Multimedia Big Data Computing for IoT Applications: Concepts, Paradigms, and Solutions*, S. Tanwar, S. Tyagi, N. Kumar (Eds.), pp. 185–215, https://doi.org/10.1007/978-981-13-8759-3_7, Springer Nature Singapore, Singapore, 2020.

23. Rastogi, R., Chaturvedi, D.K., Satya, S., Arora, N., Trivedi, P.M., Gupta, M., Singhal, P., Gulati, M., MM Big Data Applications: Statistical Resultant Analysis of Psychosomatic Survey on Various Human Personality Indicators, in: *ICCI 2018 Paper as Book Chapter, Chapter 25*, © Springer Nature Singapore Pte Ltd, Singapore, 2020.

24. Book Subtitle: *Proceedings of Second International Conference on Computational Intelligence*, 2018, https://doi.org/10.1007/978-981-13-8222-2_25.

Study of Emission From Medicinal Woods to Curb Threats of Pollution and Diseases: Global Healthcare Paradigm Shift in 21st Century

Rohit Rastogi[1]*, Mamta Saxena[2], Devendra Kr. Chaturvedi[3], Sheelu Sagar[4], Neha Gupta[1], Harshit Gupta[1], Akshit Rajan Rastogi[1], Divya Sharma[1], Manu Bhardwaj[1] and Pranav Sharma[5]

[1]*Department of CSE, ABES Engineering College Ghaziabad, UP, India*
[2]*DG, Ministry of Statistics (P&I), Govt. of India, Delhi, India*
[3]*Department of Electrical Engineering, DEI, Agra, India*
[4]*Amity International Business School, Amity University, Noida, India*
[5]*Department of Civil Engineering, DEI, Agra, UP, India*

Abstract

The methodology for the experiment was based on the data collected on various parameters on the scientific measuring analytical software tools Airveda Instrument and IoT-based sensors capturing the humidity and temperature data from atmospheric air in certain interval of time to know the patterns of pollution increment or decrement in atmosphere of nearby area. The experiment was conducted for 1 month every day, and observation was noted every hour. For experiment, Yagya was performed. Specific herbal woods, mixture of various herbs, sticks made of dried cow dung, cow ghee, dry coconut, jiggery, and sweet made of cow milk were used along with chanting of Vedic Mantra. The ingredients were converted to volatile oils and gases which reduced air pollutants.

Keywords: PM level, emission, machine learning, sensor and IoT, pollution, Yajna and Mantra, sensors, Yagya (Yajna, Hawan, Agnihotra)

**Corresponding author*: rohit.rastogi@abes.ac.in

A. Suresh, S. Vimal, Y. Harold Robinson, Dhinesh Kumar Ramaswami and R. Udendhran (eds.)
Bioinformatics and Medical Applications: Big Data Using Deep Learning Algorithms, (191–214)
© 2022 Scrivener Publishing LLC

10.1   Introduction

10.1.1   Scenario of Pollution and the Need to Connect with Indian Culture

As we take a look at the doings and actions of the Indian culture, it totally believes to take that much from the environment which it will regenerate or produce again easily. The traditional Indian cultural practices include Yajna or Agnihotra in which offerings of various medicinal herbs and medicinal entities are made for the fire which, as a result, purify the environment and decrease the amount of contaminants in the atmosphere. In Indian culture, rivers are given the importance of mothers and trees are considered as second figures which are worshipped by the people of the country [15]. In ancient Indian culture, people used to throw copper coins and some special types of coins made up of alloys which chemically purify the water and reduce the amount of impurity in the water and trees are saved as they are considered medicinal and equivalent to human life. Rainwater harvesting is also a part of such traditional practices of Indian culture. A special type of eco-friendly clothing known as khadi is widely used in India; it is totally biodegradable and causes no harm to the environment even the kitchens of India show how the country is eco-friendly by using the utensils made up of special type of clay which are used for cooking. The water containers made up of clay worked as natural refrigerators due to the pores in them. In Indian culture, people use carry bags made up of jute and also the wet curtains used at the windows are made up of jute which makes the coming air cool [4, 16].

10.1.2   Global Pollution Scenario

In this table, you can easily understand the health impact of the human body by air pollutants and their source of emission, average time, and standard level [17]. Air pollutant is a mixture of small particles in the air that can have an adverse effect on living things and ecosystems. These particles are in the form of liquid droplets, gaseous, or solid particles present in the air, like nitrogen dioxide lead, ground-level ozone, and polycyclic aromatic hydrocarbons. The standard level in microgram per cubic meter ($\mu g/m^3$) in the air is a unit of amount of chemical vapors, fumes, or dust in the ambient air (Figure 10.1) [6, 19].

World regional capital city ranking in 2018 is sorted by average yearly PM2.5. Countries from Asia and the Middle East occupy most of the capital city ranking, with Delhi found as the highest mixture in world regional

Air pollutants	Major Source of Emission	Averaging Time	Standard level	Health impact target organs
Particle pollutants PM25	Smokes, Motor engines, Industrial activities	24h	35µg/m³	Respiratory and cardiovascular diseases, CNS and reproductive dysfunctions, cancer
PM10		24h	150µg/m³	
Ground-level ozone	Industrial activities, Vehicular exhaust	1h	0.12mg/m³	Respiratory and cardiovascular dysfunction, eye irritation
Carbon monoxide	Smokes, Motor engines, burning coal, oil and wood, Industrial activities	1h	35mg/m³	CNS and cardiovascular damages
Nitrogen dioxide	Feel-burning, Vehicular exhaust	1h	100µg/m³	Damage to liver, lung, spleen, and blood
Lead	Lead smelting, Industrial activities, leaded petrol	3months average	0.15µg/m³	CNS and hematologic dysfunctions, eye irritation
Sulfur dioxide	Fuel combustion, burning coal	1h	75µg/m³	Respiratory and CNS involvement, eye irritation
Polycyclic aromatic hydrocarbons	Fuel combustion, wood fires, motor engines	1 year	1ng/m³	Respiratory and CNS involvement, cancer

Air quality standards according to the European Union, $PM_{2.5}$ is stand for PM of 2.5µ or less, PM_{10} is stand for PM of 10 µ or more. PM = Particulate matter, CNS = Central nervous system.

Figure 10.1 Standard level of criteria air pollutants and their sources with health impact based on the United States Environmental Protection Agency (Website: jmsjournal.net).

capital city ranking in 2018 in PM2.5. Second is Dhaka and third is Kabul (world regional capital city ranking, 2018) where PM2.5 stands for particulate matter. PM2.5 is dangerous and harmful to health. PM2.5 is a mixture of liquid droplets present in the air and solid particles in the air. When the number of these particles increases and penetrates deeply into the lungs; it can affect your body like breathing problems, burning, or sensation in the eyes (Figure 10.2) [3, 18, 20].

10.1.3   Indian Crisis on Pollution and Worrying Stats

The quality of air has become so poor in India that it is leading to deadly consequences for a large section of the society. This severe air pollution affects millions of people especially in the densely populated region where the people are forced to bear dense and poisonous air for long time [21]. The air pollution in Delhi and nearby areas reached the worst level on November 3 and 4, 2019, where PM2.5 levels were shown by some indices at 407 and more than 500, respectively. As per a Washington Post report (paywall) which was published in November 2018, the lifespan of people in India is reduced by 5.3 years due to the air pollution. Hence, air pollution is the biggest challenge for mankind and some additional measures should be taken in order to control it [7, 23, 30].

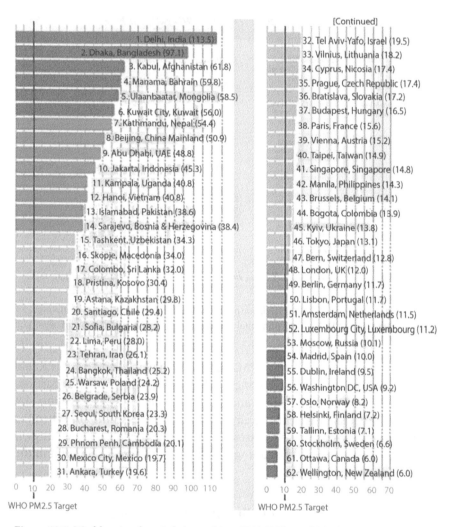

Figure 10.2 World regional capital city ranking, 2018 (Website: IQAir).

10.1.4 Efforts Made to Curb Pollution World Wide

Pollution can be in air or can be in water but pollution is pollution and exists in various forms. Pollution is the main reason for the presence of harmful contaminants in the biological ecosystem, which, in return, creates adverse and negative effects on the environment. Manufacturing operations, industrialization at global level, and the ever-increasing demand to increase the standard of living incline the graph of pollution, ultimately resulting in life loss [1, 24, 31].

Table 10.1 The different effects of Yagya on environment in studies by researchers.

Experiment	Effect on the day of Yagya
Dr. Hafkine [34] Burning of mixture of ghee and sugar in Hawan Samagri.	It destroys the bacteria of different diseases and kills the germs of certain diseases.
Trelle of France [8] On burning of mango wood and Jaggery formaldehyde	It destroys the harmful bacteria.
Tautilk [8]	It destroys germs of typhoid.
National Botanical Research Institute [13]	It reduces airborne bacteria to a large extents.
Dr. Shirowich, a Russian scientist Cow's Ghee is burn into fire Medicinal fumes emanating from Agnihotra [35]	It reduces the atomic radiation in a significant amount. These eradicate bacteria and other microorganisms.
Dr. Kundanlal M.D. in allopathic medicine [8] When 1 kg of mango wood was burnt with Hawan Samigri in open air	Bacterial count was reduced by 94%.
Chander Shekhar Nautiyal head of the division studying plant-microbes interaction [13].	On the Yagya day: Bacteria count was lower infection like T.B. and other viral infections. First day after Yagya: Bacteria count was a lower infection like T.B. and other viral infections. First day after Yagya: Bacteria count was a lower infection like T.B. and other viral infections.
The study was done by CPCB, a govt. of India body [25].	On the Yagya day: Reduction of Bacteria, 79%; Fungi, 68%; TMF, 69%; and Pathogens, 33% First day after Yagya: Reduction of Bacteria, 55%; Fungi,15%; and Pathogen, 79%. Second day after Yagya: Reduction in Pathogens, 79%; and Total micro flora had reduced, 49%. Seventh day after Yagya: Reduction of bacteria, 93%; Fungi, 88%; and Pathogen, 93%.

10.1.5   Indian Ancient Vedic Sciences to Curb Pollution and Related Disease

Effects of Hawan on Poisonous Gases: Experiment shows the observations made by distinguished scientists that are given in Table 10.1, which shows effects of Hawan on poisonous gases and disease-causing agents (Table 10.1) [5, 24].

The medicinal plants, wood, cow ghee, and sweets product used in Yagya volatilize easily and diffuse in the environment; the fumes generated in Yagya kills pathogens like bacteria, fungi, virus, and parasites like flies, ringworm, fleas, and dice. These volatile substances further subjected to photochemical reaction in sunlight and undergo through decomposition, oxidation, reduction, etc. [25, 32].

10.1.6   The Yajna Science: A Boon to Human Race From Rishi-Muni

One can easily understand the benefits of Yagya as given in Figures 10.3 and 10.4 [22, 37].

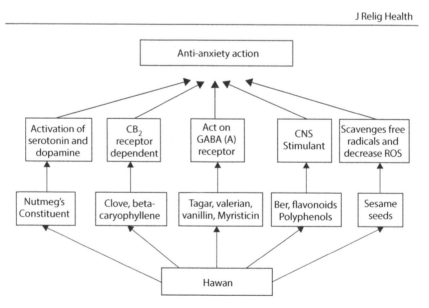

Figure 10.3 Diagrammatic representation of component of Hawan Samagri along with probable multiple mechanism of action [22].

Figure 10.4 Society residents chanting Vedic Mantras and performing community Yagya. This Yagya was organized in Ward 9 sector 29 Noida, NCR (U.P.) on World Environment Day 5, June 2017.

10.1.7   The Science of Mantra Associated With Yajna and Its Scientific Effects

An Indian scientific process through which the balance of O_2 and CO_2 is maintained in the atmosphere is termed as Yajna. In the rituals performed during Yajna, besides proper use of herbs and woods, application of Mantra is important. Mantra is usually considered as a part of cultural dimension. Recent advancements in the field of science and medicine carry the healing role of various dimensions of old age therapies like Mantras, which were originally considered as a part of the cultural traditions. Therefore, it is said that the Yajna is considered as a ritual that also has an effect on humans. This also tells us the importance of mantra in Yajna. Mantra results show us that it plays an important role in human mental capacity. Also, positive effects of mantras are seen on the plant species [26]. A study tested the effect on bacterial growth using smoke obtained from Yajna with complete procedure along with mantra chanting and using the smoke obtained from Yajna without mantra chanting. But, the effect was magnificent when the smoke obtained from Yajna with complete procedure along with mantra chanting [36].

10.1.8   Effect of Different Woods and Cow Dung Used in Yajna

It is observed that six types of gases are released from the combustion of the special types of woods, which directly reduces the bacteria. This whole process is a natural fumigation process in which these antibacterial fumes fills up the environment and disinfect it. Further, the gases and volatile substances release from the combustion of the volatile oils present in these

Figure 10.5 People in Indian and South Asian continent celebrating Holi Festival (a mass Yajna process to purify atmosphere) with cow dung, herbal woods, and spices and new barley and grains.

woods and materials further do some photochemical reactions [27]. The carbon dioxide released is also get reduced to some extent into formaldehyde due to which an amount of oxygen is also get added to the environment. Many experiments and researches regarding the checking of mineral content and medicinal content of these woods have taken place, and it is observed that the ashes obtained from the Yajna also act as a very good fertilizer because this also contains that mineral content in it. Cow dung cakes are also confirmed to have some antibacterial properties. Hence, these fumes are therapeutic in nature, naturally heal the atmosphere, and are beneficial for living creatures (Figure 10.5) [10].

10.1.9   Use of Sensors and IoT to Record Experimental Data

IoT is a source that can connect hardware and software devices very easily. It is also known as the Internet of Things. Although sensors were themselves smart enough but when we need to analyze the data, it would have become difficult without IoT. IoT is the answer to many problems, be it crime or environment. As time will pass, it is expected that, due to IoT being more and more advanced, less energy and less money will be spent in getting our tasks done [28]. We know that at this time specifically, the data is growing exponentially, and it will continue in the coming years as well. So, to control this data, to analyze it, and to store it, we need IoT. For this kind of data, traditional efforts would not bring much advantages as compared to the use of IoT devices (Figures 10.6 and 10.7) (How do Smart Devices Work: Sensors, IoT, Big Data and AI, November 4, 2018).

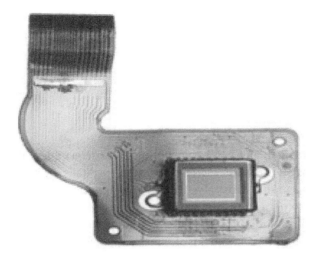

Figure 10.6 CCD image sensor for capturing images (Website: Wikipedia).

Figure 10.7 IR proximity sensor for distance measurement (Website: Flipkart.com).

10.1.10   Analysis and Pattern Recognition by ML and AI

Whenever we talk about recognition of data, then we talk about how regular the data is. By identifying the traits and characteristics of the data, we select the Machine Learning (ML) algorithm that will predict the results accurately. Recognizing these regularities plays an important role in building an efficient model. This is not only useful in the technological field but also in various fields such as e-commerce or medication [29] [Pattern Recognition (Tutorial) and Machine Learning: An Introduction, April 29, 2020].

10.2   Literature Survey

Gist

In this chapter, an attempt is made in order to determine if the emissions from the gas industry are responsible for the hospitalizations in the Darling Downs, Queensland, Australia. Outdoor air pollution especially due to the emissions from the industries has resulted in the negative health impact on humans. Air pollution is responsible for numerous diseases which include respiratory and cardiac, and it is also responsible for cancer deaths. In addition, the air pollution has reduced the human life span, and it is leading to premature deaths of humans. The hospitalization data was obtained from the Darling Downs and Health Services (DDHHS). The data is analyzed using linear regression analysis [9, 11].

Methodology Used in This Chapter

In this research paper, the data was collected via different sources. The data on admissions to the hospitals was obtained from the DDHHS for the years 2006 to 2015 [12, 14].

Instruments and Data Set used

Here, the DDHHS acute hospital admissions according to residence and year were collected. Using SPSS, linear regression analysis was performed. Linear regression is a statistical technique which is used to perform data analysis. It is used to find out the relationship between the dependent variable and one or more independent variables. The linear regression analysis was carried out on the hospital admissions data, controlled for population versus time. The circulatory conditions increased from 0.87% in 2007 to 1.86% in 2014 while the respiratory admissions increased from 0.50% in 2007 to 1.10% in 2014 [12, 27].

The Future Scope Discussed

There has been a rapid increase in the health impairment of the people due to the rapidly escalating air pollution from the heavy industries. The controls to limit exposures are not effectual as there is a growth in the hospitalization due to the acute respiratory and circulatory conditions with the increase in toxic pollutants. The acute hospitalization data indicates a danger. Further, a comprehensive investigation of the health impacts due to the unconventional gas industries in Australia can be made [2, 12].

10.3   The Methodology and Protocols Followed

This experiment was accomplished in a room by taking into consideration proper methodology in the duration of February and March 2020 at one town of Uttar Pradesh, India, on various people who were ready to perform Yagya and chant mantras by following various protocols. The Yagya was performed daily for several days for 20 minutes. Various mantras were chanted which include Vaidik Mantra of Shatkarma, Gayatri Mantra, and Mahamrityunjay Mantra [33].

Firstly, the volunteers were asked to wake up early in the morning and pray to God for the happiness and prosperity for themselves and for their family members. Hawan Kund was prepared by dropping some sand in it and putting four or five pieces of wood used in it. Ghee was poured over the woods with some camphor in it.

At the beginning of this process, water was taken in the right hands of the volunteers and some mantras were pronounced and then they were required to drink that water. Fire was set up with a matchstick in order to start the process. Then, ghee was offered to the fire 108 times with a teaspoon along with repeating the mantras. Again, Hawan Samagri was offered while reciting the Vedic mantras. At the end of Hawan, coconut kept with ghee was offered into the fire while reciting some more mantras. Finally, something was donated after the Hawan, as according to the Vedic rule, it is said that Hawan remains incomplete without the donation.

The protocol and experiment glimpses are shown in Figure 10.8.

Figure 10.8 In Yajna, besides burning material objects, chanting and praying are done to make one self-pious and mighty. It purifies air and provides fresh content through respiration.

10.4   Experimental Setup of an Experiment

The researcher developed AI with ML system to study the effect of Yagya with the aims to measure and forecast air quality and pollution levels where serious air pollution problems prevailed in Delhi region. The live data captured by sensors were deployed at Lodi Complex area of Delhi Region, the data collected with focus to test the algorithms. The researcher has tried to explore the feasibility of linking pollutant airborne particles or aerosols, present in the air to carbon control through Yagya. The specific shape and size of the Hawan Kund, specific selection of wood pieces, and the specific amount of Hawan Samagri used were all monitored for controlling chemical processing in the fire, sublimation, and chemical components for reduction of pollutants level atmosphere. This research will help to develop an ancient technique to clean air in the crowded area of a city which will help to improve the health of the population in the future.

Images of Yajna with different woods and different mantras for different expected results are provided.

Airveda and Different Sensor Based Instruments
The temperature and humidity can be accurately measured with the help of IoT temperature and humidity monitor (Rastogi, R. *et al.*, 2020). The external sensors are placed inside the room and the indicator is mounted outside the room. These kinds of sensors are used at various places like Data Centers and IT Server Rooms. These sensors help the researchers to alert remotely by the means of SMS or email. They also contain a cloud function which works with the help of a web based interface in order to view real time data transmitted by the device. They provide reports in Excel/PDF format; also, custom report designing is also possible as per the requirements of the user (Figure 10.9) [33].

10.5   Results and Discussions

Mango v/s Banyan (Bargad).

10.5.1   Mango

The following are the time series graph of the Hawan(s) done using mango wood from November 13, 2019 to November 17, 2019 every day. AQI, PM2.5, PM10, CO_2, temperature, and humidity were recorded. The Hawan was conducted between 6:30 a.m. to 6:50 a.m. Hence, a sharp change in

Figure 10.9 The IoT-based sensors capturing the humidity and temperature data from atmospheric air in certain interval of time.

values can be observed at 6:30 a.m. and 7:0 a.m. This change is of primary interest to us. Also, it should be noted that there is no significant change in the temperature due to the Hawan (Figures 10.10 and 10.11).

10.5.2 Bargad

The following are the time series graph of the Hawan(s) done using bargad wood from November 18, 2019 to November 19, 2019 every day. AQI, PM2.5, PM10, CO_2, temperature, and humidity were recorded. The Hawan

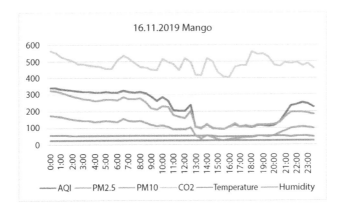

Figure 10.10 Measurement of different parameters of AQI on November 16, 2019 (Yagya was performed with mango wood at 6:30 a.m. with 20-minute protocol).

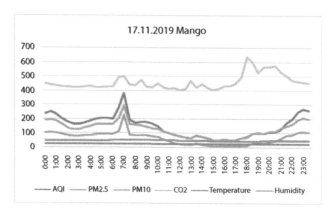

Figure 10.11 Measurement of different parameters of AQI on November 17, 2019 (Yagya was performed with mango wood at 6:30 a.m. with 20-minute protocol).

was conducted between 6:30 a.m. to 6:50 a.m. Hence, a sharp change in values can be observed at 6:30 a.m. and 7:0 a.m. This change is of primary interest to us. Also, it should be noted that there is no significant change in the temperature due to the Hawan. There is a "0" CO_2 value recorded between 16:00 and 20:30 on November 11, 2019. This can attributed to the failure of recording instrument, and it has been disregarded while using the data (Figures 10.12 and 10.13).

Comparative analysis has been depicted in graphs (Figure 10.14).

The graph is based on the comparison of the environmental conditions before the Hawan and after the Hawan. The difference mentioned above is in %age. As it is clear from the graph that, using mango wood brings an

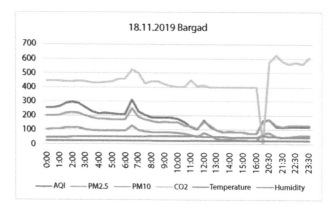

Figure 10.12 Measurement of different parameters of AQI on November 18, 2019 (Yagya was performed with Banyan wood at 6:30 a.m. with 20-minute protocol).

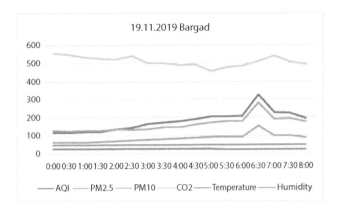

Figure 10.13 Measurement of different parameters of AQI on November 19, 2019 (Yagya was performed with Banyan wood at 6:30 a.m. with 20-minute protocol).

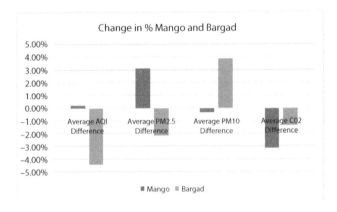

Figure 10.14 Comparative analysis of emission of different gaseous elements and AQI parameters through Yagya experiment done with Mango and Banyan woods (Yagya was performed at 6:30 a.m. with 20-minute protocol).

increase in AQI, PM2.5, and decrease in PM10 and CO2 levels on the other hand, use of bargad wood brings a significant decrease in AQI, PM2.5 and CO2 while an increase in PM10.

From Data to Insights

If Reader can refer to the working excel sheet shared in Annex and can compare it with the original sheet, they will find some additional columns that have been added. These are namely AQI Difference, PM2.5 difference, PM10 difference, and CO_2 difference. The second sheet only contains the graphs copied from the first sheet for easy understandability so it is less important. The third sheet contains the extracted data from the first sheet. These are of primary importance to us as our main goal is to identify the comparative analysis between Mango and Banyan wood emission.

The graph shows the average humidity, temperature, CO_2 levels, PM10, PM2.5, and AQI values observed when the Hawan when done with mango and bargad woods, respectively. It can be clearly seen that the levels of CO_2, PM10, PM2.5, and AQI were very high when the Hawan was done with mango wood as compared to the days when it was done with bargad wood. Also, it can be noticed that there is a small difference in the humidity levels of the both. But still, bargad is the winner here. Though, the natural weather conditions could also have contributed to the huge difference in pollution levels (Figure 10.15).

The graph contains the averaged difference measured over time in a day when the Hawan(s) were conducted. This can be a significant set of features in determining the stability of environment when the Hawan(s) are conducted using mango and bargad woods. This graph shows that CO_2, PM10, and PM2.5 levels are less stable and show more fluctuations over the day when Hawan is done using mango wood; however, the above-mentioned factors are comparatively more stable when the Hawan is done using bargad wood. However, when talking of the AQI, we can see a very huge instability when the Hawan was done using bargad wood. AQI was comparatively much more stable when the Hawan was done using mango wood (Figure 10.16).

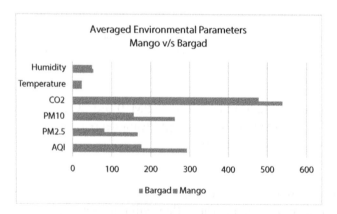

Figure 10.15 Comparative analysis of averaged environmental parameters in fume emission of different gaseous elements through Yagya experiment done with Mango and Banyan woods.

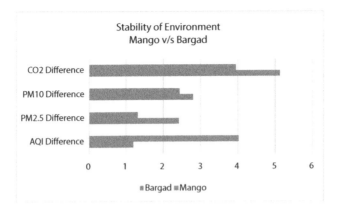

Figure 10.16 Study of the comparative analysis of stability of the environment by emission of different gaseous elements and AQI parameters through Yagya experiment done with Mango and Banyan woods.

10.6 Applications of Yagya and Mantra Therapy in Pollution Control and Its Significance

Yagya is a technique mentioned in the ancient texts including Vedas and Upanishads. When mantras are chanted along with this technique, it becomes more influential and powerful. This technique has various applications, like it purifies the environment especially the polluted air [35]. Some research shows that Yagya helps in reducing air pollution which gets generated when the SO_2 and NO_2 levels get disturbed in the environment along with biological air pollutants such as microorganisms. There are various other applications of Yagya and Mantra therapy (Figure 10.17). People are chanting mantras, which help in depression treatment and sleeplessness [33].

10.7 Future Research Perspectives

Significant findings from earlier research have proved that Yagya is the simplest, cheapest, and most potential method to purify indoor and outdoor environment pollutants such as PM2.5, PM10, and CO_2 and has laid the foundation for further research also. Future researches and studies with statistical analyses will definitely throw more vision and enlighten further the significant aspect of Yagya and how well we can control pollution [38].

Figure 10.17 Collective recital of mantra helps in depression treatment and sleeplessness.

10.8   Novelty of Our Research

According to Hinduism, while performing Hawan, we use the sound energy of mantras and thermal energy of fire which purifies the environment as well as the people around and also drives away all negative energies around us. When mango wood is burnt with Hawan Samagri, it releases formic aldehyde, a gas that kills harmful bacteria [29]. Air samples even after 24 hours showed that bacteria count goes lower by 94%. So, hawan is helpful to prevent airborne infection. Between Cosmic consciousness and human consciousness, supposedly the main link is fire. The pious fire mixed with herbal woods, medicinal spices and grains, and mixture of Sanskrit Mantra produces the combination of heat, light and thermal energy for special effects in human bio-physic structure and external nature [19].

10.9   Recommendations

Yajna with mantra has a great impact on the human body physically as well as mentally. To conduct the experiment, Yagya along with chanting Vedic mantra was performed in a fixed size room at different times on different days [20]. The data based on different parameters was collected with the help of software tools Airveda Instrument and IoT-based sensors.

The Airveda tool was used for pollution data measurement. The different AQI were measured with the help of this device. AI and ML were used in order to recognize the pattern of data. So, this experiment turned out to be fruitful in purifying the air.

10.10   Conclusions

The study indicates that emission of volatile oils and gasses from herbal woods of Banyan tree (FicusBenghalensis) and other ingredients of Hawan Samagri used in Yagya helps to reduce maximum environment pollutants such as PM2.5, PM10, and CO_2.

So, Indian culture is full of such eco-friendly and balanced practices which, if used in long term, help in sustainable development and reduction in pollution for global scan (which is published every two years) To overcome these threats, we have to recall the sayings and actions associated to our Indian culture which believes in the sustainable development and conservation of the environment because the sustainable development is the only long-term solution for these problems. So, the regression to the roots of the Indian culture is what which is needed at this time.

References

1. Apte, K. and Salvi, S., Household air pollution and its effects on health. *F1000Res.*, 5, 1, 2016, F1000 Faculty Rev-2593. https://doi.org/10.12688/f1000research.7552.1.
2. Cortés, U., Sànchez-Marrè, M., Ceccaroni, L., Artificial Intelligence and Environmental Decision Support Systems. *J. Dual Diagn. Appl. Intell.*, 13, 1, 77–91, 2000, URL link.springer.com; Spain ia@lsi.upc.es; miquel@lsi.upc.es; luigic@lsi.upc.es.
3. Chauhan, P., An overview of air pollution in India at present scenario. *Int. J. Res. Graanthalayah*, 03, 2350-0530, 1–4, Sept. 2015.
4. Dev, M., Indian culture and lifestyle for environment conservation:A path towards Sustainable development. *Int. J. Emerg. Technol.*, 8, 2249–3255, 256–260, 2017.
5. Devender, K., Air pollution mitigation through yajna: Vedic and modern views. *Environ. Conserv. J.*, 20, 3, 57–60, 2019, URL: https://environcj.in/volume-20-issue-3-20308/2019; https://doi.org/136953/ECJ.2019.20308.
6. Ghorani-Azam, A., Riahi-Zanjani, B., Balali-Mood, M., Effects of air pollution on human health and practical measures for prevention in Iran. *J. Res.*

Med. Sci., 21, 65, 2016, https://doi.org/10.4103/1735-1995.189646; http://www.jmsjournal.net/text.asp?2016/21/1/65/189646.

7. Ghosh, D. and Parida, P., Air Pollution And India: Current Scenario. *Int. J. Curr. Res.*, 7, 11, 22194–22196, 2015.

8. Gupta, S., *Hawan for cleansing the Environment*, Medium, USA, Oct.17, 2012, Retrieved 26 Feburary, 2019. Available from https://www.speakingtree.in>blog.

9. Karatzas, K., Artificial Intelligence Applications in the Atmospheric Environment: Status and Future Trends. *Environ. Eng. Manage. J.*, 9, 171–180, 2010, 10.30638/eemj.2010.026.

10. Limaye, V.G., Agnihotra (The Everyday Homa) and production of Brassinosteroids: A scientific validation. *Int. J. Mod. Eng. Res.*, 8, 2, 2249–6645, 41–51, 11 Feb. 2019.

11. McCarron, G., Air Pollution and human health hazards: a compilation of air toxins acknowledged by the gas industry in Queensland's Darling Downs. *Int. J. Environ. Stud.*, 75, 1, 171–85, Eve Sinton, 2018.

12. Rastogi, R., Saxena, M., Chaturvedi, D.K., Satya, S., Arora, N., Gupta, M., Singhal, P., Fog Data-Based Statistical Analysis to Check Effects of Yajna and Mantra Science: Next Generation Health Practices, in: *Fog Data Analytics for IoT Applications: Next Generation Process Model with state-of-the-art Technologies*, Dr. Sudeep Tanwar (ed.), 2020.

13. Nautiyal, C.S., Chauhan, P.S., Nene, Y.L., Medicine smoke reduces air born bacteria. Eve Sinton, *J. Ethnopharmacol.*, 114, 3, 446–51, Epub 2007, Aug 28, 2007 Dec 3. Rani, *et al.*, *World J. Pharm. Res.* www.wjpr.net, 8, 12, 427, 2019.

14. Oprea M., Iliadis L., An Artificial Intelligence-Based Environment Quality Analysis System, In: *Engineering Applications of Neural Networks. IFIP Advances in Information and Communication Technology*, Iliadis L., Jayne C. (eds), EANN 2011, AIAI 2011, 363, Springer, Berlin, Heidelberg, 2011, https://doi.org/10.1007/978-3-642-23957-1_55.

15. Rastogi, R., Chaturvedi, D.K., Satya, S., Arora, N., Trivedi, P., Singh, A., Sharma, A., Singh, A., Intelligent Analysis for Personality Detection on Various Indicators by Clinical Reliable Psychological TTH and Stress Surveys, in: the *proceedings of International Conference on Computational Intelligence in Pattern Recognition*, A.K. Das, *et al.* (Eds.), pp. 127–144, Singapore, (CIPR 2019) at Indian Institute of Engineering Science and Technology, Shibpur, Springer Advances in Intelligent Systems and Computing (AISC) Series.

16. Rastogi, R., Chaturvedi, D.K., Gupta, M., Singhal, P., Intelligent Mental Health Analyzer by Biofeedback: App and Analysis, in: *Handbook of Research on Optimizing Healthcare Management Techniques*, N. Wickramasinghe, (Ed.), Hershey, PA, 2020.

17. Rastogi, R., Chaturvedi, D.K., Verma, H., Mishra, Y., Gupta, M., Identifying Better? Analytical Trends to Check Subjects' Medications Using Biofeedback

Therapies', IGL Global. *Int. J. Appl. Res. Public Health Manage. (IJARPHM)*, 5, 1, Article 2, https://www.igi-global.com/article/identifying-better/240753, 2020.

18. Rastogi, R., Gupta, M., Chaturvedi, D.K., Efficacy of Study for Correlation of TTH vs Age and Gender Factors using EMG Biofeedback Technique. *Int. J. Appl. Res. Public Health Manage. (IJARPHM)*, 5, 1, 49–66, 2020.

19. Rastogi, R., Chaturvedi, D.K., Satya, S., Arora, N., Gupta, M., Verma, H., Saini, H., An Optimized Biofeedback EMG and GSR Biofeedback Therapy for Chronic TTH on SF-36 Scores of Different MMBD Modes on Various Medical Symptoms, in: *Studies Comp. Intelligence*, Vol. 841: Hybrid Machine Intelligence for Medical Image Analysis, Bhattacharya, S., *et al.*, (Eds.), 2020, https://doi.org/10.1007/978-981-13-8930-6_8.

20. Rastogi, R., Chaturvedi, D.K., Satya, S., Arora, N., Trivedi, P., Singh, A.K., Sharma, A.K., Singh, A., Intelligent Personality Analysis on Indicators in IoT-MMBD Enabled Environment, in: *Multimedia Big Data Computing for IoT Applications: Concepts, Paradigms, and Solutions*, S. Tanwar, S. Tyagi, N. Kumar (Eds.), pp. 185–215, Springer Nature Singapore, Singapore, 2020, https://doi.org/10.1007/978-981-13-8759-3_7.

21. Rastogi, R., Chaturvedi, D.K., Satya, S., Arora, N., Trivedi, P., Gupta, M., Singhal, P., Gulati, M., MM Big Data Applications: Statistical Resultant Analysis of Psychosomatic Survey on Various Human Personality Indicators. *Proceedings of Second International Conference on Computational Intelligence 2018*, 2020, https://doi.org/10.1007/978-981-13-8222-2_25.

22. Rastogi, R., Chaturvedi, D.K., Gupta, M., Singhal, P., Surveillance of Type –I & II Diabetic Subjects on Physical Characteristics: IoT and Big Data Perspective in Healthcare, @NCR, India, in: *Chapter No. 23, Internet of Things (IoT), Concept and Applications*, Alam, M., Shakil, K.A., Khan, S. (Eds.), 10 May 2020.

23. Rastogi, R., Chaturvedi, D.K., Gupta, M., Sirohi, H., Gulati, M., Pratyusha, Analytical Observations between Subjects' Medications Movement & Medication Scores Correlation Based on their Gender and Age Using GSR Biofeedback: Intelligent Application in Healthcare, in: *Pattern Recognition Applications in Engineering*, M.A. Vejar and F. Pozo (Eds.), pp. 229–257, IGI Global, Hershey, PA, 2020.

24. Rastogi, R., Chaturvedi, D.K., Gupta, M., Sirohi, H., Gulati, M., Pratyusha, Analytical Observations Between Subjects' Medications Movement and Medication Scores Correlation Based on Their Gender and Age Using GSR Biofeedback: Intelligent Application in Healthcare, in: *Pattern Recognition Applications in Engineering*, D. Burgos, M. Vejar, F. Pozo (Eds.), pp. 229–257, IGI Global, Hershey, PA, 2020.

25. Rastogi, R., Chaturvedi, D.K., Gupta, M., Exhibiting App and Analysis for Biofeedback Based Mental Health Analyzer, in: as chapter 15 in *Handbook of Research on Advancements of Artificial Intelligence in Healthcare Engineering*, p. 300, 2020.

26. Rastogi, R., Chaturvedi, D.K., Gupta, M., Computational Approach for Personality Detection on Attributes: An IoT-MMBD Enabled Environment, in: as Chapter 16 in *Handbook of Research on Advancements of Artificial Intelligence in Healthcare Engineering*, p. 300, 2020.

27. Rastogi, R., Chaturvedi, D.K., Gupta, M., Tension Type Headache: IOT and FOG Applications in Healthcare Using Different Biofeedback, in: *Handbook of Research on Advancements of Artificial Intelligence in Healthcare Engineering*, p. 300, 2020.

28. Rastogi, R. and Chaturvedi, D.K., Tension Type Headache: IOT Applications to Cure TTH Using Different Biofeedback: A statistical Approach in Healthcare, in: *Biopsychosocial Perspectives and Practices for Addressing Communicable and Non-Communicable Diseases*, Ch. 10, S.G. Taukeni (University of Namibia, Namibia) (Ed.), IGI Global, Hershey, PA, 2020.

29. Rastogi, R., Saxena, M., Maheshwari, M., Garg, P., Gupta, M., Shrivastava, R., Rastogi, M., Gupta, H., Yajna and Mantra Science Bringing Health and Comfort to Indo-Asian Public: A Healthcare 4.0 Approach and Computational Study, in: *Machine Learning with Healthcare Perspective. Learning and Analytics in Intelligent Systems*, vol. 13, V. Jain and J. Chatterjee (Eds.), pp. 357–390, Springer, Cham, 2020, Springer Nature Switzerland AG, 2020.

30. Rastogi, R., Chaturvedi, D.K., Satya, S., Arora, N., Intelligent Heart Disease Prediction on Physical and Mental Parameters: A ML Based IoT and Big Data Application and Analysis, in: *Machine Learning with Healthcare Perspective. Learning and Analytics in Intelligent Systems*, vol. 13, V. Jain and J. Chatterjee (Eds.), pp. 199–236, Springer, Cham, Springer Nature Switzerland AG, 2020.

31. Rastogi, R., Chaturvedi, D.K., Singhal, P., Gupta, M., Investigating Diabetic Subjects on TheirCorrelation with TTH and CAD: A Statistical Approach on Experimental Results, in: *Opportunities and Challenges in Digital Healthcare Innovation*, Sandhu, K. (Ed.), 2020.

32. Rastogi, R., Chaturvedi, D.K., Singhal, P., Gupta, M., Investigating Correlation of Tension Type Headache and Diabetes: IoT Perspective in Healthcare, in: *IoTHT: Internet of Things for Healthcare Technologies*, C. Chakerborty (Ed.), Springer Nature, Singapore, 2020.

33. Ritchie, H. and Roser, M., *Outdoor Air Pollution*, Published online at OurWorldInData.org. Retrieved from: 'https://ourworldindata.org/outdoor-air-pollution' [Online Resource], Delhi, India, 2019.

34. Romana, R.K., Sharma, A., Gupta, V., Kaur, R., Kumar, S., Bansal, P., Was Hawan Designed to Fight Anxiety-Scientific Evidence? *J. Relig. Health*, 59, 1, 505–521, NLM (Medline), Feb., 01, 2020, https://doi.org/10.1007/s10943-016-0345-1.

35. Saxena, M., Kumar, B., Matharu, S., Impact of Yagya on Particulate Matters. *Interdiscip. J. Yagya Res.*, 1, 01–08, 2018.

36. Sharma, P., Ayub, S., Tripathi, C., AGNIHOTRA–A Nonconventional Solution to Air Pollution. *Int. J. Innov. Res. Sci. Eng.*, 8, november issue 12 - WJPR, 1–13, 2019.
37. Sharma, P.K., Ayub, S., Tripathi, C.N., Anjavi, S., Dubev, S.K., AGNIHOTRA – A Non Conventional Solution to Air Pollution. *Int. J. Innov. Res. Sci. Eng.* 1, 2347–3207, 26 Feb. 2019, https://m.hindustantimes.com>columns.
38. Singh, R. and Singh, S., Gayatri Mantra Chanting Helps Generate Higher Antimicrobial Activity of Yagya's Smoke. *Interdiscip. J. Yagya Res.*, 1, 09–14, 2018, http://ijyr.dsvv.ac.in/index.php/ijyr/article/view/6.

11

An Economical Machine Learning Approach for Anomaly Detection in IoT Environment

Ambika N.

Department of Computer Science and Applications, St.Francis College, Bangalore, Karnataka, India

Abstract

Internet of Things (IoT) are gadgets of different capabilities provided with same platform to communicate with each other. These devices connect with each other through internet to accomplish a task. These unsupervised devices are used in many applications. A ransomware assault in IoT can be all the more obliterating as it might influence a whole scene of security administrations. Hence, precautions are to be taken to secure the devices as well as the data that is being transmitted among themselves. The threats have to be detected at the earlier stage to ensure complete security to the communication. The work is an improved version of the previous machine learning architecture. The proposal analyzes the communicating data between these devices and aids in choosing an economical appropriate measure to secure the system.

Keywords: Anomaly detection, dimensionality reduction, imputation, IoT, missing value, similarity, economical approach

11.1 Introduction

The Internet of Things (IoT) [1] is shaped by associating physical gadgets. IoT gadgets incorporate normal items from everyday life. These gadgets associate with one another to make human lives simpler. IoT gadgets are conveyed in different situations. IoT gadgets are set up in places like homes [2], workplaces, emergency clinics [3, 4], and agriculture [5, 6]. IoT has

---

Email: ambika.nagaraj76@gmail.com

A. Suresh, S. Vimal, Y. Harold Robinson, Dhinesh Kumar Ramaswami and R. Udendhran (eds.)
Bioinformatics and Medical Applications: Big Data Using Deep Learning Algorithms, (215–234)

without a doubt prompted the development of the savvy world; however, IoT gadgets are exceptionally defenseless against a wide scope of assaults. A backhanded correspondence of individual to singular shrewd gadgets additionally makes IoT helpless against different kinds of assaults. The safety efforts in IoT and the opposition of IoT gadgets against the ongoing assaults are one of the significant concern looked by IoT. IoT security [7] has been in news as of late, due to DDoS, botnet, malware, and ransomware assaults on IoT gadgets. The premature variations of ransomware started in the late 1980s.

A ransomware assault [8] in IoT is obliterating as it influences an entire scene of safety manage. The security breaches include breaching of privacy, respectability, and accessibility. It may not just outcome in monetary misfortunes; however, it may likewise bring about significant data penetration. Ransomware [9] may assume whole responsibility for information or a framework and permit constrained access for client connection with the gadgets, request a robust total as a payment, and discharge information to the client simply after effective installment. On the off chance that a client does not pay, ransomware either expands the installment time frames and payment sum or erases the information from the gadgets.

Fixing IoT gadgets may not succeed as a rule as the gadgets are as of now undermined and businessmen are left with no choice aside from paying the payment sum. To address the test, experts have to grow new techniques for primal ransomware recognition ahead the gadgets are undermined. In the event of notable ransomware assaults, the gadgets must not have the option to transfer predictable document augmentations or records having definite names as identifiers. To the other end, IoT gadget sellers can give a set rundown of information documents that are practical for performance within an IoT gadget.

The heterogeneity in IoT gadgets carries colossal difficulties to consolidate security. To completely actualize security, IoT gadgets/frameworks ought to have the option to alleviate ransomware during the whole lifecycle of the utilization process. This lifecycle starts from the establishment of security programming to make sure about the confirmation and enrollment of gadgets in IoT systems. Moreover, IoT gadgets ought to perform charging, designing, observing, controlling, and decommissioning capacities similar to the systems.

To analyze any kind of ransomware in the system, the missing qualities can be verified. The existence of missing qualities makes the dataset conflicting. It unseemly conveys the arrangement and forecast errands. The information which is taken care of by the classifiers must be liberated from missing qualities. The classifier does the arrangement task. Filling missing information in such datasets is henceforth a significant pre-preparing task. The way toward filling missing information esteems is characterized as accusation. The essential advance in any imputation procedure is processing the vicinity between record occurrences in include expanse of the dataset to decide the closest and suitable neighbor for the ascription of missing qualities. One of the most broadly theoretical separations measured to evaluate the closeness among any two cases is the Euclidean separation. The Euclidean separation unit of measurement has a few impediments.

To provide a precise missing rate and the attributes which the adversaries are looking for, the proposal is suggested. It is an addition to the previous system [10]. The initial phase in the proposed attribution strategy [10] as in any ascription procedure is to isolate all information occurrences in the dataset into two classes. The principal classification ought to contain the dataset occurrences without missing qualities (instance-feature matrix) and the subsequent class ought to contain just those cases which contain missing qualities. The datasets in the form of rows and columns are arranged. The decision label is provided for the principal classification occurrences. A marginal conditional probability is applied on the datasets for the principal classification group. The clusters of the datasets with similarity are made. They are feature-cluster matrix or transformation matrix. A reduced dimension matrix is received by computing the characteristic-cluster array with instance-feature matrix. The missing parameters in second set are substituted by zero to obtain another reduced-dimension matrix. The obtained set is known as imputed set. This is classified into training and testing instances. Marginal conditional pattern vector for each labeled attribute is obtained. The attribute pattern vectors using incremental grouping method are clustered. The performance metrics are computed.

The proposed system works on the different datasets of attributes and the frequency rates at which they are stolen from the system. In the work, four different attribute datasets are considered and four different frequency rates are margined. The different users can adopt different mechanisms based on the evaluation. The suggested measures have to be economical and serve the purpose for an organization. The proposal aids to benefit the organization. The introduction is followed by the literature survey in the subsequent section. The proposed work is detailed in Section 11.3. The analysis of the activity is given in Section 11.4. The study is summarized in the conclusion section.

11.2 Literature Survey

The section details the contributions made by various authors. The creators have utilized PowerTutor [11] to screen and test power utilization of every single running procedure in 500-ms spans. PowerTutor makes log documents containing a grouping of vitality use of each procedure at a given inspecting span. The force use tests are isolated into subsamples preceding utilizing distinctive order procedures to recognize the subsamples names. They have applied four cutting edge classifiers: k-nearest neighbor (KNN), neural network (NN), support vector machine (SVM), and random forest (RF). KNN is a straightforward and incredible classifier that looks for the K closest sample(s) and appoints most of the neighbor's name to the given examples. NN is the usage of human mind systems and for the most part, used to inexact the capacity among data sources and yield.

During the first information trade [12], the ransomware reports its interesting identifier and the casualty's IP address to the order and control, which recognizes the got data. In the subsequent trade, the reaction contains a picture containing directions for the person in question and, TOR address of the payment site page, the casualty's very own code, and an RSA 2048-piece open key that is utilized for scrambling the information. At that point, the encryption procedure begins. During the last information trade, an affirmation for the open key gathering is given.

Authors in [13] have actualized a trickiness domain to trap assailants. They screen RDP-based ransomware assaults and gather data when the event occurs. They extricate powerful hints from the screened data. They utilize programmed investigation to screen countless signs for following back the assailant. They create a document to traceback the RDP-based ransomware assailant. The work suggests tree screen layers: the system level, the host level, and the recording level. The organizing layer recognizes a remote association and gathers data including the distant IP computer address, distant station, condition tag of ports, and console design. At the point when the RDP-based assailant signs in to the server, the screen can get data and distinguish the assault without the aggressor's information. The server level screen can assemble data about the assailant's conduct and their utilization of these framework applications in the double-dealing condition.

A safe record zone has been made in framework or PC to secure documents against vindictive programming and assaults, and significant archives have been moved to this region for keeping the records from being changed by another programming. The product that is moving in the working framework [14] has restricted approach to the record framework, and entree command is given distinctly by the client. They created a safe zone framework secures the documents it holds against ransomware or different pernicious programming and ensures this insurance with a trustworthiness check. The product holds all the documents in a solitary record by packing them for making a sheltered territory. The name of this record is characterized as a "Safe Zone" and it is a ZIP record and it is controlled inside the organizer. The product deals with the substance of this document by adding another record to the ZIP record, erasing and adjusting the record. To keep the substance of this record from being denatured by different sources, it keeps the document open in relentless composing mode and the working framework keeps the document from being changed. This component is the premise of the protected region. The product likewise has a propelled logging framework. This framework logs all occasions in the protected zone. Furthermore, it begins to watch the fundamental organizer of each document added to the protected geographical area and includes the adjustments in that envelope to the log called FileWatcher. The log document is "safezone.log". In the product, there is likewise an instrument to check if the records made are in harm's way or not. This trustworthiness control instrument keeps the MD5 rundowns of the records in its SQLite database called "File.db" and checks respectability for any progressions that happen in the document "safe zone".

The work [15] utilizes ANN as disconnected IDS to assemble and break down data from a different piece of the IoT organize and distinguish a DoS assault on the system. The neurons of the ANN frame complex speculations. Assessing the hypothesis sets the info hubs in an input procedure, and the occasion streams are engendered through the system to the yield delegating ordinary or traded off. At this stage, the slope plummets push the mistake in the yield hub back through the system by a back proliferation process to appraise the inaccuracy of the concealed devices. The slope of the expense capacity would thus be able to be determined. Neural system framework experiences preparing to gain proficiency with the example made in the framework.

The proposed DRTHIS [16] uses a paired classifier, a Deep Feature Extractor (DFE), and a One-Class Classifier (OCCs), for chasing ransomware tests and recognizing their families dependent on the application grouping of exercises. At the point when a client dispatches an application, the framework records every single executed occasion that inside the initial

10 seconds of use execution and changes the caught grouping to decide whether the instance is ransomware or not. This stage alludes to as Threat Hunting. At that point, recognized ransomware tests are sent to the framework to decide the ransomware family. During Threat Intelligence, we influence the DFE segment, which utilizes a pre-prepared profound model in its first stage to separate a vector to take care of to OCCs. It gives us the capacity to recognize the group of the given ransomware test. DRTHIS plays out a Data Transformation undertaking to change printed groupings of occasions into the numerical structure. At that point, the Combining and labeling part joins input datasets into one incorporated dataset appropriate for our profound learning undertakings.

A quick Fuzzy Pattern Tree strategy was proposed [17] to improve the runtime learning. A fuzzy pattern tree contains a tree-like structure in which the internal hubs are fuzzy rationale number juggling administrators and the leaf hubs are related with fuzzy predicates on input property. At long last, the yield is submitted to its ancestor and dependent on the yield. Along these lines for malware order, the yield is isolated into limits to perceive the group of malware. During an iterative methodology, a few example trees are created for each class and toward the finish of every emphasis, the best example tree that has the least expectation mistake on the class is chosen to extend leaf hubs at the following stage. To utilize a fuzzy example tree for malware recognition, the authors have applied it to handled datasets of OpCode groupings.

Authors in [18] propose fixing plans for IoT conditions that control foundation connects. The fixing plan comprises of a few stages. In the recognizing stage, the foundation uses conventional IDS or firewalls to distinguish the presence of malware or traded off the hub. When malevolent code is seen as engendered from the undermined IoT gadgets, the fixing stage begins to examine the malware and patches the middle hubs as indicated by the fixing arrangement to forestall the enormous scope proliferation of malware. The intermediate hubs are equipped for performing asset concentrated errands and along these lines can bolster over the air (OTA) update systems. In the fixing stage, such OTA systems permit the manager to remotely introduce the necessary reports in the intermediate hubs, subsequently guaranteeing the convenient alleviation of traded off hubs. Since intermediate hubs are fundamentally less than IoT gadgets, the admin can physically fix intermediate hubs that do not bolster OTA updates.

Author in [19] explores the recognition of ransomware. They started a depiction of recognition systems found in the run of the mill business infection scanners. Discovery of malware utilizing static-based investigation implies dissecting an application's code before its execution to decide. On the off chance that the static examination finds any malignant code, the executable will be halted from propelling. The most widely recognized kind of static investigation is utilized in business infection scanners and alluded to as signature examination. In the mark investigation, code string designs (marks) are removed from the objective application's code and contrasted with a store of realized malevolent code designs. Mark put together discovery depends with respect to a huge archive of vindictive code marks. Business infection scanners have huge groups of cybersecurity specialists that constantly find, research, and concentrate pernicious marks.

FileTracker [20] is a disseminated customer server engineering. The customer comprises of a client mode examination segment and an occasion checking part module. The bit module is additionally made out of a document framework channel driver and a procedure checking driver. The channel driver gives the I/O occasion, access to crude read/compose cushion, and capacity to virtualize the I/O calls. The procedure checking module is answerable for advising process-related occasions. It plays out an occasion-based respectability output of the running procedures and document framework channel layers. The FileTracker server totals all the framework occasions from every hub and constructs a worldwide model of ordinary and irregular document access and alteration conduct. These conduct models are then common with every nearby hub at standard stretches. Highlight determination is one of the significant focuses as it straightforwardly influences the exactness and execution of the framework. Given the perception, the authors have separated the dubious highlights in three general classifications. Category 1 comprises of highlights legitimately identified with documents, Category 2 comprises of highlights identified with a procedure, and Category 3 comprises of highlights identified with sway.

Authors in [21] suggest the information assortment, which includes extraction and AI classifier periods of our test. In the information assortment stage, the system traffic tests are gathered for both malignant (ransomware) and generous Windows applications. The element extraction stage extricates the significant highlights and consolidations them to make the dataset. In the last AI classifier stage, the authors have trained and tested a few calculations in the Waikato Environment for Knowledge Analysis 3.8.1 (WEKA) AI apparatus to distinguish the ideal location model. The creators have focused on Windows ransomware organize traffic. The contaminated host will endeavor to associate with a remote assailant arrange address which could be an order and control server, installment, or dispersion site. During the AI classifiers phase of the examination that we distinguished, the AI classifier and highlight blend accomplished the most noteworthy detection rate.

Authors in [22] proposed a ransomware identification model for IoT condition dependent on ransomware correspondence attributes and traffic examinations. The discovery technique centers the traffic examination of Cryptowall [12]. The proposed model can be utilized at certain points of the doings. At the point when the framework gets and extricates TCP/IP header, it will additionally separate source IP and goal IP. The extricated information will be put away incidentally to coordinate source IP and goal IP from the boycotted IP and control servers. On the off chance that the source IP or goal IP matches with IPs recorded in order and control server boycott, then framework will square correspondence with order and control server and stops the traffic stream. The proposed model will deal with all bogus messages.

The initial phase in the proposed attribution strategy [10] as in any ascription procedure is to isolate all information occurrences in the dataset into two classes. The principal classification ought to contain the dataset occurrences without missing qualities and the subsequent class ought to contain just those cases which contain missing qualities. The datasets in the form of rows and columns are arranged. The decision label is provided for the principal classification occurrences. A marginal conditional probability is applied on the datasets for the principal classification group. The clusters of the datasets with similarity are made. They are feature-cluster matrix or transformation matrix. A reduced dimension matrix is obtained by multiplying the feature-cluster matrix with instance-feature matrix. The missing parameters in second set are substituted by zero to obtain another reduced dimension matrix. The obtained set is known as imputed set. This is classified into training and testing instances. Marginal conditional pattern vector for each labeled attribute is obtained. The attribute pattern vectors using incremental grouping method are clustered. The performance metrics are computed.

The creators have introduced a useful malware example that can bargain Arduino Yun gadgets [23], which are in the IoT field because of its minimal effort and convenience. By misusing a weakness in the asset obliged AVR chip coordinated in Arduino Yun, they demonstrated how a foe seizes the OpenWrt chip that has full availability abilities. It is conceivable because of the defects experienced in the structure of the Bridge library that conveys the two chips and that do not give get to control either confirmation. They have depicted a proof of idea worm which introduces a secondary passage and furnishes the foe with a Remote Access Tool (RAT) to the gadget. To store the information in SRAM, they have discovered an ideal couple of devices. These contraptions are incorporated with the String library and imported altogether. Arduino programs show that it is sensible that the enemy can utilize it voluntarily. As these devices are sequential in the code, they can use them recursively. To play out a product reset of the AVR bit, they employ one of the reset sources gave by the AVR design, the Watchdog reset, which builds up a break also and resets the Gallet when it lapses.

The creators characterized an assault model utilizing the ELM327 [24] order convention and a vehicle the executive's application to make an associated car condition and led hacking investigates legal automobiles. The initial step was the natural examination of the ELM327 module, and the armada board application establishes the associated vehicle condition. They dissected the correspondence procedure and the AT (Attention) order of the ELM327 through an open report and prevailing in persuasively controlling the vehicle utilizing the AT order. The powerlessness investigation was performed dependent on the working rule of the conveyance of the board application conveyed through the Android advertise and the smali code acquired by figuring out the appeal. This stage compares to the digital surveillance stage. The subsequent advance included messing with the android repackaging of the application conveyed on the Android advertise. They broke down the qualities of the ELM327 and armada the executive's applications were utilized to make an associated vehicle condition and afterward changed the dispersed business applications into noxious applications. They adjusted the AT Command, and the vehicle the executive's requisition broke down in the initial step and embeds into the machine. This stage compares to the weaponization and spread of the digital murder chain. The third stage is an assault to explore utilizing a real car vehicle. They directed a constrained move control try expecting that an altered armada the executive's application was redistributed through the underground market and on the android profit-oriented center and introduced it on the casualty's cell phone. At this stage, the scattered application conveyance and casualty's download conduct accepted by creators relates to the dispersal and abuse of the digital murder chain, separately.

The creators propose a host-based Intrusion Detection and Mitigation structure called IoT-IDM [25], which gives PC security administrations to dangers related with brilliant IoT gadgets inside the home. IoT-IDM tackles the appearance of SDN innovation, which offers organize transparency and adaptability to arrange, oversee, and secure the system distantly and the development of AI strategies in the identification of system inconsistency designs. Hence, a third substance, which has security aptitude, could assume liability to guarantee the executives for the benefit of end clients and give Security as a Service (SaaS). They consider having based

IDS to structure our answer. It restrains the volume of the system traffic that should have been dissected, as host-based IDSs screen the exercises of a solitary host of enthusiasm for dubious and noxious training. It comprises of five key modules: device manager, sensor element, feature extractor, detection, and mitigation. The IoT-IDM engineering consolidates a database to streamline the capacity and the board of a rundown of all known in-home IoT gadgets alongside the potential security dangers related to them, the location technique for known assaults, and if it is pertinent, suitable safeguard instruments. IoT-IDM structure embraces the inline sensor to screen arrangement exercises on an objective IoT gadget. When an IoT gadget enrolls for dubious practice, IoTIDM constructs a virtual inline sensor as an application on the head of the SDN controller. It makes and pushes out OpenFlow rules in primary switches trying to divert the traffic between the IoT gadget and the remainder of the system toward the sensor component. The system traffic of an enrolled IoT gadget caught by the sensor extricates includes out of it. This structure gives its client (SaaS supplier) the adaptability to choose removable fields, as the entire traffic is accessible. Along these lines, the clients of IoT-IDM can choose highlights relies upon various issue cases. The IoT-IDM structure looks at the system traffic caught by sensor components or the insights of system traffic removed from the past advance to distinguish dubious exercises. The moderation module expects to take suitable countermeasures to keep recognized assaults from having any unsafe impact.

The measurement decrease module [26] delivers constraints because of dimensionality that may prompt the creation of wrong choices while expanding the computational intricacy of the classifier. They conveyed both Linear Discriminant Analysis (LDA) and Principal Component Analysis to address the high dimensionality issue. Head Component Analysis (PCA) can include choice and extraction. Highlight determination picks a subset of all highlights dependent on their viability in the higher grouping (for example, picking progressively enlightening highlights). Highlight extraction makes a subset of new highlights by consolidating existing highlights. In TDTC, they utilized PCA as a component extraction system to plan the NSL-KDD dataset, which comprises of 41 highlights to one with a lower include space by expelling less noteworthy highlights. Since objects (tests) in the PCA-changed dataset are not perfect for order, the proposed model used another component decrease module to apply the named information in an ideal change to new measurements. LDA looks at the class marks to decrease the element of enormous working datasets, and LDA is generally utilized in various areas, for example, picture preparing and stock examination. TDTC is as of now prepared to employ the changed dataset and ordered approaching traffic using a multilayer classifier to recognize irregularities. The Naïve Bayes classifier used in a cluster of irregular conduct undergoes refinement to ordinary cases utilizing the Certainty-Factor form of KNN (CF-KNN).

The AD-IoT framework [27] utilizes a keen abnormality location technique dependent on AI calculations that can recognize assaults with diminishing the bogus positive rate. The AD-IoT framework intends to screen all IoT traffic in a dispersed mist layer and alarm the overseer or the supplier administrations in a savvy city. This methodology can identify a test of covered up undermined IoT gadgets in the enormous scope location in distributed computing. The configuration model should comprise a few parts containing a measure of IoT gadgets associated with conveyed mist arranges secretly or openly in a keen city. Identifying from this insightful model dispersed at each mist hub, it ought to recognize the new assaults to alarm the cloud server administrations. NIDS can use AI calculations to characterize and identify malicious conduct in the IoT mist systems. It should be possible by applying the NIDS framework through the utilization of the abnormality identification technique dependent on AI calculations, which utilizes measurable investigation to clean and get ready information for a wisely prescient model. This model can distinguish typical traffic and unusual assaults with decreased False Positive Rates (FPR).

The hybrid approach [28] means joining misemploy-based and abnormality based strategies. The dynamic learning strategy accomplishes high exactness utilizing as barely any named occasions as could be expected under the circumstances, subsequently limiting the expense of getting marked information. The select inquiry chooses unlabeled information dependent on specific systems. A human annotator, at that point, marks the chose information and includes it into the preparation set. The learning model alters its boundaries each time it gets new marked data. The entire learning process stops when the framework accomplishes wanted forecast exactness. Dynamic learning characterizes a stream-based specific inspecting plan and pool-based testing plan. In stream-based particular testing, the information will initially be inspected one at once from the real dispersion. The student can choose for each examined information, regardless of whether to demand its mark or dispose of it. In pool-based examining, every unlabeled datum accumulates in an information pool. The question motor will choose an information occurrence from the pool and send it to the human annotator. The choice to dispose of information in the stream-based technique is the determination of the case in the pool-based strategy. It follows particular inquiry systems that target quickening the learning procedure.

The proposal [29] is another irregularity based managed AI technique. They have utilized a deviation-based methodology, at the same time, rather than assigning a limit to characterize an interruption. It is a discriminative system that will permit us to order a specific traffic test with the interruption mark that accomplishes less recreation blunder. It depends on a restrictive variational autoencoder (CVAE). The incorporation of interruption names into CVAE decoder layers. The authors utilize a generative model dependent on variational autoencoder (VAE) ideas. This change gives numerous favorable circumstances to our ID-CVAE when contrasting it and a VAE, both as far as adaptability and execution. When utilizing a VAE to assemble a classifier, it is significant to make the same number of models as there are particular name esteems, each model requiring an individual preparation step. It utilizes, as preparing information, just the examples related to the name educated, each in turn. ID-CVAE needs to make a solitary model with remote preparing step, utilizing all preparation information regardless of their related marks. It is the reason a classifier dependent on ID-CVAE is a superior choice regarding calculation time and arrangement unpredictability. Besides, it gives better characterization results than other natural classifiers. ID-CVAE is a solo strategy prepared in a regulated way because of the utilization of class marks during preparing. More significant than its grouping results, the proposed model (ID-CVAE) can perform include remaking. ID-CVAE will get familiar with the dispersion of highlights esteems by depending on planning to its inside idle factors, from which a later element recuperation acts on account of information tests with deficient highlights. ID-CVAE can recuperate with precision over 99%. This capacity to perform includes renewal that can be a significant resource in an IoT organization. IoT systems may experience the ill effects of association and detecting mistakes that may ruin a portion of the got information. It might be especially significant for all highlights that convey gadget's state esteems.

The proposed interruption recognition framework [30] targets spots associated with IoT gadgets. Its principal objective is to distinguish potential assaults that can happen through remote interchanges. To plan proficient IDS, the authors consider together the conduct of the aggressors and clients and the dynamic development of the savvy places. It varies with the checking of remote exercises utilizing tests and on the recognizable proof of mischievous activities. The examination is sent in vital areas of the savvy place, by a security master. It comprises of two fundamental segments containing a Central Security System (CSS) and the Radio Probes. The CSS forms the perceptions gathered from the tests and actualizes the interruption location calculation to recognize ill-conceived practices.

All the assessments in the design are associated with this gadget employing a secure channel. The primary objective of the CSS is to total all the data accumulated by the tests and to process them with the neural system. The Radio Probes are sensors used to tune in to all the remote interchanges inside and around the shrewd spot. They gather explicit information illustrative of the exchange conduct, for example, the RSSI (Received Signal Strength Indication), which is a force proportion of the got sign of a radio wire. These tests guarantee the inclusion of the savvy place. Its distinctive RSSI measures realize the area of the communicate outflow. The neural system can be prepared to perceive the real territories where gadgets impart inside the savvy place. On the off chance that a transmission is from an ill-conceived location, the neural system will distinguish an assault.

The proposition [31] is a propelled interruption identification innovation utilizing AI calculations dependent on Software Defined IoT engineering. Explicitly we apply a mix of improved AI calculations includes choice and stream characterization, which are two essential strides in interruption identification. The Bat calculation improvement parts the entirety swarm into subgroups. It utilizes K-implies strategy so that every subgroup can learn inside and various populaces. Moreover, Differential Evolution builds a decent variety of people. For stream order, we advance Random woods through refreshing the heaviness of each test in the wake of building each tree iteratively and settling on the ultimate choice by utilizing the weighted democratic instrument. It catches organized parcels promotion gathers status data with brought together control. The controllers' parcels arrange bundles into streams and convey them to the upper layer. Thus, stream-based shrewd interruption discovery can be actualized utilizing AI calculations in two phases. It chooses ideal stream includes and identifies arrangement oddities by ordering each stream into fixed categories. A short time later, the controllers oversee the asset game plan and sorts out explicit activities for shielding assaults as per the order results. They consolidate two counterfeit savvy calculations in the two primary phases of interruption identification. The area and speed of each bat in space speak through paired strings. The change of estimate will guarantee the calculation with better investigation capacity at the beginning phase and higher misuse at a later stage. The division of the multitude empowers productive learning among comparative people in the region inside every subgroup in the mean time-sharing ideal data among the subgroups through the nearby minima.

The arrangement [32] separates into two sections. A gadget gathers end hubs traffic and sends it to the cloud analyzer. In this arrangement, the proposal utilizes Raspberry Pi 3 as the principle gadget for all the users. The device goes about as an interface between the application layer in the high level and the end hubs layer. Since sensors have low computational force, this administration is an increasingly appropriate way to deal with secures the end hubs in IoT arrange by watch and screen irregular practices. The subsequent part is a cloud-put together interruption locator based on RFs and NN. It gets IoT traffic from the previously mentioned gadget, performs highlights extraction, and grouping on the extricated highlights. Arbitrary Forest identifies if the information point is named interruption or not. The NN classifies the distinguished obstruction. The arrangement partitions into three modules containing data assortment module, data handling and detection module, and alarming. The proposed traffic catch calculation depends on traffic catch time and the size of the pcap record. Tshark setup permits catch external highlights of the system traffic alongside profound examination. Since the proposed model handles just numerical highlights, pcap records are prepared by BroIDS and different contents to mine the highlights, Bro-IDS is an open-source traffic analyzer, considered as a security screen and malignant exercises auditor. MySQL innovation stores the separated highlights.

The work [33] is a quick AI equipment quickening agent for IoT NIDS. A computational-effective single shrouded layer feed forward neural system model employs the least-squares solver, which is practical to help online continuous learning for IoT NIDS. Succeeding learning is the procedure to change the prepared model to limit the precision misfortune with new approaching data accordingly, a versatile and defined equipment acknowledgment is created on FPGA with 128-PE in equal working at 50-MHz devouring 0.85W influence. Exploratory outcomes have demonstrated that the proposed AI quickening agent has accomplished a decent location exactness and a data transfer capacity of 409.6 Gbps with a normal accelerate of 4.5× and 77.4× when contrasted with general CPU and installed CPU put together learning process concerning benchmark ISCX-2012. Around 113.83× and 57.75× vitality sparing are individuals watched.

The commitment is a quick and compelling two-layer irregularity based interruption identification, and avoidance component [34]. It distinguishes and forestalls broad scope of information uprightness and execution debasement assaults in the IoT frameworks. The clench hand layer of the IDPM depends on learning typical conduct of the structure utilizing RNN taking different datasets, covering both legitimate and invalid cases, as info boundaries. The prepared RNN model is then installed in the base station of the IoT framework to identify any odd conduct and forestall its proliferation. The second layer distinguishes an extended scope of IMA bugs and information honesty assaults progressively. It includes out of-bound peruse and compose gets to, stack-floods, stack-sub-currents, load floods, pile undercurrents, floods, and sub-currents in comprehensively characterized factors and direct-ordered floods/sub-currents. The proposed arrangement likewise goes about as a well-being checking framework for the IoT sensor hubs by breaking down information transmitted to the base station. As if there should arise in occurrence of any breakdown, the substantial sensor hub may either stop its activity as well as sent invalid information to the base station. The RNN model prepares to recognize such cases as an interruption and report them to the primary server. The proposed arrangement viability and execution overhead rare estimated for a current IoT framework comprising of sensor hubs transmitting information to a base station. Through the trial arrangement, it demonstrates that without legitimate security, it is conceivable to encroach into the application running on the base station. Besides, it shows that the base station effectively identified the nearness of the noxious sensor hub when the given IoT gadget empowers with the proposed IDPM.

11.3 Proposed Work

The proposal is suggested to analyze rate of the different kinds of attacks and attributes missing at various instances. The probability rates are set. Based on the margins, the different numbers of sets are created. In the work, five datasets containing different kinds of missing attributes and five datasets containing the probabilities of these attributes missing are created.

Algorithm

- The samples are collected at different instances of time to analyze the times at which the malicious activity is high or low.
- Similar to [10] two different sets are created. The first one is a dataset containing all the dumped data. The second set contains missing attributes.
- The second set two subsets. The first subset is attribute-transformation matrix. This subset is created providing the importance for certain important attributes needed during communication. The second subset is rate-transformation matrix. This subset is created to analyze how the probability rate at any instance of time.
- The margin probability rate is calculated [10].

11.4 Analysis of the Work

The work is scrutinized to understand different kinds of attributes the adversaries are looking for. The rate at which the adversaries are looking for these attributes at a particular instance is examined. The work is simulated using NS2. Table 11.1 provides the usage of different parameters in the work. Figure 11.1 denotes the analysis made w.r.t. attribute-transformation clusters. Figure 11.2 represents analysis made w.r.t. rate-transformation clusters

Table 11.1 Parameters used in simulation.

Parameters used	Description
Dimension of the network considered	200 m * 200 m
Number of IoT devices used	3
Number of samples used	100
Number of attribute-transformation datasets	4
Number of rate-transformation datasets	4
Number of adversaries used	2
Classifier used	Naïve Bayes
Simulation time	60 ms

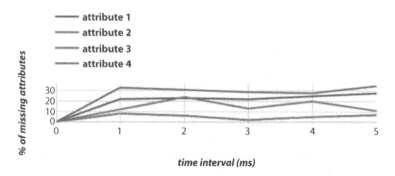

Figure 11.1 Analysis w.r.t. attribute-transformation clusters.

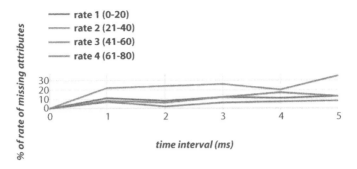

Figure 11.2 Analysis w.r.t. rate-transformation clusters.

11.5 Conclusion

IoTs are widely used in many applications to minimize human efforts. These devices belong to various categories having different competences. These devices are provided a common platform, using which they can communicate with each other and exchange huge amount of information. These devices use internet and hence can be placed wide apart. These unsupervised devices require some degree of security as they transmit confidential information. Ransomware is a threat which the work is addressing. It may assume whole responsibility for information or a framework and permit constrained access for client connection with the gadgets, request a robust total as a payment, and discharge information to the client simply after effective installment. Hence, to prevent the adversaries taking control over the data or the devices, the threats have to be detected at an early stage. One of the measures that can be adopted is analysis the communicating data. The proposal analyses the data for its missing parts. The work is further analyzed w.r.t. attributes and amount of missing parts. The outcome helps to adopt an economical solution toward securing the data and the devices against the adversaries.

References

1. Al-Sarawi, S., Anbar, M., Alieyan, K., Alzubaidi, M., Internet of Things (IoT) communication protocols, in: *8th International conference on information technology (ICIT)*, Amman, Jordan, pp. 685–690, 2017.
2. Al-Ali, A.R., Zualkernan, I.A., Rashid, M., Gupta, R., Alikarar, M., A smart home energy management system using IoT and big data analytics approach. *IEEE Trans. Consum. Electron.*, 63, 4, 426–434, 2017.

3. Ambika, N., Methodical IoT-Based Information System in Healthcare, in: *Smart Medical Data Sensing and IoT Systems Design in Healthcare*, C. Chakraborthy (Ed.), pp. 155–177, IGI Global, Bangalore, India, 2020, ch. 7.

4. Balandina, E., Balandin, S., Koucheryavy, Y., Mouromtsev, D., IoT use cases in healthcare and tourism, in: *IEEE 17th Conference on Business Informatics*, Lisbon, Portugal, vol. 2, pp. 37–44, 2015.

5. Baranwal, T. and Pateriya, P.K., Development of IoT based smart security and monitoring devices for agriculture, in: *6th International Conference-Cloud System and Big Data Engineering (Confluence)*, Noida, India, pp. 597–602, 2016.

6. Cambra, C., Sendra, S., Lloret, J., Garcia, L., An IoT service-oriented system for agriculture monitoring, in: *IEEE International Conference on Communications (ICC)*, Paris, France, pp. 1–6, 2017.

7. Ambika, N., Energy-Perceptive Authentication in Virtual Private Networks Using GPS Data, in: *Security, Privacy and Trust in the IoT Environment*, pp. 25–38, Springer, Cham, Switzerland, 2019.

8. Yaqoob, I. *et al.*, The rise of ransomware and emerging security challenges in the Internet of Things. *Comput. Networks*, 129, 444–458, 2017.

9. Bajpai, P., Enbody, R., Cheng, B.H., Ransomware targeting automobiles, in: *Second ACM Workshop on Automotive and Aerial Vehicle Security*, New Orleans LA, USA, pp. 23–29, 2020.

10. Vangipuram, R., Gunupudi, R.K., Puligadda, V.K., Vinjamuri, J., A machine learning approach for imputation and anomaly detection in IoT environment. *Expert Syst.*, 37, 5, 1–16, 2020.

11. Azmoodeh, A., Dehghantanha, A., Conti, M., Choo, K.K.R., Detecting crypto-ransomware in IoT networks based on energy consumption footprint. *J. Ambient Intell. Hum. Comput.*, 9, 4, 1141–1152, 2018.

12. Cabaj, K., Gregorczyk, M., Mazurczyk, W., Software-defined networking-based crypto ransomware detection using HTTP traffic characteristics. *Comput. Electr. Eng.*, 66, 353–368, 2018.

13. Wang, Z. *et al.*, Automatically traceback RDP-based targeted ransomware attacks. *Wireless Commun. Mobile Comput.*, 1–14, 2018.

14. Baykara, M. and Sekin, B., A novel approach to ransomware: Designing a safe zone system, in: *6th International Symposium on Digital Forensic and Security (ISDFS)*, Antalya, Turkey, 2018, pp. 1–5, 2018.

15. Hodo, E. *et al.*, Threat analysis of IoT networks using artificial neural network intrusion detection system, in: *International Symposium on Networks, Computers and Communications (ISNCC)*, Yasmine Hammamet, Tunisia, pp. 1–6, 2016.

16. Homayoun, S. *et al.*, DRTHIS: Deep ransomware threat hunting and intelligence system at the fog layer. *Future Gener. Comput. Syst.*, 90, 94–104, January 2019.

17. Dovom, E.M. *et al.*, Fuzzy pattern tree for edge malware detection and categorization in IoT. *J. Syst. Archit.*, 97, 1–7, 2019.

18. Cheng, S.M., Chen, P.Y., Lin, C.C., Hsiao, H.C., Traffic-aware patching for cyber security in mobile IoT. *IEEE Commun. Mag.*, 55, 7, 29–35, July 2017.

19. Nieuwenhuizen, D., A behavioural-based approach to ransomware detection, in: *MWR Labs Whitepaper*, pp. 1–20, April 2017.

20. Shukla, M., Mondal, S., Lodha, S., Poster: Locally virtualized environment for mitigating ransomware threat, in: *ACM SIGSAC Conference on Computer and Communications Security*, Vienna Austria, pp. 1784–1786, 2016.

21. Alhawi, O.M.K., Baldwin, J., Dehghantanha, A., Leveraging Machine Learning Techniques for Windows Ransomware Network Traffic detection, in: *Cyber threat Intelligence*, pp. 93–106, Springer, Cham, Switzerland AG, 2018.

22. Zahra, A. and Shah, M.A., IoT based ransomware growth rate evaluation and detection using command and control blacklisting, in: *23rd International Conference on Automation and Computing (ICAC)*, Huddersfield, UK, pp. 1–6, 2017.

23. Pastrana, S., Rodriguez-Canseco, J., Calleja, A., *ArduWorm: A functional malware targeting Arduino devices*, pp. 1–8, COSEC Computer Security Lab, Stanford University, California, January 2016.

24. Lee, Y., Woo, S., Song, Y., Lee, J., Lee, D.H., Practical Vulnerability-Information-Sharing Architecture for Automotive Security-Risk Analysis. *IEEE Access*, 8, 120009–120018, June 2020.

25. Nobakht, M., Sivaraman, V., Boreli, R., A host-based intrusion detection and mitigation framework for smart home IoT using OpenFlow, in: *11th International conference on availability, reliability and security (ARES)*, Salzburg, Austria, pp. 147–156, 2016.

26. Pajouh, H.H., Javidan, R., Khayami, R., Ali, D., Choo, K.K.R., A two-layer dimension reduction and two-tier classification model for anomaly-based intrusion detection in IoT backbone networks. *IEEE Trans. Emerg. Topics Comput.*, 7, 2, 314–323, November 2016.

27. Alrashdi, I. *et al.*, Ad-iot: Anomaly detection of iot cyberattacks in smart city using machine learning, in: *9th Annual Computing and Communication Workshop and Conference (CCWC)*, Las Vegas, NV, USA, pp. 0305–0310, 2019.

28. Yang, K., Ren, J., Zhu, Y., Zhang, W., Active learning for wireless IoT intrusion detection. *IEEE Wireless Commun.*, 25, 6, 19–25, December 2018.

29. Lopez-Martin, M., Carro, B., Sanchez-Esguevillas, A., Lloret, J., Conditional variational autoencoder for prediction and feature recovery applied to intrusion detection in iot. *Sensors*, 17, 9, 1–17, August 2017.

30. Roux, J., Alata, E., Auriol, G., Nicomette, V., Kaâniche, M., Toward an intrusion detection approach for IoT based on radio communications profiling, in: *13th European Dependable Computing Conference (EDCC)*, Geneva, Switzerland, pp. 147–150, 2017.

31. Li, J., Zhao, Z., Li, R., Zhang, H., Ai-based two-stage intrusion detection for software defined iot networks. *IEEE Internet Things J.*, 6, 2, 2093–2102, November 2018.

32. Mohamed, T., Otsuka, T., Ito, T., Towards machine learning based IoT intrusion detection service, in: *International Conference on Industrial, Engineering and Other Applications of Applied Intelligent Systems*, Montreal, QC, Canada, pp. 580–585, 2018.

33. Huang, H., Khalid, R.S., Liu, W., Yu, H., Work-in-progress: a fast online sequential learning accelerator for iot network intrusion detection, in: *International Conference on Hardware/Software Codesign and System Synthesis (CODES+ ISSS)*, Seoul, South Korea, pp. 1–2, 2017.

34. Saeed, A., Ahmadinia, A., Javed, A., Larijani, H., Intelligent intrusion detection in low-power IoTs. *ACM Trans. Internet Technol. (TOIT)*, 16, 4, 1–25, December 2016.

12

Indian Science of Yajna and Mantra to Cure Different Diseases: An Analysis Amidst Pandemic With a Simulated Approach

Rohit Rastogi[1*], Mamta Saxena[2], Devendra Kumar Chaturvedi[3], Mayank Gupta[4], Puru Jain[1], Rishabh Jain[1], Mohit Jain[1], Vishal Sharma[1], Utkarsh Sangam[1], Parul Singhal[1] and Priyanshi Garg[1]

[1]ABES Engineering College, Ghaziabad, India
[2]Min. of Statistics, P&I, GoI, Delhi, India
[3]Dayalbagh Educational Institute, Agra, India
[4]Tata Consultancy Services, Kobe, Japan

Abstract

There has been a great interest of researchers in Vedic knowledge using the symbol of OM, and this word Om is considered to be the beginning and end of the past and future. Mr. Slogan's motive is a subtle understanding of the human body, mind, and the world of reality. Emotions, Thoughts and Beliefs in our lives are important characteristics. In accordance with the Indian philosophy, OM which is a spiritual symbol is also called Atman Brahman (reality, God, supreme soul, truth, cosmic principles, world, and knowledge). The research is a symbol of Global OM. The main aim of this research was to calculate the effects of Gayatri Mantra and Ohm readings on human health. The Gayatri Mantra is a very potential mantra mentioned in Rigveda. This research was performed on some patients (male = 4) and (female = 7) in the age range 44 to 70 years. All the patients were trained to read the Gayatri Mantra for 3 days. We used basic data. Participants at the Mantra Gayatri Meeting and Om Conference attended for approximately 15 minutes on two consecutive days. The order of meetings was randomly assigned to participants. This previous study showed that both Gayatri's mantra and comfort are of interest, as measured by Stormwork. However, Mantra Gayatri's work was much more numerous than Om's

Corresponding author: rohit.rastogi@abes.ac.in

A. Suresh, S. Vimal, Y. Harold Robinson, Dhinesh Kumar Ramaswami and R. Udendhran (eds.) *Bioinformatics and Medical Applications: Big Data Using Deep Learning Algorithms*, (235–268)
© 2022 Scrivener Publishing LLC

reading. The manuscript also provides an analysis of the well-being index before and after the Yaina process and radiation analysis of various devices.

Keywords: Diabetes mellitus, insulin and non-insulin–dependent diabetes, gestational diabetes, tension type headache (TTH), obesity, machine vision, Rudrakash, Homa therapy, aroma therapy, GSR, radiation, Yajna science and Mantra science, happiness index, artificial intelligence and machine learning in healthcare, Internet of Things and big data in healthcare, Yagyopathy, OM chanting, medical images and analysis, Gayatri mantra (GM), ECG, EEG

12.1 Introduction

12.1.1 Different Types of Diseases

12.1.1.1 Diabetes (Madhumeha) and Its Types

Madhumeha (sweet urine disease, diabetes) is a disease that has plagued humans for centuries, especially in developed countries. In this disease, Indian doctor Charaka observed honey polyuria and urine as early as 400 BC. He described the disease as "Madhumeha". This means honey in the urine. Madhumeha was declared an ancient Ayurvedic scholar, KastaSadi (unwieldy), and even Asadija (unbearable) [7]. They have explained that all types of prameha (diabetes), if left or partially treated, convert into Kashtasadhya Madhumeha [difficult to treat diabetes, that is type 2 diabetes mellitus (T2DM)], and later on, if not treated properly, a period comes when it converts to Asadhya Madhumeha (incurable diabetes), i.e., type 1 diabetes mellitus (T1DM). It is still a challenge for every system of medicine to treat this disease. It seems to be the largest "silent killer" in the world today. T1DM is nearer to Dhatukshyajanya Madhumeha, while T2DM resembles Avarana Janya Madhumeha [9, 10].

Major types of diabetes:

- Insulin-Dependent Diabetes (T1D): In T1D, the immune system destroys and attacks insulin-producing pancreatic cells.
- Non-Insulin–Dependent Diabetes (T2D): In T2D, the body becomes insulin resistant and blood sugar levels rise.
- Prediabetes: Sugar levels in blood are higher than normal in prediabetes.

Gestational Diabetes:
This type of diabetes increases blood sugar levels during pregnancy [1, 4, 12].

12.1.1.2   TTH and Stress

The main reasons for types of headaches are smoking, colds, fatigue, alcohol, eye strain and dry eye, sinus infection, caffeine, poor physical condition, and mental stress [24–26, 29].

12.1.1.3   Anxiety

Anxiety is the body's natural effect to TTH. This is the fear of the future. On the first day of school, most people may feel anxious during a job interview or lecture. However, if you have a very severe anxiety that lasts more than 6 months and interferes with your life, you may have an anxiety disorder [21, 23, 27].

Common anxiety symptoms are as follows:

- Heart rate has increased
- Breathe fast and continuously
- Restless
- No focus
- Hard to sleep [6].

12.1.1.4   Hypertension

High blood pressure is commonly known as hypertension. Blood pressure is the force that presses blood into vessels of blood. It turns out that almost half of the adults in the US have problems of high blood pressure and many do not know it. Blood pressure management is really very important. Prevention of high blood pressure is very important. First of all, since this is the first step, everyone needs to change their lifestyle. You need to do it with this regular exercise. People use certain drugs to treat high blood pressure. Doctors also recommend to use low or optimal doses of the medications as they can result in side effects also. By following heart-healthy diet, hypertension can be cured [5, 28, 31, 32].

12.1.2   Machine Vision

Machine vision (MV) is a technology and technique commonly used in the industry for automated inspection and image-based automated analysis of applications such as automated inspection and robot guidance [2, 39].

12.1.2.1 Medical Images and Analysis

Medical image analysis is the science that solves and analyzes medical problems based on various imaging and digital imaging techniques [13].

- Analysis method
- Various image methods
- Geometry
- X-ray: 2D and 3D
- MR images: 2D, 3D, 4D, etc.
- Tomography procedure
- Microscopic image
- Standard (coloring required)
- HMC (Huffman Modular Contrast)
- SPECT (radioactive isotope)
- Ultrasound
- Different composite images (heart bull's eye)

The Vital Role of medical images in treatment and diagnosis are now known to all and many important applications have been designed on it. Medical images play a very important role in care of patient. It is useful for early detection, disease prevention, treatment, and diagnosis. It is essential for almost all the major medical conditions and illnesses [33–35, 39].

12.1.2.2 Machine Learning in Healthcare

Machine learning (ML) has recently become popular in medicine. In order to help to detect cancerous tumors in mammograms, Google has developed a very efficient ML algorithm. To detect skin cancer, Stanford University also uses and intensively written ML algorithm. According to JAMA paper reports, the output of a ML algorithm detects the diabetic retinopathy in retinal images. In the need of clinical decision, ML is clearly another very most important factor.

However, ML is good for processes that perform better than other processes. The algorithm can provide utilities for repeatable or standard processes. Radiology is also suitable for large datasets of image such as pathology and cardiology. ML can improve all of these processes by iden-tifying anomalies, displaying images and training to indicate interested areas. In the long run, ML reaches your bedside physician or trainee. ML provides objective insight and can improve efficiency, reliability, and accuracy.

12.1.2.3   *Artificial Intelligence in Healthcare*

Artificial intelligence (AI) aims to mimic the cognitive functioning of humans. This provides a fast access to healthcare data and analytics technology, shifting the paradigm shift to healthcare. The current status of AI applications in healthcare helps us to aim for a better future. AI can be applied to many types of medical data (unstructured and structured). Common AI technologies include ML techniques for the structured data such as traditional support vector machines and the neural networks, modern deep learning, and natural language processing of unstructured data. The main areas of disease that use AI tools are cancer, neurology, and heart disease. Next, we will take a closer look at the three major areas of stroke, diagnosis and early diagnosis, treatment, and AI applications for prognosis and outcome prediction. Finally, we discuss pioneering AI systems such as actual deployment barriers for AI and IBM Watson [36].

12.1.3   Big Data and Internet of Things (IoT)

Big data is an evolving term for huge amounts semi-structured, structured, and unstructured data that can extract information and is used in ML projects and other very advanced analytic applications. It also includes different types of data, such as structured data in data warehouses and SQL databases, unstructured or unstructured SQL, and the semi-structured data such as the stream files and web servers. Moreover, big data contains many concurrent data sources, which are not otherwise integrated.

Internet of Things is a system of machines, counting devices, digital machines, animals, objects, or individuals that are connected through a network without human or human-to-human interaction and is a unique identifier [37, 40].

12.1.4   Machine Learning in Association with Data Science and Analytics

ML is a method of analysis of data that helps to automate the process of construction of analytical models. It is a branch of AI based on the idea that the system can perform its learning from data, identification of patterns, and decision-making with the minimal human intervention. Many algorithms of ML have been around for a long time, but the ability to automate sophisticated calculations of math on big data (automatic and fast) is a recent development. Here are some extensive examples of ML applications.

- Extreme and exciting Google car? The essence of ML.
- Are there any online tips like Amazon or Netflix? ML programs for everyday life.
- Do you know what Twitter customers say about you? A combination of ML and language method development.
- Would you like to detect fraud? One of the most important applications in the world today [38, 40–42].

12.1.5 Yajna Science

Yagya Vigyan is working on the head of Yagya. The Yajna is originally played by the amazing sage-munis in the cave. At that time, not only saints, citizens, and some men, rich and poor, but all played Yoga. All of them had respect and belief in Yajna. He spent at least a third of his life playing with Gaia. At that time, people believed that a yagna was necessary to refine Brian's human life from the instinct of animals [11, 56] (as per Figure 12.1).

12.1.6 Mantra Science

When the Yajna is complete, look at it, touch the material with your hands, and sing the mantra. We sing, praise, pray, and uplift God with the mantra motto. The use of Yajna is described in the mantra text. So, the application is a reminder and a reminder. She has also been remembered for her mantra several times for the motto. People know about God and do not become atheists. All good deeds must begin with prayer to God. That is why the mantra motto is essential [43–46, 56].

- Increase Vitality In the Air and All forms of life
- Increase Anti-oxidants
- Cleaning of Environment
- Purifies water
- Aroma therapy
- Reduction in Radiation
- Purifies Blood
- Helps in Diabetes, High blood pressure
- Relieves stress
- Removes Negative emotions like anger, jealousy, hatred etc.
- Biological - Removal of Pathogens
- Increases –ve ions
- Parjanya Varsha - Soil nourishment
- Subtle effect – removes animal instincts and awakens Divinity
- Yagyopathy– Inhale smoke of medicinal herbs to cure different diseases, especially mental diseases

- Make Pitrues happy

Figure 12.1 Benefits of Yagya or Yagyopathy [56].

12.1.6.1   Positive Impact of Recital of Gayatri Mantra and OM Chanting

It is said that the entire mantra spiral through the cosmos is the deepest part of the center of liturgy-demanding peace and goodwill. Gayatri Mantra invites and inspires us. Simply put, the mantra says, "Let God's light shine on our hearts and lead us to the path of the right person". The Vedas cleanse the Chanter for the Gayatri Mantra motto. It purifies the listener to hear Gayatri's mantra. But this beautiful mantra is more than just refining. It opens your mind and broadens your horizons. Gayatri Mantra helps open up new opportunities. Most Hindus regard Gayatri as the awakening of the God of heart and soul, the awakening of fire. There is an association of collective consciousness—a place to accept Brahman. Gayatri's simple mantra power is close to touching God. One common interpretation of Gayatri Mantra is "Gaia" means important energy, "essence or triple"—meaning preservation, protection, and release [46–49].

12.1.6.2   Significance of Mantra on Indian Culture and Mythology

The logic behind the mantra and ritual is the support of all true seekers who believe in their effectiveness, power, and glory. He can be any caste, creed, climate, or sect. All that really matters is the faith and purity of his heart. Gayatri Mantra, also known as Savitri Mantra, is a highly respected mantra of Rig Veda dedicated to the sun god Savitr. Gayatri is the name of the Vedic meter in which the poem is composed [49–51].

Vishwa Mitra Mantra is said to have founded or written Gayatri. Mantra Gayatri is an unimaginable spiritual armor, a true fortress that protects and protects voting, turns him into God, and blesses him with the best spiritual light and spiritual awakening. Hindu young male rituals have long been read by dvija men as part of their daily rituals. Gayatri, Gita, Ganga, and Cattle are the four pillars of Indian culture. Of these, Gayatri is the best. All the sacred books, denominations, elders, etc., declare that Gayatri has a very important message for humanity all over the world. In Atawala Weda, Gayatri Meditation blesses his devoted life with a healthy long life, strong vitality (prana), sacred energy, fame, wealth, and God's satisfaction It is said [52–54].

12.1.7   Usefulness and Positive Aspect of Yoga Asanas and Pranayama

In Hinduism, Sanskrit yoga means "yoking" or "combining" means or techniques that change the consciousness and achievement (moksha) of karma and reproduction (Samsara). It is an action "in the sense that the spiritual seeker aims to (1) regulate nature and make the soul conducive to an eternal soul (true self or Atman Brahm or "God") connection, (2) God. This is the rebirth of the soul and liberation from death. Yoga is widely known as a program of physical exercise (asana) and breathing exercises (pranayama) [3].

Yoga health benefits:

- Improve posture
- Increased flexibility
- Strengthen muscle strength
- Promote metabolism, etc. [55]

12.1.8 Effects of Yajna and Mantra on Human Health

In all aspects, including positive impacts at the physical, mental, and spiritual levels, Yagya is very helpful in carrying out yogi's actions. Yoga is part of your practice, and you can do it now by eliminating your negative karma and strengthening your positive future karma. Yagya will help neutralize problems in your life and increase your chances. This will help you succeed in secular and spiritual problems (Brahmavarchas, 1994). While some Yajna can improve your life to ultimate salvation, while others are done to attract secular and desires. Yagya is very helpful in getting rid of the obstacles in your life. If you want to run Yagya or Pooja to avoid and eliminate life obstacles, choose Yagya to avoid life problems. There are challenges and problems for everyone. This Yagya is considered the best Hindu yajna skyline to protect against all obstacles. The Vedas contain mantras, and these mantras have no illusions and contain only truth because God fully recognizes them. However, sentences edited by ordinary humans are not completely true and may not be fantastic. Of course, sentences from Apa (a person who has complete knowledge of the subject, is neutral and will benefit society) can be trusted. But such people rely only on ordinary text, not [56, 15].

12.1.9 Impact of Yajna in Reducing the Atmospheric Solution

There are two ways to get purified air and good rain respectively.

- God's creation
- Human creation [59]

When God creates the sun, the flowers and plants smell good and the water evaporates from the sea. The two mix well to form a cloud. In the

Table 12.1 Yagya decreases air pollution [60].

Time of sample	Sulfur dioxide (SO$_2$) content	Nitrogen oxide (NO) content	Bacterial count
Before Yagya	3.36	1.16	4,500
During Yagya	2.82	1.1.4	2,470
After Yagya	0.8	1.02	1,250

second method, humans create yaga and clouds are formed. According to Dayananda Saroswati, the atmosphere is combined with good atoms, bad atoms, and molecules. So, the rain we get and the plants, fruits, and vegetables are also combined with good and bad atoms. For this reason, this food, as well as the energy and body formed, have mediocre properties. Because of this existence, power, courage, courage, etc., are essentially mediocre. The reason is that "causative substance properties are always the result".

Pollution in the atmosphere is not the fault of God, but humans are harming it. Humans create all kinds of soil in nature and pollute the atmosphere. We bring milk for milk and transport (as per Table 12.1) [13, 60, 61].

12.1.10   Scientific Study on Impact of Yajna on Air Purification

The various changes in chemical take place in order to have an idea. It is very important to know about the various objects presented in Yagya. As explained below: Wood: Depending on the size of the altar or "Acnicunda" called "Samida", the wood is cut into pieces. There are several types of agar, sandal wood, tagger, deoda, mango, duck, parachute, Bilba, Paypal, etc. In addition to wood, different types of havivia or havan clams are provided in yaga and divided into four groups.

- Aroma substances: saffron, musk, agar, tagger, cast iron, coconut, difarboytri, and camp brain.
- Substances containing healthy ingredients: These are grains such as butter, milk, fruit, wheat, rice, barley, crown, cango, mung beans, chana, alhal, masseur, or peas.
- Sweet ingredients: These are usually sugar, dried grapes, honey, or coffler.
- Herbs: These herbs are used for special needs: Rixos Murata or Guilloy, shank pushpins, Nagsal, Baheda, Mulhati, Chandan Red, Hard, etc. [60].

12.1.11 Scientific Meaning of Religious and Manglik Signs

- The average energy of the mosque is 12,000 bovis. The energy level of Tibetan temples is 14,000 bovis. The Buddha's stupa has around 12,000 Bovis energy measured. The cycle rotated during the worship of Tibetans produces around 12,000 to 14,000 Bovis energy.
- Manglik signs used in the house are not only for decoration, but behind them, the blessings of sages and sages are flowing in the Ganges of Indian knowledge. Who, after hard work in ancient times, have made today's human beings easily accessible without any greed. Regards to those scholars and take advantage of their research done for your good. Actual energy of Ghritavghranjal is 50,000,000 Bovis or 5 million units!!!! [57].

12.2 Literature Survey

According to Narottm Kumar, the scientific study also found that mantra yoga and religious slogans have a positive effect on the vibration of the body's physiological and psychological functions. He revealed the gayatri mantra chanting resulted in significant improvement on performance or attention in school children, the whole population was divided into two groups: one is an experimental group and the second is the control group.

The author has proposed the following methodology in which the subject consisted of 60 high school students, including 30 boys and 30 girls, ranged in age from 12 to 14 years, during which they taught five days of Gayatri Mantra. According to him, they were evaluated in the same time liturgy (10 minutes) and poetry line (10 minutes) immediately before and after the two DLST sessions. Fifty percent of the participants read GM on the sixth day and the rest recited PL. Gayatri Mantra chanting invokes the capacity to influence thinking compared to random thinking. Previous studies reported that practice of Om chanting is effective in improving pulmonary function and vital capacity in healthy individual; 82 subjects were participated in this study divided into two study group (SG) consisting 41 participants and control group (CG) consisting 41 participants; SG practiced Om chanting per day for the period of 6 days for two weeks and CG did not asked to practice.

He found the result that there is significant improvement in peak expiratory flow, forced expiratory flow, and significant improvement in slow vital capacity. A period of mental chanting "OM" shows that there is significant reduction in heart rate and a subtle change in mental state indicated by a decrease in skin resistance. The author investigated changes in autonomy in respiratory variables of prayer, autonomy, and experienced mediators (5 to 20 years of experience). Each subject was examined in two types of session meditation. This is a trial session using controls in the OM mental slogan and non-target thinking courses. Meditation showed a significant decrease in heart rate. Different types of Japanese prayer and Buddhist scriptures showed different brain activations. The reading of Nembutsu prayer activates the frontal cortex and the reading of Trans-Buddhism activates the right frontal cortex and the right partial cortex. Control study of the Vedic hymns chanting showed that there is an improvement in memory and sustained attention in teen ager school students. Sixty students participated in this study in the age group of 13 to 15 years, the whole population divided into two chanting experience groups and non-chanting experience group. The sustained attention assessed by SLCT and memory was assessed by using delayed recall tests. Effect of Hare-Krishna Mahamantra on mental health indicators of participants have been checked and it is found to be quiet effective. Five subjects were assessed during 1-week baseline and 4-week intervention chanting phase. He also revealed that there is a significant reduction in stress, depression, and verbal aggressiveness [16].

The paper is written by Devashish Bhardwaj, Veenit K. Agnihotri, and Pranav Pandya titled as clinical evaluation of an Ayurvedic Formulation in the management of Avaranajanya Madhumeha (T2DM) [17].

According to him, in this study, a research plan was developed to solve the problems associated with Avaranajanya Madhumeha (T2D). This research project is based on Ayurvedic therapy (ancient Indian medicine) and use of the research tools as modern scientific methods.

They used the following methodology in which special preparations for medicinal and mineral herbs are prepared in the form of gansat (solid extract). Rejuvenation effect (RASAYANA) of eight selected plants and one mineral and antihypertensive agent (PRAMEHA HARA) and antihypertensive agent (MEDOHARA) as described in the classic aerodynamic method. Fifteen patients diagnosed with T2D were selected by random sampling. He has prescribed Ayurvedic formulation for 1 year with restrictions on diet. The parameters of diagnosis of these patients were monitored every 3 months, including fasting blood glucose (FBS), postpartum blood glucose (PPBS), glycated hemoglobin (HbA1C), and fasting urine sugar, before and after measurement of intervention.

12.3 Methodology

- Participants: 11 Diabeteic patients in the age group of 38 to 70 years were recruited from Chetna Kendra in Noida. The study was approved by the ethics committee of Chetna Kendra. All participants are classified according to gender, age, and weight variables. They signed a consent form before studying.
- Study design: This study was a self-test (control) that included two sessions: a test session (Mantra Gayatri) and a control session (Om recitation). All participants were trained in GM reading and Om reading for 3 days prior to the start of the study. Two sets of measurements were taken on consecutive days. They were asked to close their eyes and sit comfortably on the first floor. All participants were asked to recite Mantra Gayatri for the first 15 minutes of the day, and the same participant was invited to practice the second day.
- Interventions: During the Mantra Gayatri test session, I was asked to recite Mantra Gayatri for about 15 minutes. During the Gayatri Mantra, eyes were closed and the slogan was read out in a traditional way. Om bhurbhuvahsvah tat Saviturvarenyambhargodevasyadhimahidhiyoyo nah prachodayat. During the Om Mantra control session, the same person was asked to read On for about 15 minutes (Om ... Om ... Om).
- Controlling the collision process requires attention to the brain. The reaction time reflects the attention of the brain. The Stroop effect is used to represent mental and attention processes. This strict task gives a score for colored words. Stroop test scores and responses were recorded in the computer of each participant. Some patients were improved in all sections.

Read the Surabaya Tri Mantra 24 times, 30 minutes of prime Nadi I witness. Mix the hawan clam quass twice a day. A lung function test (LFT) was performed on December 18 to measure the effects of vascular disorders, and the use of vascular disorders was started according to the above instructions (once daily) from the 24th day of 18 years of age. Approximately, two and a half months, the results obtained after receiving one daily treatment of daily vascular injury show significant improvement in lung function parameters was shown. It was twice a day.

They obtained the data using statistical analysis, and a paired t test was used. FBS, PPBS, HbA1C, and fasting blood glucose levels decreased significantly in patients with T2D who successfully completed the clinical trial. Therefore, they concluded that aerodynamic prescription leads to a significant reduction in blood sugar and urine. No adverse effects were observed during the study of glucose levels in patients with T2D. The author has suggested that its aerodynamic formulation had a very good hyperglycemic effect as evidenced by clinical improvement and chemical biological analysis of diabetes parameters in the treatment of T2D [17].

According to Ruchi Singh today, its usefulness is increasing year by year due to environmental degradation and the danger of widespread pollution. In fact, there are polluted emotions and motives that dominate all living creatures. She has got a result: illness, anxiety, and friction are everywhere. The only effective scientific solution to this problem has emerged in the form of Yagia. Yaguni produced by hybrid energy or vitality and raw materials may seem clearly a religious practice, but its power and effects are surprising, and this is based on extensive and successful experiments over the past 20 years, as proven by scientist [18].

The author has revealed about yoga. This is an ancient tradition that brings balance and harmony between body and mind. This effect can be seen through a study of yoga and all its benefits to the human body. In China, people have learned and loved yoga since the 1980s. According to recent reports, yoga is an optional course at some universities. In 2015, the first Indian Chinese Yoga College (ICYC) was established. Since then, yoga has focused not only on body and mind but also on exchanges between nations, understanding between people, culture mixing and coexistence. ICYC trains yoga teachers to teach yoga in China and leads the way in teaching yoga in China, providing a platform for cultural exchange between the two countries. They described the ICYC should continue for centuries as a bridge between our two countries in modern society. They concluded during the study and concluded the paper's efforts to portray yoga as a messenger and portray yoga as a link to physical health, spirit, culture, and cultural exchange [19]. The author has developed a lot of knowledge about world symbols.

This syllable is one of the most important symbols of world religion and is often found in Vedic, Upanishad, and other ancient texts. It is a sacred spiritual motto built between spiritual texts, prayers, rituals, weddings, meditations, and yoga readings.

The author published his current study; morphological studies were conducted to investigate levels of rhododendron (Elaeocarpus ganitrus). Microscopic studies have observed that Om symbols are present on the surface of different cells in the spine, indicating that Om is present on the cell surface. Suniljawala also explained that this study further strengthens the belief that there is a universal Om symbol [22].

The paper "Ethno-medicinal and Ayurvedic Approach in the Management and Treatment of Asthma (Swash Roga)" was written by Kaushal Kumar and Avnish K. Upadhyay. According to him, In Ayurveda, Asthma is known as "SwasRoga". According to Ayurveda's "Planbayu", the pathogenesis of Schwas Loga is related to the aging "Duke of Kappa" in the lungs causing obstruction of the "Srotas Butterfly" (respiratory system). They found the results in breathable and painstaking breathing known as "ChausaRoga". Asthma is a chronic disease involving the airways, which sometimes contracts, becomes inflamed, overloads with mucus, and often responds to one or more stimuli. These episodes are reduced by exposure to environmental stimuli (or allergens), cold, hot air, humid air, exercise or exercise or stress. Ayurvedic medicines are very safe and cure the problem to a great extent. Researchers of various disciplines are working on this problem to find out the solutions. Various modern means and measures havebeen discovered in this regard. Even then the effective drug without any side effects has not been established yet. Ayurveda is the rich source of the therapeutic measures that can control the disease. Out of such therapeutic measures, various herbs, poly-herbal and herbo-mineral compounds were selected in different studies for the benefit of the increasing number of asthma patients and have been found to be effective.

They have described the aims of the present review are to establish the importance of Ethno-medicinal and Ayurvedic approach in the management and treatment of Asthma and explore any new interventions needed [20].

The paper was written by Santa Mishra and Jyoti Satpathya titled as "Correlation of Age, Yoga and Circadian Rhythm on Attention".

She has described that the field of investigation was conducted concerning the impact of Yoga practice and Circadian Rhythmic impact on Span of Attention of the subjects. The proposed methodology used by her followed in which all the subjects were randomly selected from different Yoga practicing centers throughout Orissa. They are divided into two groups like Yoga practicing groups (n = 40) and Non-Yoga practicing groups (n = 40). All the subjects are tested individually four times in a day like morning, noon, and evening, for their span of attention test.

According to her analysis of results, biasing on their average span of attention score revealed that both the groups differed significantly with regard to their circadian Rhythmic impact. However, interaction impact is not found to be statistically significant which revealed the idea that the activity and arousal level may have certain other physiological aspects to be explored further.

On November 23, during a meeting in Shantikunj on Homeopathy, chaired by Dr. Pranav Pandya, Professor Rostov volunteered to voluntarily test its effects. He consulted with Dr. Vandana Srivava and was advised to seek treatment: Yagyopathy twice a day at times of sunrise and sunset with 3:1 Havan Samagali for normal semolina and asthma. Read the Surabaya Tri Mantra 24 times, 30 minutes of prime Nadi I witness. Mix the hawan clam quass twice a day. A lung function test (LFT) was performed on December 18 to measure the effects of vascular disorders, and the use of vascular disorders was started according to the above instructions (once daily) from the 24th day of 18 years of age. Three important parameters are measured during the LFT. Protective vital capacity (FVC): measurement of lung volume or air volume after deep breathing Forced 1 second volume (FEV1): Respiratory measurement. FEV1/FVC: Percentage of lungs that expire in seconds (FVC) approximately two and a half months, the results obtained after receiving one daily treatment of daily vascular injury show significant improvement in lung function parameters. It was twice a day.

12.4   Results and Discussion

I consulted Dr. Banana Srivava and was advised to seek treatment: The ratio of goat opathy, asthma to normal sagari twice a day at times of sunrise and sunset is 3:1 with 24 readings of the Surya Gayatri Mantra and 30 minutes of reading the NadiShabangPaliyam. Mix the Hawan Clam Kvass twice a day. To measure the effects of vascular disorders, I performed a lung function test (LFT) on 18 December and started vascular disorders on December 24 according to the instructions above (or once a day) (as per Table 12.2).

Compare the results. After continued treatment of vascular disorders and keratitis once a day, LFT was repeated on March 19 and comparison results were obtained.

Table 12.2 Comparison of results.

Parameter (unit)	Predicted/ reference value	% of Predicted value (normal)	Values obtained on 18 Dec 18	Values obtained on 05 Mar 19
FVC (liters)	3.5	≥80	85	94
FEV1 (liters)	2.86	≥80	73	80
FEV1/FVC (%)	78.4	≥70	70.9	89

12.5 Interpretations and Analysis

There was significant improvement in both Gm and Om session. But analysis showed that there was improvement in Gayatri mantra than the Om chanting session (Table 12.3 and Figure 12.2).

Some patients are taking high levels of diabetes medication. Got out of this place is an increase in its sugar level after the time of YAGYOPATHY treatment for 4 months. The accessible level has now been captured and has fallen below the normal limit. Now, doctor has authorized the medicine and names of all the parties. Sugar level without taking any medicine was drastically reduced.

HBA1c has come down from 9.29 to 7.6 in the period of 2 months. He has stopped B.P. medicine totally and B.P. level is within limit (Table 12.4).

The blood sugar graph shows FBST PRANDAL. Research is conducted among the different groups of age in society (both men and women) (Figure 12.3).

In this graph, Professor Rohit Rastogi, in addition, you can see FBST PRANDAL before and after your blood sugar level changes.

The graph shows weight change, fasting sugar, P.P. sugar, and HBA1C over a period of 4 months. A survey of Mr. JP Sharma is being conducted to calculate these quantities (as per Figure 12.4). Mr. Sharma has taken many medications for diabetes, despite fluctuations in his blood sugar levels. But after 4 months of treatment for menopause, his blood sugar level has been stabilized and is lower than normal.

This graph shows weight change, fasting sugar, P.P. sugar, and HBA1C w.r.t. different dates (in Figure 12.5 and Figure 12.6).

This data is given by Mr. S.K. for 32 years, Agarwal used diabetes medicines to the fullest. However, the Chinese were out of control.

Table 12.3 Yagyopathy experiment on diabetic patient.

Yagyaopathy experiments
Chetna Kender Noida evaluation done on May 11, 2019

S. no.	Name of patients	Gender/ weight	Fasting blood sugar		FBST Prandal blood sugar		Improvement in other symptoms
			B.T.	A.T.	B.T.	A.T.	
1	Mr. Anil Mishra	M/68 years	200	88	400–450	261	Improved in all sections
2	Smt. Geeta Mishra	F/56 years	300	183	400	272	Improvement in knee pain and body weight
3	Shri J.P. N upadhaya	M/60 years	180	117.5	220	259	Positive thoughts have increased
4	Mrs. Sahkumbals Gupta	M/53 years	RBS-160	112.3	RBS-160	102.3	Improvement in energy level
5	Mr. O.P. Yadav	M/44 years	RBS-136	128	RBS-136	210	Improvement in chronic constipation
6	Mrs. Parmila Saxe Smt. Ananda Devina	F/69 years	100	136	166	220	Improvement in blood sugar

(Continued)

Table 12.3 Yagyopathy experiment on diabetic patient.

S. no.	Name of patients	Gender/ weight	Fasting blood sugar		FBST Prandal blood sugar		Improvement in other symptoms
			B.T.	A.T.	B.T.	A.T.	
7	Smt. Renu Bala Singh	F/70 years	RBS-155	131	RBS-155	219	Improvement in body weight from 93 to 88.2 kg
8	Smt. Ananda Devi	M/65 years	RBS-	137.6	RBS-324	325.4	Improvement in blood sugar
9	Mr. D.D. Gupta	M/38 years	RBS-213	213.7	RBS-202	275.4	Positive thinking has increased
10	Smt. Neelam	F/60 years	RBS-324	106	RBS-354	125	Improvement in body weight 65 to 64 kg
11	Shri Kedarnath	M/68 years	RBS-135	107	RBS-135	127	160/85/130/75

Table 12.4 Final result.

S. no.	Name of patient	Problem	Progress
1	M.l. Gupta	Prostate, joint pain, cholesterol	75% relief
2	Prem Devipareek *	Joint pain, high B.P.	75% relief
3	Govind Narayn Pareek *	Prostate, B.P., joint pain	50% relief
4	Roshani Devi *	B.P., allergy, headache	90% relief
5	Prem Devichaudhry	B.P., depression	50% relief
6	L.R. Sharma	Asthma	50% relief

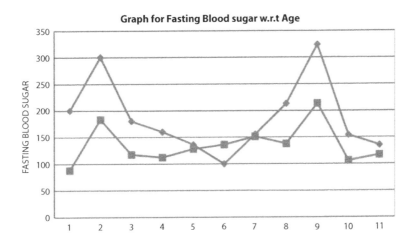

Figure 12.2 Graphical analysis for fasting blood sugar with the respect to the age.

Since the seventh day of treatment, their medication has decreased by 50%, which is well controlled. HbA1c decreases from 9.29 to 7.6 in 2 months.

Various electronic devices, such as cell phones, chargers, tablets, and laptops, emit different levels of radiation, some of which have been exposed for extended periods of time. The graph above shows the change in radiated emissions of electronic devices. You can see that the amount of radiation levels changes significantly after menopause. The above experiment involves the use of several technologies, the data of the above experiment

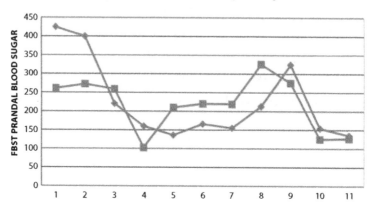

Figure 12.3 Graphical presentation for FBST PRANDAL blood sugar with the respect to the age.

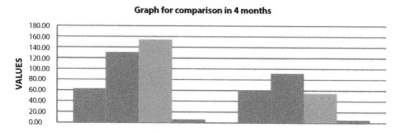

Figure 12.4 Graphical representation to compare the sugar level results in 4-month duration on different parameters.

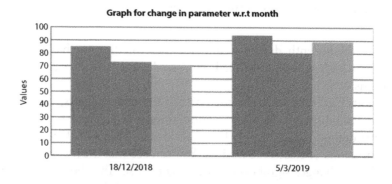

Figure 12.5 Graphical representation to compare the FVC and FEV1 on parameters.

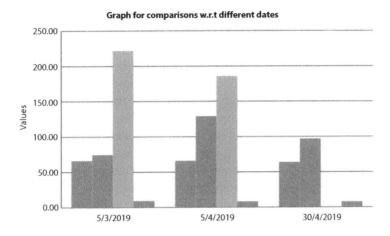

Figure 12.6 Graphical representation to compare subject's data on different dates.

is stored and evaluated using large data, the readings are taken using IoT sensors, and the data using ML and AI are processed and analyzed (Figure 12.7).

Readings of the subject matter of the above experiments were conducted in rural areas of Delhi Metropolitan City and Uttar Pradesh. The subjects of the study were between 5 and 75 years old.

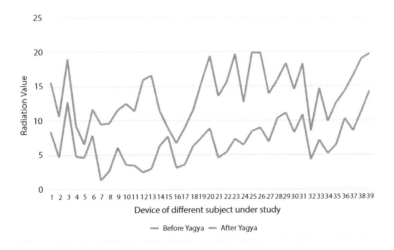

Figure 12.7 Radiation variation of different electronic gadgets of subjects (laptop, mobile, earphone, charger, etc.).

The happiness index varies from person to person and depends on many factors but is still considered a developing philosophy. The graph above shows an analysis of the happiness index of individuals tested to test the happiness index. On average, left-hand readings show a significant change in an individual's well-being index after attending Yagya. You can see that big data allows you to store and evaluate data, and IoT technology allows you to store measurements, which helps indepth analysis of the data collected by ML and AI (Figures 12.8 and 12.9). Subject readings were made for the above experiments in the city of the capital city Delhi and the rural area of Uttar Pradesh. Subjects were in the age group of 5 to 75 years.

The graph above shows an analysis of the happiness index of people tested to test the happiness index. On average, reading your right hand after participating in yoga shows a big change in people's well-being index. The above experiment involves the use of several technologies, the data of the above experiment is stored and evaluated using large data, the readings are taken using IoT sensors, and the data using ML and AI are processed and analyzed. There is. Readings of the subject matter of the above experiments were conducted in urban and rural areas of Delhi, Uttar Pradesh. Subjects were in the age group of 5 to 75 years. Subjects included men and women attending Yagya (as per Figure 12.10).

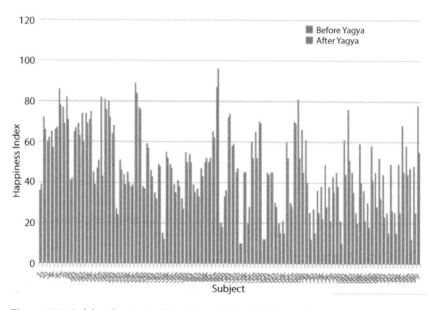

Figure 12.8 Left-hand analysis of happiness index of different subjects.

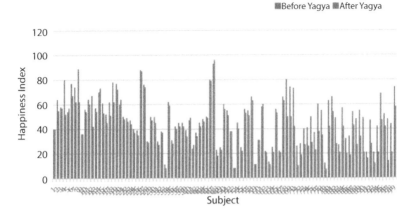

Figure 12.9 Right-hand analysis of happiness index of different subjects.

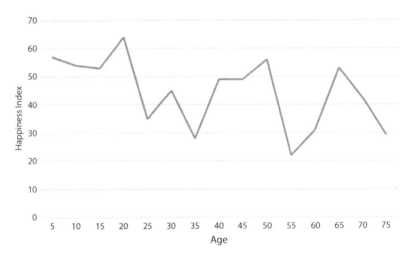

Figure 12.10 Age vs. happiness index (right hand).

Indicators of well-being depend on a variety of factors, no matter how old one is, the variety of stresses, responsibilities, challenges, and conflicts that they face can usually be traced to patterns. To analyze this case, the versatility of a big data consumer enables data storage and evaluation, and IoT technology enables deep data analytics to read storage, ML, and AI. It increasingly collected help. The above experiments involved the use of several technologies, the test data above was stored and evaluated using large data, the readings were taken using IoT sensors, and the data using ML

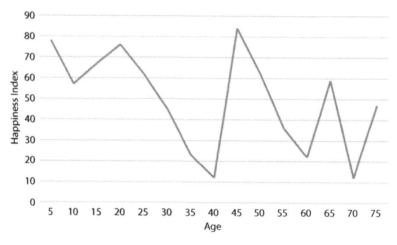

Figure 12.11 Age vs. happiness index (left hand).

and AI are processed and analyzed.(as per Figure 12.10). Readings of the subject matter of the above experiments were conducted in rural areas of Delhi Metropolitan City and Uttar Pradesh. The subjects of the study were between 5 and 75 years old.

The graph above uses domain 5 and has been investigated for the age group 5 to 75. This image shows overall diversity of happiness index (left hand) according to age. Reading the happiness index examined above, it was taken after Goaia. The above tests involve the use of several technologies, the above test data is stored and evaluated using large data, readings are taken using IoT sensors, and data using ML and AI are processed and analyzed (as per Figure 12.11). Readings of the subject matter of the above experiments were conducted in rural areas of Delhi Metropolitan City and Uttar Pradesh. The subjects of the study were between 5 and 75 years old.

12.6   Novelty in Our Work

All activities in the infinite expansion of the world are said to have come from the great immortal Yana (Yagya). Atharva Veda explains Yaga as follows: Ayam Yajna Vishvasya Bhuvanasya Nabheehiâ implies Yagya as a basic process of natural appearance. During the Yajna, the energy of the water of the Pranita Patra, which is dripping during the AajYahudi, is displayed on the Bovis meter on the high unit, what is the secret behind it?

Phonology says that the sound waves of the mantra have such strength that it can produce the desired result by stirring the word waves in natural atoms. Ghee is the carrier of both energy and waves, when the word of the mantra strikes with ahuti, in the oxidation method of fire, the natural atoms of the ghee explode from the combined contact of fire and mantra, in the same explosive state, it is dropped into where the water goes. Which also causes an expected explosion in the natural atoms of water? Ayurveda, homeopathy, and modern science know that the more you break the atoms, the more energy will be increased manifold. This sequence also works in it because the ghee explodes into atoms and it explodes into water atoms as well as the ultrasound waves of the mantra of the mantle produce high energy [56].

12.7 Recommendations

Arun Jaitley started with Diabetes mellitus and excessive weight gain. He had bariatric surgery for weight reduction (September, 2014).

- Lead to leak in after surgery
- Lead to septicemia
- Lead to renal kidney shut down led to kidney transplant (14th May 2018)
- Lead to immunosuppressive drugs
- Lead to cytomegalovirus infections
- Lead to soft tissue sarcoma
- Lead to metastasis all over the body by lymphatic and blood streams
- Lead to loss of life

Smt. Sushma Swaraj has similar stories about diabetes, renal failure, transplantation, and myocardial infarction. Two major deaths have been reported. Water dilutes high energy and makes that really good for the humans. After sacrificing again, the hand of the fire regains the unpleasant mantra, and the soul mixes with the stream of hands, is destroyed again by the fire, and is immediately destroyed. Therefore, delicate energy is mixed into the respiration, and reaches to lungs and to the whole of the body from there, making particles of iron in the blood and releasing the energy. It transmits kind of electric current. When you see this water from hundreds of millions of photo cameras, you can notice the rays [44].

Major two reasons why we do not recommend drinking this water directly.

Currently, not all humans have the capacity to digest the materials of high energy. If the person is not at the level of Seeker, this force cannot be handled. Currently, checking the status of former job seekers is a daunting task. Therefore, how to mix it in the natural life should be done with the olfaction. Water which is placed near the Yajna Kunda, during the Yajna, other gases with carbon dioxide which rise up and down due to being heavier than oxygen, the water near the Yajna kunda absorbs the carbon and other water, which Trees are good for vegetation, but Magar is not for humans. Therefore, it is forbidden to drink water placed near the Yagna Kund.

Now, you will be really amazed to find that the real energy of GritavGrangajal is 5 million units or 50,000,000 bovis!!!! Pranic energy can also be measured via Bovis. Our research can be very helpful for all of us, take all precautions to prevent onset of diabetes and, if diabetes is already there, then take it seriously from the start to prevent complications as the best of healthcare is not going to help once the cascade of complications sets in [58] and [14].

12.8   Future Scope and Possible Applications

Yagya or agniYagya is a powerful medicine against the mental and physical illnesses and mental disorders also. It is carried out by choosing the right wood and mortar. It is really much more powerful than just an excellent process for cleaning the environment. Excellent program of health is promised by the proper selection of the schedules, modes and mantras etc. In addition to important medical and physical uses such as physiotherapy, environmental cleansing, and improving vitality and physical fitness, vascular disorders are widely used in the treatment of mental health problems. Mental illnesses are invisible but far more widespread and severe than any of the physical illness. Almost all human societies suffer from these forms in some of the ways. More than 90% reasons of physical illness are hidden in the mind of patient. Hallucinations, confusion, anger, fear, excitement, suspicion, and weird behavior are common mental disorders for most of us.

Lack of control increases the silence and stability and can make others middle or normal aged. Insomnia, depression, and various psychological and psychological conditions are more painful than physical: poverty, relapse, insult, negligence, peroxidation, oxidation, abrasions, forgetfulness, dullness, inefficiencies, and other types of distressing mental illness. The important substances for sublimation and herbal therapy inhaled in yoga reach to the brain first, then to the lungs and to other parts. Hence, its effect is to directly treat brain complications and diseases.

The body absorbs heat of fire of victim and inhales the transcendental plants vapors through the holes and breaths in the skin. It increments the amount of free radicals in terms of the antioxidants, anions, and neurons, eliminating the root cause of the mental stress. Precise energy flow with gore sharks, headaches, migraine, holes from cold to mental movements, mental disorders, intolerance, depression, epilepsy, insomnia, schizophrenia, and precise mantras from various diseases and sickness. The test was performed by the Central Pollution Control Council (CPCB) [58].

12.9   Limitations

The survey used tools such as Aura Meter, Chakra Energy Meter, Human Energy Meter, Consciousness, Mental, and Index Happiness Index. Checkers were very expensive and time consuming. This study is performed on large sample sizes and randomized control designs using powerful tools. After Havan, jump to Bovis again from 4,000 to 8,000. However, drinking Greta and Jagran Jal will immediately increase your energy by minimum of 30,000 bovis. This is great. The energy of fresh water is around 13,000 bovis, and fresh fruits are about 13,000 to 20,000 liquors, and most bakery products are negative.

It is between 8,000 and 11,000 fresh cooked chilled vegetables, but when older says, it has 2 days of negative energy. The energy of hot milk tea is very negative. The energy of my home in my bedroom where the professor sees resurrection and colleagues. Taking a daily towel will cost you 24,000 to 31,000 buoys after Chandra, which used to be 24,000 buoys. The energy of the water stored in Havan is 18,000 Havan, which is very high in Ghritagrahankal.

12.10   Conclusions

Deep Yagya training is an amazingly practical application that is at least easy to use and exciting and has a great impact on delicate thinking and emotions. Fire of yagya is scientific method that spreads the possible positive effects of matter as energy on the atmosphere of surrounding, and its impact on Mantra Shakti's incomparable empathy is very necessary. Mantra Syntax The Vedic paradigm originates from a deeper study of secondary sounds, music, and knowledge (by Rishi) that is deeper than consciousness. The superb combination of precise mantra, yoga energy, and Yajka's superior autonomy in the Yaga process creates a very wonderful furnace. This evil melts the evil and then evaporates it. These vulgar instincts cleanse the mind by removing the weaknesses, evil desires, and other emotional anger, weaknesses, excitement, jealousy, fear, craving, anxiety, and stress.

Results of treatment of once-daily menopause for approximately 2.21 months indicate a significant improvement in the parameters of lung function. Results can be improved by incrementing the therapeutic dose up to twice daily.

12.11 Acknowledgments

Prof. Rohit Rastogi *et al.* would like to thank the experts of ABES Engineering College, Ghaziabad, DEI Institute, Agra Seniors, and Tata Consulting Services for excellent cooperation in this research process. Infrastructure and research samples were collected from various laboratories. We sincerely thank all authors, and all direct and indirect fans.

References

1. Nall, R., *An overview of diabetes types and treatments*, Medical News Today, Retrieved from https://www.medicalnewstoday.com/articles/323627.php, USA, 2018, November 8.
2. Brazier, Y., *What is obesity and what causes it?*, Medical News Today, Retrieved from https://www.medicalnewstoday.com/articles/323551.php, USA, 2018, November 2.
3. Chopra, D., In: *The Seven Spiritual Laws of Yoga*, N.J. Hoboken (Ed.), John Wiley and Sons, United States, USA, 2004.
4. Barnes, P.M., Bloom, B., Nahin, R.L., *Natl Health Stat Report*, National Center for Health Statistics, pp. 1–23, USA, 2008 Dec 10.
5. Felman, A., *Everything you need to know about hypertension*, Medical News Today, USA, Retrieved from https://www.medicalnewstoday.com/articles/150109.php, USA, 2019, July 22.
6. Felman, A., *What to know about anxiety*, Medical News Today, USA, 2018, October 26, Retrieved from https://www.medicalnewstoday.com/articles/323454.php.

7. Zimmet, P.Z., Diabetes and its drivers: The largest epidemic in human history? *Clin. Diabetes Endocrinol.*, 3, 1, 2017.

8. VidhyadharShukal, A., CharakaSamhita of Agnivesh (1996). Elaborated by Charaka and Dridhbala, Volume – 1, with, in: *Charaka-Chandrika Hindi commentary, TriaishaniyaAdhyaya*, Fourth edition, 1996, Chaukhambha Subharati Prakashan, Varanasi, Sutrasthan, 11/54.

9. Anjana, R.M., Deepa, M., Pradeepa, R., Mahanta, J., Narain, K., Das, H.K., Prevalence of diabetes and prediabetes in 15 states of India: Results from the ICMR-INDIAB population-based cross-sectional study. *Lancet Diabetes Endocrinol.*, 5, 585–96, 2017.

10. Unwin, N., Whiting, D., Guariguata, L., Ghyoot, G., Gan, D. (Eds.), *The IDF Diabetes Atlas*, 5th edition, pp. 7–12, International Diabetes Federation, Brussels, Belgium, 2011.

11. Brahmavarchas, (Ed.), Yagya – Ek Samagra Upachar Prakriya (Hindi) (Yagya - A Holistic Therapy), in: *Pandit Shriram Sharma Achrya Samagra Vangamaya -* Volume 26, Akhand Jyoti Sansthan, Mathura, Uttar Pradesh, India, 2012.

12. Brahmavarchas, *Yagya Chikitsa (Hindi)*, First Edition 2010, Published by Shri Vedmata Gayatri Trust (TMD), Shantikunj, Haridwar, Uttarakhand, India, 1994.

13. Brahmavarchas, Yagya Chikitsa (Hindi), in: *Chap.5 Diabetes kiVishishta Hawan samagri*, First Edition 2010, p. 103, Published by Shri Vedmata Gayatri Trust (TMD), Shantikunj, Haridwar, Uttarakhand, India, 2010.

14. Shrivastava, V. *et al.*, *A Case Study-Management Of Type II Diabetes Mellitus (T2DM) Through Herbal Medicinal-Smoke (Dhoom-Nasya)*, pp. 103–118, Dev Sanskriti Vishwavidyalaya, Haridwar, 2016.

15. Lisa, A. and Gustafson, D.H., The Role of Technology in Healthcare Innovation: A Commentary. *J. Dual Diagn.* Author manuscript; available PMC 2014 Jan 1, 9, 1, 101–103, 2013, *J. Dual Diagn.*

16. Kumar, N., Immediate Role of Two Yoga Based Mantra Recitation on Selective Attention in Undergraduate Students. *Dev. Sanskriti: Interdiscip. Int. J.*, 13, 1–7, 2019

17. Bhardwaj, D., Agnihotri, V.K., Pandya, P., Clinical evaluation of an Ayurvedic Formulation in the management of Avaranajanya Madhumeha (Type 2 Diabetes Mellitus). *Dev. Sanskriti: Interdiscip. Int. J.* 01, 50–64, 2012.

18. Singh, R., Yagya–Vedic way to Prevent Air pollution. *Dev. Sanskriti: Interdiscip. Int. J.*, 01, 29–35, 2012.

19. Chen, L. and Lu, F., Yoga - A Link for Healthy Body, Culture and Cultural Exchange. *Dev. Sanskriti: Interdiscip. Int. J.*, 2019-07-28, 10, 01–10, 2017.

20. Avnish, K. and Kumar Upadhyay, K., Ethno-medicinal and Ayurvedic Approach in the Management and Treatment of Asthma (Swash Roga). *Dev. Sanskriti: Interdiscip. Int. J.*, 7, 1–11, 2016.

21. Misra, S. and Satpathy, J., Correlation of Age, Yoga and Circadian Rhythm on Attention. *Dev. Sanskriti: Interdiscip. Int. J.*, published 2019-07-25, 4, 01–07, 2014.

22. Durg, V.R., Jawla, S., Bajpai, S., The Study of Rudraksha Bead showing a Symbol of OM. *Dev. Sanskriti: Interdiscip. Int. J.*, 8, 08–13, 2016.

23. Chauhan, S., Rastogi, R., Chaturvedi, D.K., Arora, N., Trivedi, P., Framework for Use of Machine Intelligence on Clinical Psychology to study the effects of Spiritual tools on Human Behavior and Psychic Challenges. *Proceedings of NSC-2017 (National system conference)*, DEI, Agra, Dec. 1–3, 2017, 2017.

24. Rastogi, R., Chaturvedi, D.K., Satya, S., Arora, N., Yadav, V., Chauhan, S., Sharma, P., SF-36 Scores Analysis for EMG and GSR Therapy on Audio, Visual and Audio Visual Modes for Chronic TTH, in: *the proceedings of the ICCIDA-2018 on 27 and 28th October 2018, CCIS Series*, 28 Oct. 2018, Springer, Gandhi Institute for Technology, Khordha, Bhubaneswar, Odisha, India.

25. Sharma, A., Rastogi, R., Chaturvedi, D.K., Satya, S., Arora, N., Trivedi, P., Singh, A., Singh, A., Intelligent Analysis for Personality Detection on Various Indicators by Clinical Reliable Psychological TTH and Stress Surveys, in: *the proceedings of CIPR 2019 at Indian Institute of Engineering Science and Technology*, Shibpur, 19th-20th January 2019, Springer-AISC Series, 2019.

26. Sharma, P., Rastogi, R., Chaturvedi, D.K., Satya, S., Arora, N., Yadav, V., Chauhan, S., Analytical Comparison of Efficacy for Electromyography and Galvanic Skin Resistance Biofeedback on Audio-Visual Mode for Chronic TTH on Various Attributes, in: *the proceedings of the ICCIDA-2018 on 27 and 28th October 2018, CCIS Series*, Springer, Gandhi Institute for Technology, Khordha, Bhubaneswar, Odisha, India, 2018.

27. Rastogi, R., Chaturvedi, D.K., Arora, N., Trivedi, P., Mishra, V., Swarm Intelligent Optimized Method of Development of Noble Life in the perspective of Indian Scientific Philosophy and Psychology. *Proceedings of NSC-2017(National system conference)*, DEI Agra, Dec. 1–3, 2017, 2017.

28. Vyas, P., Rastogi, R., Chaturvedi, D.K., Satya, S., Arora, N., Singh, P., Statistical Analysis for Effect of Positive Thinking on Stress Management and Creative Problem Solving for Adolescents. *Proceedings of the 12th INDIACom*; 2018, pp. 245–251, 2018.

29. Gulati, M., Rastogi, R., Chaturvedi, D.K., Satya, S., Arora, N., Singhal, P., Statistical Resultant Analysis of Spiritual & Psychosomatic Stress Survey on Various Human Personality Indicators, in: *The International Conference proceedings of ICCI 2018*, 2018.

30. Agrawal, A., Rastogi, R., Chaturvedi, D.K., Sharma, S., Bansal, A., Audio Visual EMG &GSR Biofeedback Analysis for Effect of Spiritual Techniques on Human Behavior and Psychic Challenges. *Proceedings of the 12th INDIACom*; 2018, pp. 252–258, 2018.

31. Yadav, V., Rastogi, R., Chaturvedi, D.K., Satya, S., Arora, N., Gupta, M., Chauhan, S., Sharma, P., Book chapter titled as Chronic TTH Analysis by EMG & GSR Biofeedback on Various Modes and Various Medical Symptoms Using IoT, in: *Advances in ubiquitous sensing applications for healthcare, Book-Big Data Analytics for Intelligent Healthcare Management*, 2019.

32. Singh, P., Rastogi, R., Chaturvedi, D.K., Arora, N., Trivedi, P., Vyas, P., Study on Efficacy of Electromyography and Electroencephalography Biofeedback with Mindful Meditation on Mental health of Youths. *Proceedings of the 12th INDIACom*; 2018, pp. 84–89, 2018.

33. Singh, V., Rastogi, R., Chaturvedi, D.K., Satya, S., Arora, N., Sirohi, H., Singh, M., Verma, P., Which One is Best: Electromyography Biofeedback Efficacy Analysis on Audio, Visual and Audio-Visual Modes for Chronic TTH on Different Characteristics, in: *the proceedings of ICCIIoT- 2018*, 14–15 December 2018, ELSEVIER- SSRN Digital Library, NIT Agartala, Tripura, 2018.

34. Saini, H., Rastogi, R., Chaturvedi, D.K., Satya, S., Arora, N., Verma, H., Mehlyan, K., Comparative Efficacy Analysis of Electromyography and Galvanic Skin Resistance Biofeedback on Audio Mode for Chronic TTH on Various Indicators, in: *the proceedings of ICCIIoT- 2018*, 14–15 December 2018, ELSEVIER- SSRN Digital Library, NIT Agartala, Tripura, 2018.

35. Yadav, V., Rastogi, R., Chaturvedi, D.K., Satya, S., Arora, N., Bansal, I., Intelligent Analysis for Detection of Complex Human Personality by Clinical Reliable Psychological Surveys on Various Indicators, in: *the national Conference on 3rd MDNCPDR-2018*, DEI, Agra, 06–07 September, 2018, 2018.

36. Yadav, V., Rastogi, R., Chaturvedi, D.K., Satya, S., Arora, N., Yadav, V., Sharma, P., Chauhan, S., Statistical Analysis of EMG & GSR Biofeedback Efficacy on Different Modes for Chronic TTH on Various Indicators. *Int. J. Adv. Intell. Paradig.*, 13, 1, 251–275, 2018.

37. Gupta, M., Rastogi, R., Chaturvedi, D.K., Satya, S., Arora, Verma, H., Singhal, P., Singh, A., Comparative Study of Trends Observed During Different Medications by Subjects under EMG & GSR Biofeedback. *ICSMSIC-2019, ABESEC*, Ghaziabad, 8–9 March 2019, vol. 8, issue 6S, IJITEE, pp. 748–756, 2019, https://www.ijitee.org/download/volume-8-issue-6S/.

38. Singhal, P., Rastogi, R., Chaturvedi, D.K., Satya, S., Arora, N., Gupta, M., Singhal, P., Gulati, M., Statistical Analysis of Exponential and Polynomial Models of EMG & GSR Biofeedback for Correlation between Subjects Medications Movement & Medication Scores. *ICSMSIC-2019, ABESEC*, 8–9 March 2019, vol. 8, issue 6S, IJITEE, Ghaziabad, pp. 625–635, 2019, https://www.ijitee.org/download/volume-8-issue-6S/.

39. Saini, H., Rastogi, R., Chaturvedi, D.K., Satya, S., Arora, N., Gupta, M., Verma, H., An Optimized Biofeedback EMG and GSR Biofeedback Therapy for Chronic TTH on SF-36 Scores of Different MMBD Modes on Various Medical Symptoms, in: *of Hybrid Machine Intelligence for Medical Image*

Analysis, Studies Comp. Intelligence, vol. 841, Springer Nature Singapore, Singapore, Pte Ltd, 2019.

40. Singh, A., Rastogi, R., Chaturvedi, D.K., Satya, S., Arora, N., Sharma, A., Singh, A., Intelligent Personality Analysis on Indicators in IoT-MMBD Enabled Environment, in: *Chapter 7 of Multimedia Big Data Computing for IoT Applications: Concepts, Paradigms, and Solutions,* pp. 185–215, Springer Nature, Singapore, 2019.

41. Gulati, M., Rastogi, R., Chaturvedi, D.K., Sharma, P., Yadav, V., Chauhan, S., Gupta, M., Singhal, P., Statistical Resultant Analysis of Psychosomatic Survey on Various Human Personality Indicators: Statistical Survey to Map Stress and Mental Health, in: *Chapter 22 of Handbook of Research on Learning in the Age of Transhumanism,* pp. 363–383, IGI Global, Hershey, PA, 2019.

42. Chaturvedi, D.K., Human Rights and Consciousness, International Seminar on Prominence of Human Rights in the Criminal Justice System (ISPUR 2012. *Proceedings of Organized Ambedkar Chair, Dept. of Contemporary Social Studies & Law,* 30–31 March 2012, Dr. B.R. Ambedkar University, Agra, p. 33, 2012.

43. Chaturvedi, D.K. and Arya, M., Correlation between Human Performance and Consciousness. *IEEE-International Conference on Human Computer Interaction,* 23–24 Aug. 2013, Proceedings of Saveetha School of Engineering, Saveetha University, Thandalam, Chennai, IN, India, 2013.

44. Chaturvedi, D.K. and Satsangi, R., The Correlation between Student Performance and Consciousness Level. *Proceedings of International Conference on Advanced Computing and Communication Technologies (ICACCT™-2013),* 16 Nov. 2013, Asia Pacific Institute of Information Technology SD India, Panipat (Hariyana), Souvenir – pp. 66, proc., pp. 200–203, 2013.

45. Chaturvedi, D.K., Science, Religion and Spiritual Quest, in: *Edited book on Linkages between Social Service, Agriculture and Theology for the Future of Mankind,* pp. 15–17, DEI Press, Agra, India, 2004.

46. Chaturvedi, D.K. and Rajeev, S., The correlation between Student Performance and Consciousness Level. *Int. J. Comput. Sci. Commun. Technol.,* 6, 1–5, 2014.

47. Chatruvedi, D.K. and Lajwanti, Correlation between Energy Distribution profile and Level of Consciousness. *ShiakshkParisamvad, Int. J. Educ., SPIJJE,* 4, 1, 1–9, 2014.

48. Chaturvedi, D.K. and Arya, M., A Study of Correlation between Consciousness Level and Performance of Worker. *Ind. Eng. J.,* 6, 8, 40–43, 2013.

49. Chaturvedi, D.K. and Lajwanti, Dayalbagh Way of Life for Better Worldliness. *Quest J., J. Res. Hum. Soc. Sci.,* 3, 5, 16–23, 2321-9467, 2015.

50. Chaturvedi, D.K., Arora, J.K., Bhardwaj, R., Effect of meditation on Chakra Energy and Hemodynamic parameters. *Int. J. Comput. Appl.,* 126, 12, 52–59, September 2015.

51. Chaturvedi, D.K., Relationship between Chakra Energy and Consciousness. *Biomed. J. Sci. Tech. Res.,* 15, 3, 1–3, 2019.

52. Richa, Chaturvedi, D.K., Prakash, S., The consciousness in Mosquito. *J. Mosq. Res.*, 6, 34, 1–9, 2016.

53. Richa, Chaturvedi, D.K., Prakash, S., Role of Electric and Magnetic Energy Emission in Intra and Interspecies Interaction in Microbes. *Am. J. Res. Commun.*, 4, 12, 1–22, 2016.

54. Chaturvedi, D.K., Lajwanti, Chu, T.H., Kohli, H.P., Energy Distribution Profile of Human Influences the Level of Consciousness. *Towards a Science of Consciousness, Arizona Conference Proceeding*, Tucson, Arizona, 2012.

55. Tsai, H.C., Cohly, H., Chaturvedi, D.K., Towards the Consciousness of the Mind, Towards a Science of Consciousness. *Dayalbagh Conference Proceeding*, Agra, India, 2013.

56. Saxena, M., Sengupta, B., Pandya, P., A study of the Impact of Yagya on Indoor Microbial Environments. *Indian J. Air Pollut. Control*, VII, 1, 6–15, March 2007.

57. Saxena, M., Sengupta, B., Pandya, P., Comparative Studies of Yagya vs. Non-Yagya Microbial Environments. *Indian J. Air Pollut. Control*, VII, 1, 16–24, March 2007.

58. Saxena, M., Sengupta, B., Pandya, P., Effect of Yagya on the Gaseous Pollutants. *Indian J. Air Pollut. Control*, VII, 2, 11–15, September 2007.

59. Saxena, M., Sengupta, B., Pandya, P., Controlling the Microflora in Outdoor Environment: Effect of Yagya. *Indian J. Air Pollut. Control*, VIII, 2, 30–36, September 2008.

60. Saxena, M., Kumar, B., Matharu, S., Impact of Yagya on Particulate Matters. *Interdiscip. J. Yagya Res.*, 1, 1, pp. 01–08, Oct. 2018.

61. Saxena, M., Sharma, M., Sain, M.K., Bohra, G., Sinha, R., Yagya reduced level of indoor Electro-Magnetic Radiations (EMR). *Interdiscip. J. Yagya Res.*, 1, 2, 22–30 Oct. 2018.

13

Collection and Analysis of Big Data From Emerging Technologies in Healthcare

Nagashri K.*, Jayalakshmi D. S. and Geetha J.

Computer Science and Engineering, Ramaiah Institute of Technology, Bangalore, India

Abstract

Big data in healthcare is a fast advancing area. With new diseases being continuously discovered, for instance, the COVID19 pandemic, there is a tremendous surge in data generation and a huge burden falls on the medical personnel where automation and emerging technologies can contribute significantly. Combining big data with the emerging technologies in healthcare is the need of the hour. In this chapter, first, we focus on the collection of big data in healthcare using emerging technologies like Radio Frequency Identification (RFID), Wireless Sensor Networks (WSN), and Internet of Things (IoT) along with its applications in medical field. We then explore the issues and challenges faced during data collection. Next, we bring out the different data analysis approaches. Then, the challenges and issues during data analysis are explored. Finally, the current research trends going on in the field are summarized.

Keywords: RFID, WSN, IoT, healthcare, big data

13.1 Introduction

Big data has been a focus of significant attention over the past 20 years due to its immense potential in various real-life applications. Big data is generated, collected, and analyzed by numerous public and private sector enterprises in order to enhance the services offered by them. In the healthcare sector, hospital reports, patient health records, medical test reports, and IoT applications

---

Corresponding author: nagashri27@gmail.com

A. Suresh, S. Vimal, Y. Harold Robinson, Dhinesh Kumar Ramaswami and R. Udendhran (eds.)
Bioinformatics and Medical Applications: Big Data Using Deep Learning Algorithms, (269–288)
© 2022 Scrivener Publishing LLC

are different sources of big data. A huge proportion of big data pertaining to public healthcare is also produced by biomedical research. To extract relevant insights, such data involves significant monitoring and analysis. Proper management, study, and understanding of big data will be a game changer by building unique pathways for the modern-day healthcare system. This is precisely why different sectors, including the medical field, are adopting aggressive measures to transform the opportunities for improved services and monetary gains. Advanced healthcare organizations will eventually revolutionize medical treatments and customized treatment with a thorough convergence of biomedical and healthcare information [1, 2].

There are many healthcare data sources worth studying due to the advancement of digitalization, including Electronic Health Records (EHR) and personal health information. In order to enhance patient care quality and appropriate therapies, having access to the vast data and transforming it into medical data, analytics plays a pivotal role. By implementing a broad range of healthcare activities, involving disease monitoring, clinical decision support systems, and patient medical management, Big Data and Analytics (BDA) promises to make the maximum utilization of huge volumes of data. By offering a more succinct overview of an enormous volume of healthcare data, the BDA further aims to minimize healthcare costs while increasing healthcare quality [3].

Big data generated using emerging technologies like RFID, WSN, IoT, and remote sensors are playing a big role in bioinformatics research. The applications of such technologies in the collection of data from healthcare-related domains must be clearly understood. This data collected might be of heterogeneous nature which needs systematic managing techniques to overcome various challenges posed in the data collection process. It is important to address such challenges and provide solutions to analyze the accumulated data. Needless to say, it is of utmost importance to ensure privacy and security of the data collected failing which leads to serious data breaches.

Figure 13.1 shows a taxonomy of topics presented in this chapter. The topics discussed broadly fall into two parts: data collection and data analysis. Under data collection, we discuss the emerging technologies like RFID, WSN, and IoT and their applications in the healthcare domain. We also identify the issues and challenges faced during the data collection from these technologies. Under data analysis, we concentrate on the approaches to analyze the big data to obtain meaningful insights and draw conclusions. We also look into the issues and challenges arising during data analysis. Finally, the current research trends in this field will be inspected to understand the ongoings of the latest technologies in medical big data analytics.

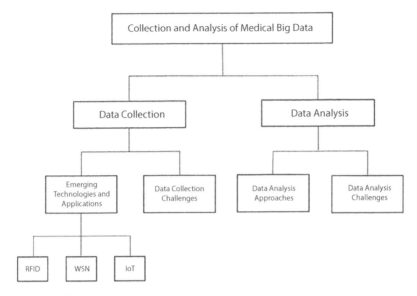

Figure 13.1 Taxonomy.

13.2   Data Collection

Medical big data can be collected from multiple sources. Out of these, data collection from some of the emerging technologies in healthcare like RFID, WSN, and IoT is discussed along with its applications. Some of the issues and challenges during data collection from these technologies are also put forth in this section.

13.2.1   Emerging Technologies in Healthcare and Its Applications

Emerging wireless technologies have revolutionized the development of human healthcare services. Wearable technologies are being used predominantly in the medical sector. They are employed to constantly communicate health data, mitigate the possibility of injuries, and enhance the quality of interaction between doctors and patients. They even deliver overlooked sensory attributes, like physiological process monitoring as well as biofeedback [3, 4].

Several wearables are now getting increasingly prominent among the common man. Numerous mobile applications working on medical and health gadgets like smartwatches, sports wristbands, and smartphones have evolved in the recent past. Such wearables provide a computational capability for the consumer to track or monitor necessary information. Wearable computing technologies have significantly promoted Mobile device-based healthcare; several wearables are being developed with disease surveillance and body awareness capabilities [5].

From the perspective of cognitive infrastructures, smart and pervasive sensor-based devices are significant in the healthcare domain. This should be combined with other capabilities like data mining methods, stream processing, and real-time processing methods which analyze and interpret the data to derive meaningful information [6].

Some of the emerging technologies which are the sources of medical big data in healthcare are described below.

13.2.1.1   RFID

RFID technology has gained prominence in the healthcare domain. It makes use of radio waves to obtain data and transmit it. In addition to locating objects and people, it also renders precise accessibility to healthcare data for medical personnel. It is considered to be a great invention for the future for automatically collecting data and to track equipment [7].

Some of the applications of RFID in healthcare [7] are given below.

- Tracking: Hospital equipment, medical devices, and apparatus must be tracked in large quantities. It can not only track accessories but also hospital personnel and patients who require constant monitoring like infants, people with Alzheimer's, old patients, and those who need medical assistance very frequently. It can also precisely locate accidents, emergency locations, and casualty. In addition to assets and human tracking, prescribed drugs from the manufacturing unit to the receiver end can be tracked in the pharmaceutical industry by enabling the RFID tags with the drugs container [8].
- Identification and Verification: Identifying a drug, personnel, or patients wrongly is a possibility among human beings; RFID removes this disadvantage by accurate identification. Patients are provided with smart wristbands on scanning which the patient's details like name, birth date, admission number, insurance details and other information can be known. Scanning the medical assets, like syringes, helps in identifying the name, quantity, manufacture, and expiry date and related information. The assets linking to

the patients will remove manual errors of giving the wrong dosage to the wrong patient [9].

- Sensing: To obtain data from sensors and performing computations, RFID tag enables in providing the interfacing ability of a chip to the sensor. Sensing RFID devices must be incorporated with both physical as well as chemical sensors to log logistics data and it must be integrated with gas sensors for food logistics. Other sensing includes chemical, temperature, and humidity to name a few. To detect contaminated blood, sensing temperature comes into picture which helps to manage blood supplies in hospitals and blood banks [10].

13.2.1.2   WSN

WSN comprises a huge set of spatially distributed independent nodes. The sensor nodes send the data to a designated sink node having greater memory capacity and processing ability [11, 12]. The sensor nodes are less expensive, consume less power, and can be deployed quickly; they have self-coordinating and collaborative data processing abilities. They are used for tracking and noting the various attributes required in healthcare like measuring the patient's temperature, blood pressure, heartbeats, etc. With the rapid technology growth, the healthcare sector is shifting toward many new advancements and infrastructures including nanosensors. Nanosensors can be worn by patients which helps in recognizing, locating, and processing different kinds of biomedical feedback including heartbeat surveillance using electrocardiogram (ECG) sensor, brain response signals using electroencephalogram (EEG) sensor, muscle activation using electromyogram (EMG) sensor, blood pressure (BP) using a BP sensor, trunk placement check using tilt sensor, and many more [13].

Some of the applications of WSN in healthcare [11, 14] are given below.

- Patient Monitoring in the Hospital Environment: To obtain data from patients through various sensors attached to the body, wireless body area networks (WBAN) is used. It is increasingly becoming essential to monitor different parameters of such clinical data to provide continuous and real-time care which helps in better understanding of a patient's health condition rather than by using just one sensor.
- Patient Monitoring From Home: It is extremely necessary for monitoring the aged and chronic (heart disease, respiratory

problems, diabetes, etc.) patients living alone. Sensors to detect fall are useful for elderly; heartbeat sensors to warn if the heartbeat increases than the normal and various other sensors are included here. It reduces the monetary expenses incurred and avoids the trouble of an in-person visit to the healthcare centers.

- Acquiring Long-Term Data in the Hospital Environment: The sensors help to collect data which can be transformed into a form that may be used for data processing, storing and analyzing to get meaningful insights. By observing the data collected from sensors, appropriate decisions about the patient's situation can be decided. The previously gathered data can be used to predict a similar situation arising in the future.

13.2.1.3 IoT

IoT is a technology which has enabled communication between commonly used devices and also with human beings. IoT may be perceived as an extension to the Internet; there is a logical connection between the smart devices which can identify, locate, sense, and communicate among each other. Some such smart systems like smartphones, digital assistants, and tablets in addition to sensors, RFID tag systems are able to exchange data with each other to create a digital connection. IoT systems can also be deployed using typical WSNs. The IoT is indivisible from wearable devices as well as remote mobile applications [6, 12].

Some of the applications of IoT in healthcare [15] are given below.

- Real-Time and Remote Health Monitoring Systems: IoT gathers data and transmits it to the cloud. They further transmit the data to the concerned medical personnel for monitoring patients mainly suffering from chronic disorders. Such real-time monitoring systems reduce the appointments with the doctors since remotely the condition of the patient can be supervised [16].
- Prevent and Diagnose Diseases: In preventive care, the aim is to promote healthy lifestyles among people, rather than finding a cure after the disease is diagnosed. In chronic care, the aim is for efficient handling of patients' health thereby decreasing acute situations. In acute care, the aim is for providing appropriate and proper information during therapy,

post which the aim is for building protected, convenient, and reduced monetary expenses for patient rehabilitation.

- Emergency Notification Systems: A growing demand is noticeable in the recent past for immediate, quick, and proper medical assistance in case of unexpected events like accidents or other health emergencies. Some systems are coming into existence to handle this scenario using IoT for alerting the concerned people about the patient's condition to take necessary actions [16].

The architecture of remote monitoring also known as telemedicine has three layers; layer 1 is the user where the data is collected from different technologies attached to the patients, layer 2 is the base station which sends the data collected from layer 1 to layer 3 which is the server and is used by medical professionals like doctors and nurses to analyze the data. The data generated by wearables are in signals form which needs processing to convert to samples on which the medical practitioners perform analysis to understand vital body changes or disruptions if any in the patient's body to make conclusions and decisions can be taken accordingly. The three-layer architecture for remote health monitoring is shown in Figure 13.2. In layer 1, a patient is attached with multiple sensors, say, temperature, pulse rate, and motion sensors. From the sensors, the data is sent to base stations like a mobile or laptop which is in layer 2. The patient may also have a personal digital assistant whose data will be sent to a smart personal robot which is in layer 2. From layer 2 base stations, the signals will be transmitted to the server in layer 3 using wireless technologies like Bluetooth, internet, Zigbee, and Wi-Fi where the data can be stored and analysis can be done; also in case of emergencies, alert systems will notify the caretakers of the patient and hospitals about the criticality of the patient to take immediate actions [17].

For collecting the big data from different sources or technologies, the six V's are explained below in terms of the healthcare data [17, 18].

- Volume: It indicates the quantity of data produced by the different emerging technologies which are the data sources; there has been a tremendous surge in the data being generated nowadays. The data might be population health records, or per patient's multiple physiological aspects; this volume of data is reaching extreme heights.
- Velocity: It means how often the data is getting generated which would need further processing and analysis. Since a

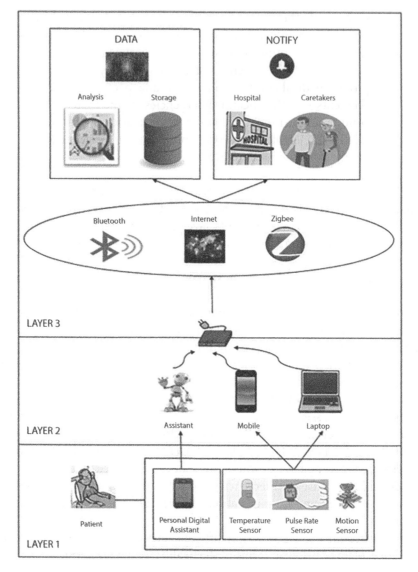

Figure 13.2 Three-layer architecture for remote health monitoring.

patient's condition has to be continuously monitored, the velocity is high.

- Variety: With just one biomarker, a patient's condition cannot be concluded. Multiple sensors sense the data and send them to the destination. Such data comes from various sources leads to the gathering of a variety of heterogeneous data.

- Value: The data collected will have some weight or value associated with it in terms of the information it provides like identifying the patients, determining emergency situations, and assessing patients' health and so on.
- Variability: Different kinds of data in the form of textual, image, audio, video, and signals are generated which are essential in addressing several types of medical situations to draw conclusions by finding hidden patterns from the data.
- Veracity: This includes consistent and trustworthy data. Sometimes, due to faulty sensors, precise values might not be obtained from them and they might not be trustable. Also, using the Internet, Bluetooth, Zigbee, Wi-Fi, Ethernet, or other similar technologies to establish a connection between the layers may result in inconsistent data. During analysis in layer 3, some questions may arise like whether the data was obtained from the right medical care center and was it collected from the right patient, were the diagnosis made accurately, and so on.

13.2.2   Issues and Challenges in Data Collection

During the data collection from multiple sources, many issues and challenges may arise which are described below.

13.2.2.1   Data Quality

Reliable accurate devices with almost no flaws must be used to collect data under proper conditions. Sensor data is collected without in-person monitoring which could cause problems if the device is faulty or corrupted when used over a period of time. The medical big data suffers from poor quality, inconsistent, and volatile data; it requires continuous wireless technology (Internet, Bluetooth, and so on) connection to collect data of high quality [18–20].

13.2.2.2   Data Quantity

Big data need huge storage space and computational capacity and may suffer from data transmission delays. The amount of data collected from different sources in IoT is so massive that it is causing chaos due to the sudden surge in IoT devices. To improve treatments and patient experience, hospitals gather a tremendous amount of heterogeneous data [20, 21].

13.2.2.3   Data Access

One of the main challenges in data collection is obtaining the patient's consent to use their sensitive information. Collecting the patient's data without permission leads to privacy concerns. Several countries have their own restrictions and regulations for data access. Some hospitals do not allow sharing of data with other hospitals which leads to the same data being collected again and again whenever necessary, thereby increasing redundancy [18–20].

13.2.2.4   Data Provenance

Patient-Generated Health Data (PGHD) means that the creation, recording, gathering, and inferring of data are done by patients or caretakers for handling a health issue consisting of patients medical history, health variations, the background of therapies, and their way of living. Data captured from emerging technologies are also part of PGHD. Tracking and maintaining the origin of PGHD when it arrives in the system is called data provenance; it needs proper standardization with well-structured infrastructures [20].

13.2.2.5   Security

The data collected from the source and transmitted to the destination must be transmitted through a secure pathway as it contains user sensitive data which when exposed may lead to trust issues, data breach and misuse of information [11]. Some of the security issues are described below.

13.2.2.5.1   WSN Attacks

The layer data collects data consists of RFIDs, sensors, and actuators; they are tampered so as to send the data to some other wrong nearby devices leading to data integrity and confidentiality issues. Attacks can be performed in the following ways [12].

- Sensor Jamming: This type of attack is used for denial of communication between the devices. A hacker manipulates a device to stop the communication with the other devices by introducing a malicious device causing the man in the middle attack.

- Eavesdropping: By doing a packet sniff, the attacker can listen to what the devices are communicating with one another; the data thus obtained can be used for further attacks or to misuse.
- Spoofing: The hacker can make the devices believe that it is interacting with an authenticated device but replaces it with a malicious one similar to the actual device. Detecting the attack is hard since the attacker masquerades the device like the original by generating authentication credentials to override the authenticated device [8].

13.2.2.5.2   Data Aggregators Vulnerabilities

Data aggregators include desktop health monitors, smartphones, and mobiles built specifically for healthcare affiliated applications. Healthcare-related application configurations are done in such devices well in advance enabling the communication with the sensor devices. Any mistakes during the configuration make it vulnerable to attacks. Malware attacks are also a possibility in this scenario due to the internet connection. When the security is hampered, the hacker can transmit wrong data using the device.

13.2.2.5.3   Social Engineering

For gaining physical or remote access into the system, social engineering methods may be used. A hacker can determine the working of a hospital IT system using rogue techniques by disguising himself as a patient thereby gaining access to the hospital.

13.2.2.6   *Other Challenges*

Despite the appealing upsides of RFID over various other identification technologies, it can still take quite some time for adopting and using it in a full-fledged manner. Although it can aid in improving the safety of patients and accomplish effective operational capabilities, it poses difficulty during the interfacing of healthcare equipment and has a dearth of proper standardization [7].

Due to the capacity constraints of a sensor node connecting through a narrow network link, issues while transmitting the data from the source node to the destination node may arise. If the distance between the source nodes to the destination node is more, then data has to traverse through multiple nodes in the path, thereby increasing the latency. Gathering a large amount of data in a densely distributed sensor network poses performance and energy efficiency issues [11].

IoT may have issues like scalability, high response time, bandwidth, availability, and longevity. All of these factors affect the data collection process. Integration of the IoT systems with other applications like web and software needs several middleware applications to manage big data which increases system complexity [21].

13.3   Data Analysis

BDA aims to find patterns and understand how the data obtained are correlated. They use several data mining methods like association rule, classification, clustering, anomaly detection, feature extraction, summarizing, and visualizing to capture hidden information from the dataset for finding the associations and patterns in the data [22]. Describing the data, converting it to human-understandable form, finding correlations and predicting necessary information is a part of the analytics process. The management of the heterogeneous data obtained from different sources is a daunting task and analyzing them to find meaningful information is a necessary step [23]. The raw unprocessed data collected from the emerging technologies are first converted to required formats such as text, image, audio, and video to perform analysis.

13.3.1   Data Analysis Approaches

There are various approaches to analyze different kinds of data. Some of the approaches are described below.

13.3.1.1   Machine Learning

Different methods of Machine Learning (ML) can be used for analysis. ML for BDA can use supervised, semi-supervised, and unsupervised learning algorithms for predicting future trends. In supervised learning, a prediction of a target output is made based on the training dataset belonging to different classes and predictions are made on the testing dataset. Semi-supervised learning is a combination of a small labeled dataset and a large unlabeled dataset which is used for balancing performance and precision. In unsupervised learning, patterns are found from the data which has no target labels [19]. ML classification algorithms like k-nearest neighbors, support vector machines, naïve Bayes, decision trees, and logistic regression; clustering algorithms like K-means, density-based, principal components–based, and spectral methods; regression algorithms like linear and logistic can be used as predictive methods. Reinforcement learning is an advanced ML technique which learns by trial and error, by gains and losses [23]. Other modern ML algorithms facilitate analysis over a combination of data types like images collected from X-ray scanning device and text (medical reports) to enhance the decision-making ability. Emerging technologies can be used for lifestyle data captures like activity or mood tracking that cannot be accurately captured otherwise. Recommendation applications alert about the patient's situation and provide suggestions to manage the disease using such data [20].

13.3.1.2 Deep Learning

Deep learning algorithms like convolutional neural networks (CNN), deep neural networks, recurrent neural network, and artificial neural networks are used to extract knowledge with high abstraction level (representing unstructured higher-level data in a human-understandable format) which deploys techniques imitating the human brain for complex processing of signals [23]. Such techniques can be used to analyze data with high complexity like text, video, image, or such unstructured data. It helps healthcare personnel like radiologists who mainly rely on outputs from images data [20].

13.3.1.3 Natural Language Processing

Text analysis is an analysis technique where Natural Language Processing (NLP) can be used. Text is unstructured data. Using IoT devices, the speech or audio data can be captured which helps in collecting information like what and how a patient is talking; this can help in identifying disorders like mental stability and depression. Text analytics tools like Apache cTAKES and MetaMap are available for this purpose [20].

13.3.1.4 High-Performance Computing

For vast data generated by devices for CT scan, PET scan images, or other omics data like genomics, data analytics using high-performance computing architectures having high computation power, high storage, and communication can be effective. They help in faster and better analysis of such data [18].

13.3.1.5   Edge-Fog Computing

Nowadays, cloud, fog, and edge computing analytics are gaining prominence in medical data. Sensitive data from wearables, RFID devices, and sensors will be used for capturing, processing, and performing analysis on the devices itself, thereby reducing the transfer of data produced, resulting in reduced resource utilization like bandwidth, processing, computation power of the cloud, as well as minimizing the response time and delay, curbing the privacy and security issues which are of high importance. This is achieved by introducing a fog layer between the edge devices (RFID, WSN, and IoT devices) and the cloud for lightweight processing; instead of sending all the raw data collected from the edge devices to the cloud, it is sent to the fog layer which has a small storage capacity and also can do lightweight computation. But some computations which require high computation and memory are performed at the cloud [18, 24].

13.3.1.6   Real-Time Analytics

It is one of the important analysis methods that help in saving lives during critical life and death situations. As soon as the data arrives from any of the sensors or IoT devices, there is a need to analyze the data and gain information especially in ICUs and alarms can be triggered. Real-time analytics approach analyzes and provides information using both existing and freshly arriving data. Data stream mining approach analyzes and provides insights about data as and when it arrives from the devices, instead of storing and making use of it later [20].

13.3.1.7   End-User Driven Analytics

Monitoring applications developed in combination with IoT devices where data can be visualized on smartphones, tablets, or other digital media can be used by either patients or healthcare practitioners to check on the patient's health status. In this case, the patient can self-monitor their health by getting updates about different biomarkers (temperature, blood pressure, pulse rate, etc.) collected from different devices attached to them. Such an analysis technique helps the patients who do not have in-depth technical knowledge about statistical analysis or data processing but can only understand data through visualizations or interactive easy to use tools using Question-Answer with the help of chatbots [20].

13.3.1.8 Knowledge-Based Analytics

This technique can be used for prescriptive analysis (giving suggestions and recommendations based on the knowledge-base). For example, to track the availability of the number of drugs in a hospital using RFIDs, the suggestions are done on how much quantity of drugs might be further required [20].

13.3.2 Issues and Challenges in Data Analysis

During the data analysis from multiple sources, many issues and challenges may arise which are described below.

13.3.2.1 Multi-Modal Data

There are different kinds of data: structured data such as EHR and unstructured data such as readings obtained by multiple sensor devices like EEG, text data from reports by medical experts, image, and omics data. Obtaining insights from all kinds of heterogeneous data are essential to provide it to the doctors about the patient's background to make an informed decision [20].

13.3.2.2 Complex Domain Knowledge

Clinical data has high complexity. It comprises in-depth information about the patient at different stages, therapies and medications, existing medical research works, biobanks, clinical trials, and so on. The complexity in healthcare metadata must be considered for optimal analysis to predict outcomes and for backing medical decisions taken [20].

13.3.2.3 Highly Competent End-Users

Data analytic tools will be used by well-trained professionals like doctors, clinicians, or scientists who have a lot of responsibilities on them; therefore, they expect highly trustable tools which match the quality standards. To meet their expectations, standard and reliable analytic tools are necessary that give output in a readable form which should also enable the cross verification of results smoothly [20, 25].

13.3.2.4 Supporting Complex Decisions

Complex medical data are to be analyzed for taking important decisions regarding patients. Such data might have missing values, noises, outliers, and, sometimes, inaccurate values due to lack of physical monitoring during data collection from devices which has a major impact on decision-making. Always an optimal result cannot be promised, be it by a human or technologies; but minimizing the error rate is the challenge. Smart assistants as discussed in the three-layer architecture for remote health monitoring in Section 13.2.1 can be highly beneficial in the future along with the emerging technologies which can make patients' lives better [20, 26].

13.3.2.5 Privacy

Sensitive medical data are subjected to legal standardizations and protection. Developing the analytic tools incorporating the privacy statements issued by law is of utmost significance for the practical implementation in the health sector [20].

13.3.2.6 Other Challenges

While handling a huge amount of medical data, there may also occur many issues such as wrong values collected due to human errors, misinterpretation of the data, integrating with the data captured from multiple sources, and different formats used by various healthcare organizations due to lack of standardizations. Apart from these, high dimensionality (number of records being more than the number of features) is also an issue, which may include omics data such as genomics, metabolomics, diseasomics, EHR, and biomedical data of individuals among others [22, 27].

13.4 Research Trends

Many works are going on the emerging technologies due to their major contribution toward healthcare data. Some such works are discussed below.

Healthcare information system based on IoT using WSN is proposed by Kashyap [12]. The design methodology is provided in the perspective of future users and the contract owners by taking into consideration their requirements making it more user-driven; this aids the patients or ageing people living independently, who find it challenging to handle their day to day activities. Firstly, the body and home sensor networks are monitored. To provide a connection, a gateway like base stations are used to send signals using communication networks like Ethernet, Wi-Fi, Internet, and GSM to the server, where the medical professionals make use of the data for analyzing the patient's condition.

IoT big data analytics is a growing research area which can be combined with fog and cloud computing. Activity recognition is one such application which can be done for finding any health complications. A model to integrate IoT with cloud and fog is shown by Yassine *et al.* [28] to decrease decision-making time, where fog layer does as much computation as it can handle to reduce the burden on the cloud; in addition to this, design and development with automation can be done, thereby increasing the performance and memory and decreasing redundancy in the systems. A systematic literature survey of different research trends where the medical IoT applications make use of fog computing is provided by Mutlag *et al.* [29].

Another significant application which the health sector needs is automation. Once a person is infected by some incurable diseases like certain kinds of cancer and it reaches a certain level, there are no proper treatments yet to cure the disease. To detect the stage of the disease well in advance to allow better therapies, the medical researchers are eyeing on automated systems. Deep learning can aid in medical image processing to diagnose the scanning reports; a research conducted by Sekaran *et al.* [30] combines CNN with Gaussian mixture for predicting the level of pancreatic cancer in the body.

To couple medical big data with fog computing, some challenges of fog computing must be addressed and improvements on existing parameters will enhance the analytics; in this regard, Li *et al.* [31] introduced virtualization (creating new resources like hardware, storage, and network) in fog environment where they achieved lesser delay and jitter. By introducing virtual fog layers, their system also increases interoperability, is more flexible, has less latency, low cost, and effective energy utilization, increased scalability, and can deploy heterogeneous objects which can be handled, dynamically enabling sharing with multiple tenants and systems.

Traditional ML and data mining techniques find it challenging to manage the large quantity of data being generated at a high rate in the medical sector. Cano [32] provided a survey on processing significantly bigger data where Graphics Processing Units (GPUs) have shown promising results since they have high parallelism which increases the scalability of the algorithms. They provide extremely quick decision-making ability which is a must in healthcare to save patient lives. Sometimes, even GPU fails to manage the big data, multi-GPU and distributed GPU is a solution, which works by combining multiple resources to scale up for a larger dataset. Performance hindrance can be overcome by integrating MapReduce and GPU.

13.5   Conclusion

The manual burden on healthcare is increasing day by day, leading to the inventions of new technologies. Replacing humans whenever possible with smart intelligent advanced technologies have many benefits like increased speed and reduced errors and effort by medical staff, which are a must to handle huge volumes of data being generated. There is a need to combine big data with emerging technologies in healthcare. In this chapter, we discussed the data collection with emerging technologies like RFID, WSN, and IoT with its applications and challenges. Next, we focused on the data analysis approaches and the challenges faced in the data analytics process. We also explored some of the research works in the field.

References

1. Dash, S., Shakyawar, S.K. *et al.*, Big data in healthcare: management, analysis and future prospects. *J. Big Data*, 6, 54, 2019.
2. Hong, L., Luo, M. *et al.*, Big Data in Healthcare: Applications and Challenges. *Data Inf. Manage.*, 2, 175, 2018.
3. Wu, J., Li, H., Lin, Z., Goh, K.-Y., How big data and analytics reshape the wearable device market – the context of e-health. *Int. J. Prod. Res.*, 55, 5168, 2015.
4. Wu, J., Li, H., Lin, Z., The promising future of healthcare services: When big data analytics meets wearable technology. *Inf. Manage.*, 53, 1020, 2016.
5. Ma, X., Wang, Z. *et al.*, Intelligent Healthcare Systems Assisted by Data Analytics and Mobile Computing. *Wirel. Commun. Mob. Comput.*, 2018, 1, 2018.
6. Mukherjee, A., Pal, A., Misra, P., Data Analytics in Ubiquitous Sensor-Based Health Information Systems, in: *6th Int. Conf. NGMAST*, pp. 193–198, 2012.
7. Yao, W., Chu, C.-H., Li, Z., The use of RFID in healthcare: Benefits and barriers. *Int. Conf. on RFID-Technology and Applications*, China, IEEE, pp. 128–134, 2010.
8. Sundaresan, S., Doss, R., Zhou, W., RFID in Healthcare – Current Trends and the Future, in: *Springer Series in Bio-/Neuroinformatics*, Adibi, S. (Ed.), pp. 839–870, 2015.
9. Haddara, M. and Staaby, A., RFID Applications and Adoptions in Healthcare: A Review on Patient Safety. *Proc. Comput. Sci.*, 138, 80, 2018.
10. Fosso Wamba, S., Anand, A., Carter, L., A literature review of RFID-enabled healthcare applications and issues. *Int. J. Inf. Manage.*, 33, 875, 2013.
11. Kim, B.-S., Kim, K.-I.I. *et al.*, Wireless Sensor Networks for Big Data Systems. *Sensors*, 19, 1565, 2019.

12. Kashyap, R., Applications of Wireless Sensor Networks in Healthcare, in: *IoT and WSN Applications for Modern Agricultural Advancements*, pp. 8–40, 2020.

13. Dorj, U.-O., Lee, M. *et al.*, The Intelligent Healthcare Data Management System Using Nanosensors. *J. Sens.*, 2017, 1, 2017.

14. Minaie, A., Sanati-Mehrizy, A. *et al.*, Application of Wireless Sensor Networks in Healthcare System. *ASEE Annu. Conf. Expo. Proceedings*, 2013.

15. Saheb, T. and Izadi, L., Paradigm of IoT Big Data Analytics in Healthcare Industry: A Review of Scientific literature and Mapping of Research Trends. *Telemat. Inform.*, 41, 70, 2019.

16. Priyanka, A., Parimala, M. *et al.*, BIG data based on healthcare analysis using IOT devices. *IOP Conf. Ser. Mater. Sci. Eng.*, 263, 042059, 2017.

17. Kalid, N., Zaidan, A.A. *et al.*, Based Real Time Remote Health Monitoring Systems: A Review on Patients Prioritization and Related "Big Data" Using Body Sensors information and Communication Technology. *J. Med. Syst.*, 42, 1, 2018.

18. Vitabile, S., Marks, M. *et al.*, Medical Data Processing and Analysis for Remote Health and Activities Monitoring, in: *High-Performance Modelling and Simulation for Big Data Applications*, Lect. Notes Comput. Sci., vol. 11400, J. Kołodziej and H. González-Vélez (Eds.), p. 186, Springer, Cham, 2019.

19. Lee, C.H. and Yoon, H.-J., Medical big data: promise and challenges. *Kidney Res. Clin. Pract.*, 36, 1, 3–11, 2017.

20. Mayer, M.A., Heinrich, A. *et al.*, Big Data Technologies in Healthcare. Needs, opportunities and challenges, in: *Big Data Value Association*, 2016.

21. Aziz, F., Chalup, S.K., Juniper, J., Big Data in IoT Systems. *Internet of Things (IoT): Systems and Applications*. Pan Stanford Publishing Pte. Ltd., ArXiv, abs/1905.00490, 2019.

22. Ristevski, B. and Chen, M., Big Data Analytics in Medicine and Healthcare. *J. Integr. Bioinform.*, 15, 3, 2018.

23. Raeesi Vanani, I. and Majidian, S., Literature Review on Big Data Analytics Methods, in: *Social Media and Machine Learning*, IntechOpen, Rijeka, Croatia, 2020.

24. Chen, X., Zhu, H. *et al.*, Merging RFID and Blockchain Technologies to Accelerate Big Data Medical Research Based on Physiological Signals. *J. Healthcare Eng.*, 2020, 1, 2020.

25. Wang, Y., Kung, L., Byrd, T.A., Big data analytics: Understanding its capabilities and potential benefits for healthcare organizations. *Technol. Forecast. Soc. Change*, 126, 3, 2018.

26. Wu, J., Li, H., Liu, L., Zheng, H., Adoption of big data and analytics in mobile healthcare market: An economic perspective. *Electron. Commer. Res. Appl.*, 22, 24, 2017.

27. Djedouboum, A.C., Abba Ari, A.A. *et al.*, Big Data Collection in Large-Scale Wireless Sensor Networks. *Sensors*, 18, 4474, 2018.

28. Yassine, A., Singh, S. *et al.*, IoT big data analytics for smart homes with fog and cloud computing. *Future Gener. Comput. Syst.*, 91, 563, 2018.

29. Mutlag, A.A., Abd Ghani, M.K. *et al.*, Enabling technologies for fog computing in healthcare IoT systems. *Future Gener. Comput. Syst.*, 90, 62, 2019.

30. Sekaran, K., Chandana, P. *et al.*, Deep learning convolutional neural network (CNN) With Gaussian mixture model for predicting pancreatic cancer. *Multimed. Tools Appl.*, 79, 10233, 2020.

31. Li, J., Jin, J., Yuan, D., Zhang, H., Virtual Fog: A Virtualization Enabled Fog Computing Framework for Internet of Things. *IEEE Internet Things J.*, 5, 121, 2018.

32. Cano, A., A survey on graphic processing unit computing for large-scale data mining. *WIREs: Data Min. Knowl. Discovery*, 8, 1232, 2017.

14

A Complete Overview of Sign Language Recognition and Translation Systems

Kasina Jyothi Swaroop[1]*, Janamejaya Channegowda[2] and Shambhavi Mishra[3]

[1]Indian Institute of Technology (Indian School of Mines), Dhanbad, India
[2]Ramaiah Institute of Technology, Bangalore, India
[3]CBP Government Engineering College, Delhi, India

Abstract

Sign Language Recognition and Translation systems involve the usage of the human body pose and hand pose estimation. Sign Language Recognition has been conventionally been performed by some preliminary sensors and later evolved to various advanced Deep Learning–based Computer Vision systems. This chapter deals with the past, present, and future of the Sign Language Recognition systems. Sign Language Translation is also briefly discussed here, giving insights on Natural Language Processing techniques to accurately convert Sign Language to translated sentences.

Keywords: Sign language, sensor-based systems, vision-based

14.1 Introduction

Sign Language is the language of performing signs using hands, human body pose, facial expressions, etc., to communicate with each other. This is prevalent among the deaf and the mute communities which constitute about 5% of the world's population. With a language that is practiced only among certain communities, the socialization of those community people becomes very difficult. Active research in the fields of Sign Language

---

*Corresponding author: kasina.18je0405@ee.iitism.ac.in

A. Suresh, S. Vimal, Y. Harold Robinson, Dhinesh Kumar Ramaswami and R. Udendhran (eds.)
Bioinformatics and Medical Applications: Big Data Using Deep Learning Algorithms, (289–314) © 2022 Scrivener Publishing LLC

Recognition and Translation is being taken up over various Sign Languages to help and address the above problems.

Sign Languages themselves are very diverse differing from countries depending on the various factors taken into consideration while performing the sign like using single or a dual hand sign language, involvement of facial expressions in the Sign Language, etc.

14.2 Sign Language Recognition

14.2.1 Fundamentals of Sign Language Recognition

Sign Language Recognition on a simplified note is the process of recognizing the Sign performed by a signer (a person practicing sign language is often referred to as a signer). Sign Language Recognition is the method employed to detect the signs and further process and convert them into a text or speech output. Sign Language Recognition is a task that has been an active area of research over many years. The initial research was predominantly in the American Sign Language (ASL); later on, research interest toward others Sign Languages like the German Sign Language (GSL), Brazilian Sign Language (BSL), and Indian Sign Language (ISL) was observed. The diversity in these Sign Languages lies in the fact that the Sign Languages of various countries sometimes within the country to change a lot based on considerations like number of hands used, human pose, eye movements, and facial features.

Sign Language Recognition, sometimes, is also considered as the task of jointly recognizing the type of Sign Language (i.e., whether the data obtained depicts the Signs belonging to ASL or ISL, etc.) first and then classifying the Sign as a particular word in that Particular Sign Language. The latter part is the primary area of focus among many researchers in the field, owing to the fact that Sign Language Recognition systems are developed regionally and thus would have the capability to detect the Sign Language of a particular region only and trying to expand them to intra regions might prove to be very resource heavy yet there has been some research going on toward that end to make Sign Language Recognition Systems more robust.

Sign Language Recognition Systems age back to the 1990s. During this period, the most significantly used approaches were dependent upon hardware-based approaches due to the limited computational resources and not many methods pertaining to images were present during the time. Hardware-based methods predominantly included the process of the signer performing a particular Sign and recording the gesture through the certain type of mechanical sensors [1] (as shown in Figures 14.1 and 14.2) and further processing this sensor data through various processing networks, and finally, output is obtained. This method lacks the capability to capture other body movements during performance of a Sign so only the hand posture

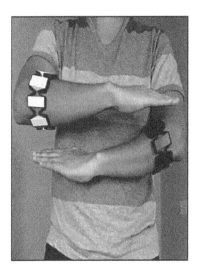

Figure 14.1 The Myo armbands usage for Sign Language Recognition.

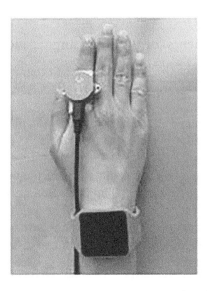

Figure 14.2 Smart ring + watch setup to detect movements of the finger during the process of signing by a signer.

can be captured. Taking this into account, Image Recognition–based systems were an alternative approach of research. Initial Image Recognition–based systems mostly relied on using conventional methods like Hidden Markov Models (HMMs) [2]. HMMs were initially used along with sensor data also and have been proven to be quite accurate in Sign Language Recognition Systems. Image Recognition Systems capture the image using a camera, and based on the collected datasets, the models are trained to identify the signs using pose estimation, gestures, and facial recognition, where these features are extracted and learnt by architectures like Neural Networks.

Sign Language Recognition systems can further be also thought to be of two kinds: static and dynamic. This classification completely depends on the architecture being used and the dataset. Sign Language Recognition systems with the ability and architectures to capture gestures in motion (e.g., gesture of Alphabets J and Z are motion gestures) are commonly known as the dynamic systems. These systems can be used to capture the signs in real time and thus have found applications highly in Real-Time Sign Language Recognition Systems. Further, networks with the capability to capture the frame-to-frame differences in time have been proven to be effective for capturing the temporal data and thus improve the accuracy of existent systems. Static systems are those where in the architectures are limited to processing only the static signs generally all the Alphabets excluding the J and Z.

14.2.2 Requirements for the Sign Language Recognition

Major requirements for the Sign Language Recognition systems that are explained in this section are as follows:

- Sensor logging data for sensor-based systems
- Images, videos for vision-based systems

The basic requirement for the vision-based recognition systems is image/video data. Data in the field of Sign Language Recognition is highly diverse and, sometimes, is readily available or created. Primarily, Sign Language Recognition Systems with sensor data requires the sensor reading which are to be recorded for experiments and is not so diversely available. Also, Sign Language being variant based on regions becomes difficult to have various datasets for various regions, and thus, designing a Universal Sign Language Recognition is highly difficult. Further, problem with the sensor datasets is that the sensors must be calibrated properly and if the sensors are not highly accurate, and thus, noise introduction occurs; hence, these kinds of datasets further will require signal processing.

Sign Language Recognition systems based on images have datasets which are highly diverse. As mentioned in the previous section, the datasets can be collected only for the static Alphabets which will contribute toward the training of static systems or the collection of datasets related to dynamic signs be it individual alphabets or words will help in designing dynamic architectures. The most processed and abundantly available dataset for theimage-based methods is the ASL. Most of the recognition systems around the globework on ASL owing to its abundance properly labeled and very diverse data.

Certain robust networks have been also developed on other Sign Language Datasets apart from the ASL which are GSL, ISL, Arabic Sign Language (ArSL) [3], etc. SLR's data might involve just the images of the person performing the static signs, person wearing color coded gloves, and person recording images for easier segmentation of the hand (varies based on model architectures) or for dynamic recognitions videos are recorded. Apart from the major recognition system architecture, sometimes, additional networks based on HOG features, segmentation features must be extracted from these image datasets; thus, developing such networks can be stated as a further requirement.

14.3   Dataset Creation

In the task of Sign Language Recognition as already stated above, diverse methods and thus diverse datasets areavailable and/or need to be created. This section describes about the various existing datasets and how the datasets can be obtained. The major datasets discussed here will be related to ASL, considering it is the most widely developed dataset. Additionally, we shall consider ISL, ArSL, and GSL.

14.3.1   American Sign Language

ASL is one of the most extensively used for research toward Sign Language Recognitions, Translations, and various other tasks. It is the most developed dataset with a huge amount of datain the form of images, videos, sensor data, etc.

American Sign Language Lexicon Video Dataset (ASLLVD) [4] is one of the largest datasets available. This was started out as a project in 2008 to curate resources for ASL thus progressing research toward Computer

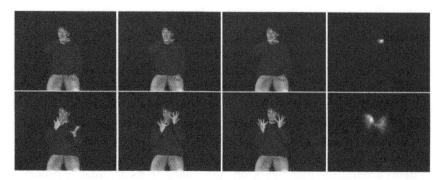

Figure 14.3 Figure shows the start, middle, and end frames along with the motion energy model for two different signs [4].

Vision–based methods for Sign Language Recognition. Additionally, this dataset served as a look up dictionary for various symbols in ASL for non-signers to easily understand and interpret signs. This dataset basically contains sequences of videos of thousands of Signs of ASL along with indications of start and end of signs, gloss, signerID, and whether the sign is single handed or double handed. The isolated videos captured are labelled using the glossary from the Gallaudet Dictionary of American Sign Language [5]. Four different camera views are inculcated in the dataset along with having a dedicated camera for the facial region as shown in Figure 14.3. This dataset was further used to create a lookup project where in the signer signs in front of the camera, and based on the Motion Energy Models, the nearest Sign in the Lexicon Dataset is retrieved.

American Sign Language Image Dataset (ASLID) is another dataset developed extracting frames from Gallaudet Dictionary of American Sign Language and the previously stated ASLLVD. This was developed for evaluation of Deep Learning–based pose estimation for Sign Language Recognition [6]. This dataset basically described seven locations in the upper body, namely, left hand, left elbow, leftshoulder, head, right hand, right shoulder, and right wrist. A separate visualization tool was also developed to show the annotations in the frames as shown in Figure 14.4.

This dataset contained a set 809 images as training dataset and 479 images as test dataset. Figure 14.5 furthershows variation in the training and test datasets among the frames.

The next dataset is the MS-ASL [7], a large-scale dataset comprising about 25,000 images of the ASL with annotations. The dataset was collected in real-life settings with over 200 signers across 1,000 different signs of ASL. This dataset has been developed to test the State-of-the-Art Computer

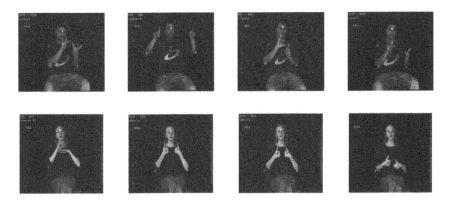

Figure 14.4 Images showing annotations of various images extracted from ASLLVD and Gallaudet Dictionary of ASL [6].

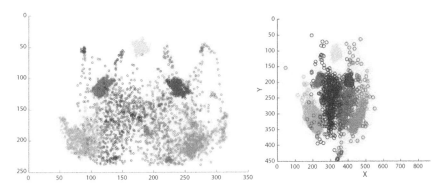

Figure 14.5 Image showing variation in the training and test set images. The various colors are the seven locations in the upper body as annotated in the images. Yellow, head; violet, right shoulder; blue, left shoulder; cyan, right elbow; green, left elbow; black, right hand; red, left hand [6].

Vision Techniques for SLR without the use of depth images. This dataset also includes a review of various other smaller datasets that were studied as a part of the Literature Survey. This work basically extracted their images from publicly available ASL videos uploaded on community platforms using techniques like Optical CharacterRecognition to extract the frames and the captions associated. This dataset also proves to be challenging, and thus, the models can be trained better in the fact that it involves various lighting conditions, a diverse number of signers, same word representing different sign due to the variability in dialects, etc. Apart from the above datasets some datasets involve only 26 letters and 10 digits.

Depth-based images are also collected generally using the Microsoft Kinect Sensor. As 3D image collection andimplementation is a computational heavy process, they are generally only collected for specific works. Such specific depth-based images are as presented in the works [8–10].

Similar to depth, due to the diverse number of sensors present and various functionality wise datasets of some ofthe sensor-based, glove-based, etc., are as presented in the works [10–12]. Glove-based detection methods will be discussed in the next section.

14.3.2   German Sign Language

GSL is yet another sign language gaining research interest and thus led to development of standard datasets for DGS. Many major research methods for the task of SLR have been applied to DGS and gained some highly good results [13].

SMILE Swiss German Sign Language Dataset [14] is a part of the SMILE Project (Scalable Multimodal Sign Language Technology for Sign Language Learning and Assessment) where the system aims at generating feedback based on the signs performed by the signer. For this purpose, Deep Learning–based methods were used, and thus, this required a bigger dataset to process; thus, Swiss German Sign Language Dataset was developed involving 11 L1 signers and 19 L2 signers. The dataset was obtained for 100 different words and the cameras used for capturing included a Microsoft Kinect v2 sensor, 2 Go Pro cameras, and 3 webcams, as shown in Figure 14.6.

Since this dataset was being developed to train the SLR systems, measures were taken to prevent blank frames without any sign being performed. Further, the sentences were gathered from DSGS Online Gloss [15]. Figure 14.7 represents the entire contents of the SMILE Swiss Language Dataset describing the resolution, frame rate, file type, etc.

The next dataset in the GSL is the RWTH-PHOENIX Weather 2014 T Continuous Sign Language Recognition and Translation benchmark dataset [16]. Developed by the Human Language Technology and Pattern Recognition Group, this work involved collecting weather forecast TV airing featuring   Sign Language Interpretations and annotating them based on gloss. Videos were also recorded using a single camera where signers would wear dark clothes and perform the signs against a gray background.

SIGNUM Database [17] is one more significant dataset in the DGS. This corpus consisted of signs of 450 general words in GSL like nouns and verbs used frequently in daily life. Using these isolated words further, sign

Figure 14.6 Image showing the capturing system used in the SMILE Swiss German Sign Language Dataset using six cameras [14].

Modality	File Type	Resolution	Content
Kinect Color Video	.MP4 Video File	1920×1080 Pixels @ 30 FPS	24bpp Image Sequence
GoPro Color Video [HD]	.MP4 Video File	3840×2160 Pixels @ 30 FPS	24bpp Image Sequence
GoPro Color Video [HS]	.MP4 Video File	1280×720 Pixels @ 240 FPS	24bpp Image Sequence
Webcam Color Videos	.MP4 Video File	1280×720 Pixels @ 30 FPS	24bpp Image Sequence
Depth Map	.RAR Binary File	512×424 Pixels @ 30 FPS	16bpp Image Sequence
User Mask	.RAR Binary File	512×424 Pixels @ 30 FPS	8bpp Binary Image Sequence
Kinect Pose Information	.CSV File	25 Joints	3D Joint Coordinates and Angles
Body Pose Information	.JSON File	18 Joints	2D Joint Coordinates and Confidences
Facial Landmarks	.JSON File	70 Joints	2D Joint Coordinates and Confidences
Hand Pose Information	.JSON File	2×21 Joints	2D Joint Coordinates and Confidences
iLex Annotations	.XML File	(not applicable)	Linguistic Annotations

Figure 14.7 Image showing the contents of SMILE Swiss German Sign Language Dataset [14].

language videos were recorded for 780 continuous word sentences. The corpus in total includes 25 signers. Figure 14.8 shows the method of data acquisition used for the SIGNUM Database.

14.3.3 Arabic Sign Language

ArSL is also one sign language which has gained research interest in the recent times and many Arab Journals involve Advanced Computer Vision–based methods to detect ArSL.

Figure 14.8 Figure representing the recording procedure for the SIGNUM corpus [17].

ArASL is one such ArSL image-based dataset which includes 54,049 images collected from 40 participants for 32 different Signs of the Arabic Language. The dataset collection method involved signers standing in front of RGB camera and performing the signs,

Additionally, datasets containing ArSL benchmark for various sensors are also available [19]. This dataset was collected using the Microsoft Kinect, Leap Motion Sensor. The contents of this dataset are represented in Figure 14.9.

14.3.4   Indian Sign Language

ISL is unique from many other datasets out there in the fact that ISL generally uses both the hands to represent sign of a word. Thus, datasets developed also generally include two hand signs.

The dataset involving the two hands is Two-Hand Indian Sign Language (THISL) [20]. This dataset comprises of 9,100 images for 26 alphabets and 350 images per alphabet. The images were collected using a DSLR camera.

Further, this THISL dataset was tested for many Machine Learning methods, and accuracies were obtained.

In the context of ISL, the dataset availability is low, and new and emerging datasets are being created dynamically.

Input Arabic Alphabet Sign classes with their lables and number of images.

#	Letter name in English Script	Letter name in Arabic script	# of Images	#	Letter name in English Script	Letter name in Arabic script	# of Images
1	Alif	(أَلِف)	1672	17	Zā	(ظَاء)	1723
2	Bā	(بَاء)	1791	18	Ayn	(عَين)	2114
3	Tā	(تَاء)	1838	19	Ghayn	(غَين)	1977
4	Thā	(ثَاء)	1766	20	Fā	(فَاء)	1955
5	Jīm	(جِيم)	1552	21	Qāf	(قَاف)	1705
6	Hā	(حَاء)	1526	22	Kāf	(كَاف)	1774
7	Khā	(خَاء)	1607	23	Lām	(لَام)	1832
8	Dāl	(دَال)	1634	24	Mīm	(مِيم)	1765
9	Dhāl	(ذَال)	1582	25	Nūn	(نُون)	1819
10	Rā	(رَاء)	1659	26	Hā	(هَاء)	1592
11	Zāy	(زَاي)	1374	27	Wāw	(وَاو)	1371
12	Sīn	(سِين)	1638	28	Yā	(يَا)	1722
13	Shīn	(شِين)	1507	29	Tāa	(ة)	1791
14	Sād	(صَاد)	1895	30	Al	(ال)	1343
15	Dād	(ضَاد)	1670	31	Laa	(لا)	1746
16	Tā	(طَاء)	1816	32	Yāa	(يَاء)	1293

Figure 14.9 The figure represents the 32 alphabets and the number of images obtained along with the English Letter [18].

14.4 Hardware Employed for Sign Language Recognition

This section briefly describes the various hardware-based approaches employed for the task of SLR. We focus on the following:

i) Glove/sensor-based systems
ii) Microsoft Kinect–based systems

14.4.1 Glove/Sensor-Based Systems

Glove/sensor-based systems, as the names suggests, are conventionally sensor-based data collection methods for the task of Sign Language Recognition. This section outlines some of the prominent sensors used in the glove-based approaches and also provides insights about the processing methods used for the sensor data.

The sensors that have been used for the process of Hand Gesture Recognition which further helps in Sign Language Recognition include light-based photovoltaic way back from the 1970s. Further, flex sensors were used which basically measured the bend in the fingers and were wired to a microcontroller to process the data, and then, these data were used to model Sign Language Recognition systems. The flex sensors were not quite accurate since these sensors could only detect the bend at one position of the finger. They further include the disadvantage of being wired to the microcontrollers, thus making them bulky and inconvenient for experimentation. Also, these flex sensors were unable to measure certain important characteristics like the contact of thumb with other regions of the hand and also relative twist and pose of wrist, etc. Thus, later on, to add these functionalities, touch sensors were additionally employed on the gloves. Additionally, Inertial Measurement Unit (IMU) Sensors were employed which could measure the acceleration value along three perpendicular axes, thus enabling us to detect the location and pose accurately. Further, sensors like Hall effect sensors and capacitive extension sensors were used to record the finger flexions, extensions, etc.

The development of more and more precise sensors found applications into SLR. Cyber Glove developed at Center for Design Research at the Stanford University is a glove sensor system containing in total of 22 sensors which are piezoresistive sensors (sensors whose resistance and thus the current drawn changes with respect to the pressure experienced by the sensor) was one of the major glove-based methods used for SLR. Figure 14.10 shows a table describing various gloves that were developed for SLR.

The readings obtained from these sensory glove systems are used to estimate the pose of the hand and the bends and extensions pretty accurately, and then, in some cases, these sensor data are modeled using design software applications, and the Hand Model is regenerated and fed to Machine Learning systems for SLR. Some other systems simply build classification models based on the collected sensor data and annotating a range of the values to belong to a particular sign. One of the drawbacks with the sensor-based systems can be pointed out to be that they only consider the hand pose and do not take into account the other parts of the body which are quite essential in the context of SLR. These drawbacks are mitigated by the vision-based systems which will be discussed in the next section.

14.4.2 Microsoft Kinect–Based Systems

This section deals with briefly describing the Microsoft Kinect Sensor application toward Sign Language Recognition systems. Microsoft Kinect is essentially a depth camera sensor which is used extensively in various research applications like pose estimation, gesture recognition, and many other image-based and depth-based applications. Furthermore, Microsoft Kinect Sensor being a motion capture system too can be used to capture dynamic signs and thus be implemented in the Dynamic Sign Language Recognition.

Also, the depth-based images captured by the sensor were further used for applications like 3D reconstruction-based pose estimations, estimating joint angles from the depth-based images [22], thus contributing toward better sign language recognition systems, etc.

Device	Technology	Sensors	Sensor Precision	Records/sec	Interface	Advantages/Disadvantages
Digital Entry Data Glove	N/A	4 Flex C	n/a	n/a	n/a	Legacy Equipment
Data Glove (MIT, VPL Inc.)	Fiber Optic	5-15 flex C	12 bits	30-160 Hz	Serial	good amount of literature/ non-linear mapping between joint movement and intensity of reflected light, no abduction-adduction sensors, sampling inadequate for time-critical applications, difficult to capture thumb movement, calibration required for every new user
Power Glove	Piezo Resistive	4 Flex C	2 bits	n/a	serial	very low cost/low precision, calibration required for new users
Cyber Glove	Piezo Resistive	18-22 flex C	8 bits	150 Hz - Unfiltered, 112 Hz - Filtered (18 sensors)	serial	equipped with abduction-adduction sensors, good amount of literature, wireless version/1 size, difficult recording from thumb, calibra-tion required, very expensive
5 DT, 16DT Glove	Fiber Optic	5 (5DT), 16 (14DT) flex C	8 bits	200 Hz (5DT), 400 Hz (16DT)	serial, USB Adapter available	left-right handed models available, wireless version, MRI compatible, fair amount of literature, equipped with abduction-adduction sensors/ 1 size, calibration required
Accele Glove	dual axis accelerometers	6 C/No. C	6.5 deg	100 Hz	serial	no calibration, external tracking not required, low cost/cannot detect horizontal postures
StrinGlove	Magnetic	24 flex C	12 bits	30 Hz	serial	washable, 3 sizes, embedded DSP based encoding system/fragile sensors, calibration required
Chording Glove	switches	5 C	1 bit	N/A	N/A	portability/non-trivial training to learn chords

Figure 14.10 This table summarizes some glove sensor systems among which systems like Cyber Glove and Digital Entry Data Glove were used for SLR in ASL, Australian Sign Language, Japanese Sign Language, etc. [21].

Kinect Sensor is also one of the preferred and widely used because the depth information obtained paired with certain software extract a depth-based skeletal systems of the human body, thus contributing to accurate pose estimation without the variability of the accuracy of the prediction systems since the system now only depends on the skeletal system extracted and is not at all associated with the person, background, etc. [23].

Additionally, as described before, Kinect is also a motion capture system; hence, it allows for capturing the signs performed in the temporal dimension and also thus finding its applications in sequential-based Sign Language Recognition and Translation systems [24].

In the context of ISL Recognition where the grammar rule is in a sequen-tial complex order and systems developed in classifying the Sign Language

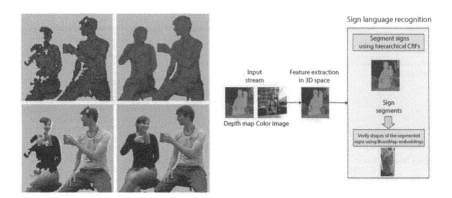

Figure 14.11 Image showing the 3D reconstruction through Kinect-based images. Image showing Kinect-based SLR methods [26].

are highly rule-based, the Kinect-based recognition system was found to be quite efficient [25].

Certain other systems include using the depth-based information and the 2D image information to extractcustom features and use these features for the Sign Language Recognition systems using methods like Conditional Random Fields and have gained good accuracies [26]. Figure 14.11 shows this procedure.

14.5   Computer Vision–Based Sign Language Recognition and Translation Systems

This section is dedicated to the discussion of advancement in Sign Language Recognition and Translation systems using Computer Vision–based methods. Computer Vision can be considered as a branch of Machine Learning primarily dealing with image data to be further precise dealing with the color properties of physical objects. Image data being more precise when compared to the sensor-based systems had helped to build highly accurate Sign Language Recognition pipelines.

14.5.1   Image Processing Techniques for Sign Language Recognition

Initially, Image Processing techniques were employed to extract certain features from images like the following:

i) SIFT features (Scale-Invariant Feature Transform) which provides the advantage that local imagedescriptors are found which are invariant to any kind of transformations, and thus, these features will remain the same even though the object orientation in the image changes.

ii) HOG (Histogram of Gradients) is predominantly used to extract human-based features in images and thus suitable for SLR systems. Gradients are obtained for the pixels in the image in a fixed frame size and the obtained gradient orientations are sorted into nine gradient bins, and thus, we obtain the feature vector.

iii) LBP (Local Binary Patterns) which extract features related to facial expression. This system employs making the value of all the pixels into binary by some comparison metric and these binarydigits form a decimal number and they are further used for facial feature detections. Thus, this method becomes helpful in facial expression detection which plays a key role in certain SLR systems.

The above listed are some of the feature extraction methods which are widely used for the task of Sign Language Recognition. The features obtained from these above techniques are sometimes belonging to higher dimensions, and thus, a famous technique called Principal Component Analysis is used to reduce the features into a two-dimensional space, and these features are then classified using the Support Vector Machine (SVM) classification systems.

Some features which were extracted formed clusters, i.e., nearby pixels belonging to a certain class upon extraction and plotting, represent close clusters. In such cases, cluster-based classification methods were employed like the K-Nearest Neighbors and K-Means. Sometimes, when features extracted from certain class of images are transformed into a high-dimensional space there due to the similarities, they may form clusters and similar methods can be employed.

With the advancements in Machine Learning systems specifically the Neural Networks, they found significant applications in the classification systems in many cases, thus giving improved accuracy results upon the previously mentioned SVM and Clustering-based techniques. Artificial Neural Networks, basically a nonlinear algorithm, was fed with these extracted features and the classification scores were obtained. Figure 14.12 shows an ANN for extracting features from images in an ISL context.

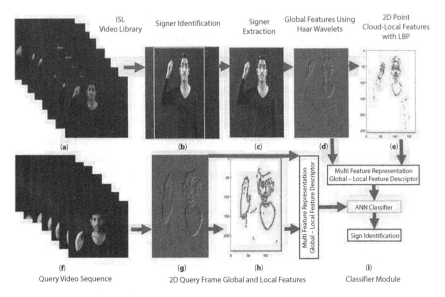

Figure 14.12 Figure representing usage of multi-feature extraction from an image and an ANN classifier employed for the classification of Indian Sign Language [27].

14.5.2 Deep Learning Methods for Sign Language Recognition

The next improvements in the Computer Vision–based methods are definitely the Deep Learning–based techniques to extract features and classify them. Convolutional Neural Networks are the most popular systems to deal with images. Convolution operation is performed by matrices on the image pixels and the models extract various features and, furthermore, unlike the Image Processing techniques, where the operational values, i.e., the parameters in the operation matrix are fixed numbers in CNNs; these values are actually learnt, and thus, instead of a universal kind of features, they can better extract features for an image based on the factors in the image pertaining to the lighting conditions of the image, occlusion, edge detections, etc.

In Sign Language Recognition, most CNN-based methods are employed to the hand region and not the entire body since focusing on just the hands, which is the Region of Interest in many cases, helps the CNN in learningthe features better and thus attain higher accuracies. Furthermore, this CNN extracted features that are then fed intothe classification systems mentioned before, and the classification results are obtained. The results obtained were definitely better using the CNN-based systems [28]. Certain improvised networks from the conventional methods like the Capsule

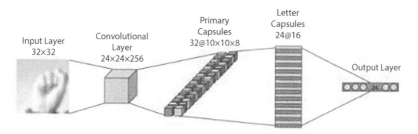

Figure 14.13 Capsule network for the Sign Language Recognition task [29].

networks (as shown in Figure 14.13) are also used for the Sign Language Recognition task [29].

All the methods described above deal with recognition of only the hand regions or, in some cases, include the facial expressions, but now, we also focus on one more important concept in the aspect of Sign Language Recognition, i.e., the Pose Estimation.

14.5.3   Pose Estimation Application to Sign Language Recognition

Human Pose Estimation is the task of localizing the various joint locations using 2D or 3D images and thus detect the (x, y) or the (x, y, z) coordinates. Pose Estimation methods generally take the RGB/RGBD images as an input and provide the interconnected skeletal points as outputs. Pose Estimation in the context of SLR can be said to be in two ways: Hand Pose Estimation only and the entire Human Pose Estimation. Hand Pose Estimation basically deals with the relative pose of the hand with respect to the wrist and the Human Pose Estimation deals with a multitude of factors like the head pose, hand pose, and relative finger poses. In the following, we shall discuss some of the popularly used Human Pose Estimation models which were employed in SLR.

1. Pose Net [30]: This Pose Estimation system is a CNN-based six-DOF system with applications toward the real-time systems and thus can be applied to Dynamic Sign Language Recognition systems, too [13].

2. Open Pose [31]: Open Pose is a widely used network in 2D Pose Estimation using Part Affinity Fields. This model can also be employed in real-time and is a multi-person tracking system. Applications of this system have been found to

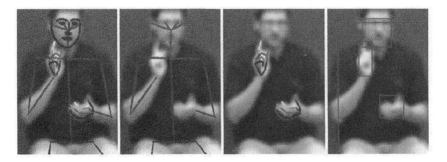

Figure 14.14 Real-Time Sign Language Recognition system using Pose Estimation and the Bounding Box Approach [13].

extract features [32] like relative distances and thususe these for Sign Language Recognition task. Figure 14.14 shows application of Open Pose into SLR.

Coming to the task of Hand Pose Estimation, the above specified models can be used, but some other novel methods like detecting the hand pose based on the edge detections, color segmentations, and key point estimations have also been employed [33]. Various other methods can also be found wherein the Encoder-Decoder type of networks are employed, and also, some visual-based features like overlay of heatmaps are used [34].

14.5.4 Temporal Information in Sign Language Recognition and Translation

The following section discusses about the spatio-temporal analysis for the Sign Language Recognition systems. In the previous sections, the major focus was on the image datasets and the image-based recognitionsystems. This section deals with the video datasets, and Real-Time Sign Language Recognition in the spatio-temporal data and also in 3D images will be discussed in detail.

In Real-Time Sign Language Recognition systems, for example, Detecting Sign Language using Mobile Applications, and Sign Language Recognition in Video Call Meetings, the data format is a video which is essentially a sequence of images with relation between one image and the next, i.e., if there is a hand movement to perform a dynamic sign, the relative position of the hand varies from one frame to the other, and this movement has to be captured to predict accurate gestures. This type of

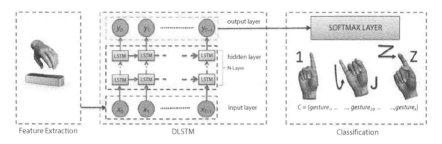

Figure 14.15 Network showing the feature extraction and the usage of LSTM to perform classification of gesture [35].

information can be accurately captured using Sequential-based networks and Attention-based networks like Long Short-Term Memory (LSTM) (as shown in Figure 14.15), Gated Recurrent Unit (GRU), and Transformer-based networks. These networks are used to accurately capture the co relation between the sequences of frames in the time domain. First, the video systems are sampled at a fixed frame rate, and then, these obtained frames are passed through a network like CNN to extract the desired featured and further can be passed through the sequential networks to model this time-based data.

After solving this task of the temporal data, the next advanced approaches were based on the 3D image data obtained from the Kinect Sensor or the Intel Image Real Sense.

Methods like the 3D CNN networks were employed to the 3D depth images obtained from the sensors and were further processed using the required processing techniques. Some methods also included a Query Search–based networks where the given image was first processed using the 3D CNN, and then, this obtained image was mapped to the already available database of processed images, and then, based on the closeness to the clusters, the tag is assigned to the query image [36].

14.6   Sign Language Translation System— A Brief Overview

The entire chapter till now had described Sign Language Recognition systems based on the sensor data, images, their processing techniques, etc. In this last section, the concept of Sign Language Translation is briefly discussed, and some of the methods used to perform Sign Language Translation are outlined.

Sign Language Translation systems are those in which the semantics and the grammar is also taken into accountalong with the Sign Language Recognition Systems. Every language has a certain order that is followed or the intricate semantics and rules to be followed to frame meaningful. The Mere Sign Language Recognition systemscannot perform this task as it can output a sequence of words but they cannot understand the rules of a Sign Language. Figure 14.16 shows a clear difference between Sign Language Recognition and Translation.

Sign Language Translation systems are based on the understanding of Natural Language Processing (NLP). NLP systems are basically those which are based on language processing techniques and have advanced quitewell understanding of the internal structure of language capturing and help in predictions using Attention-based methods and sequential methods.

Transformer-based methods like Encoder-Decoder structures (shown in Figure 14.17) are also employed to the task of SLR. We use state-of-the-art sequence-to-sequence (seq2seq)–based Deep Learning methods to learn the spatio-temporal representation of the signs, the relation between these signs (in other words, the language model), and how these signs map to the spoken or written language [37].

Further recent advancements included development and usage of Multi-Stage Transformer networks for the multiple channels of information like the hand pose, facial features, and body pose and thus developed these multi-channel networks with the Multi-Stage Transformer head (as shown in Figure 14.18). The use of Transformer-based networks also mitigates the problem of vanishing gradients [38].

Figure 14.16 Difference between a Sign Language Recognition and a Sign Language Translation system [37].

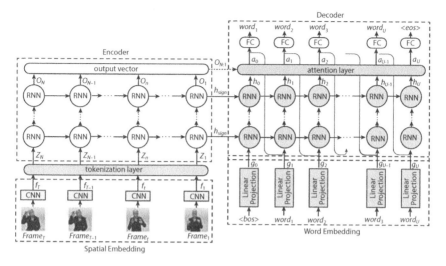

Figure 14.17 Image showing the Neural Sign Language Translation by employing sequential-based Encoder-Decoder networks [37].

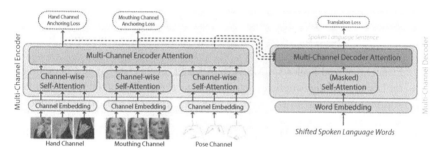

Figure 14.18 Image showing the different human body parts take into account and a multi-channel transformer network to process these images [38].

14.7   Conclusion

To summarize the chapter, the end goal for the upcoming vision-based systems must be to generate data suitable for Sign Language Recognition methods, to recognize signs taking into account various human body features, to further leverage the methods of above-described Attention-based methods, and thus to build a Sign Language Translation [39]. The modern evolving methods like adversarial attacks research is also applied to make the systems more robust [40]. Hence, we finally have the entire pipeline for understanding signers and accurately reproducing their language and build systems to help the deaf and mute people to communicate and socialize better, thus improving their quality of life.

References

1. DiPietro, L., Sabatini, A.M., Dario, P., A Survey of Glove-Based Systems and Their Applications. *IEEE Trans. Syst. Man Cybern., Part C (Appl. Rev.)*, 38, 4, 461–482, July 2008.

2. Wang, H., Leu, M., Oz, C., American Sign Language Recognition Using Multidimensional Hidden Markov Models. *J. Inf. Sci. Eng. - JISE*, 22, 1109–1123, 2006.

3. Ibrahim, N.B., Selim, M.M., Zayed, H.H., An Automatic Arabic Sign Language Recognition System (ArSLRS). *J. King Saud Univ. – Comput. Inf. Sci.*, 30, 4, 470–477, https://doi.org/10.1016/j.jksuci.2017.09.007, 2018.

4. Athitsos, V., Neidle, C., Sclaroff, S., Nash, J., Stefan, A., Yuan, Q., Thangali, A., The ASL Lexicon Video Dataset. *CVPR 2008 Workshop on Human Communicative Behaviour Analysis (CVPR4HB'08)*.

5. http://gupress.gallaudet.edu/bookpage/GDASLbookpage.html

6. Gattupalli, S., Ghaderi, A., Athitsos, V., Evaluation of Deep Learning based Pose Estimation for Sign Language, *Proceedings of the 9th ACM international conference on pervasive technologies related to assistive environments*. arXiv Prepr, 2016.

7. Joze, H.R.V. and Koller, O., MS-ASL: A Large -Scale Data Set and Benchmark for Understanding American Sign Language. *Proceedings of the 9th ACM international conference on pervasive technologies related to assistive environments*, arXiv:1812.01053 [cs], Dec. 2018.

8. Zafrulla, Z., Brashear, H., Starner, T., Hamilton, H., Presti, P., American sign language recognition with the Kinect, in: *Proceedings of the 13th international conference on multimodal interfaces*, pp. 279–286, 2011.

9. Hassan, S., Berke, L., Vahdani, E., Jing, L., Tian, Y., Huenerfauth, M., An Isolated-Signing RGBD Dataset of 100 American Sign Language Signs Produced by Fluent ASL Signers, in: *Proceedings of the LREC2020 9th Workshop on the Representation and Processing of Sign Languages: Sign Language Resources in the Service of the Language Community, Technological Challenges and Application Perspectives*, 2020, May, pp. 89–94.

10. Oz, C. and Leu, M.C., American sign language word recognition with a sensory glove using artificial neural networks. *Eng. Appl. Artif. Intell.*, 24, 7, 1204–1213, 2011.

11. Brashear, H., Starner, T., Lukowicz, P., Junker, H., Using multiple sensors for mobile sign language recognition. *Proc. IEEE Int. Symp. Wearable Comput.*, pp. 45–52, 2003.

12. Mehdi, S.A. and Khan, Y.N., Sign language recognition using sensor gloves. *Proceedings of the 9th International Conference on Neural Information Processing, 2002. ICONIP '02*, Singapore, vol. 5, pp. 2204–2206, 2002.

13. Moryossef, A., Tsochantaridis, I., Aharoni, R., Ebling, S., Narayanan, S., Real-Time Sign Language Detection using Human Pose Estimation, In: *European Conference on Computer Vision*, pp. 237–248, Springer, Cham, 2020.

14. Ebling, S., Camgoz, N., Braem, P., Tissi, K., Sidler-Miserez, S., Stoll, S., Hadfield, S., Haug, T., Bowden, R., Tornay, S., Razavi, M., Magimai-Doss, M., SMILE Swiss German Sign Language Dataset, 2018.

15. https://signsuisse.sgb-fss.ch/

16. Camgöz, N.C., Hadfield, S., Koller, O., Ney, H., Bowden, R., Neural Sign Language Translation. *IEEE Conf. on Computer Vision and Pattern Recognition*, Salt Lake City, UT, 2018.

17. https://www.phonetik.uni-muenchen.de/forschung/Bas/SIGNUM/

18. Latif, G., Mohammad, N., Alghazo, J., AlKhalaf, R., AlKhalaf, R., ArASL: Arabic Alphabets Sign Language Dataset. *Data Brief*, 23, 103777, 2019, 10.1016/j.dib.2019.103777.

19. Alfonse, M., Ali, A., Elons, A.S., Badr, N.L., Aboul-Ela, M., Arabic sign language benchmark database for different heterogeneous sensors. *2015 5th International Conference on Information & Communication Technology and Accessibility (ICTA)*, Marrakech, pp. 1–9, 2015.

20. Teja Mangamuri, L.S., Jain, L., Sharmay, A., Two Hand Indian Sign Language dataset for benchmarking classification models of Machine Learning. *2019 International Conference on Issues and Challenges in Intelligent Computing Techniques (ICICT)*, GHAZIABAD, India, pp. 1–5, 2019.

21. Ahmed, M.A. *et al.*, A Review on Systems-Based Sensory Gloves for Sign Language Recognition State of the Art between 2007 and 2017. *Sensors (Basel, Switzerland)*, 18, 7, 2208, 9 Jul. 2018.

22. Dong, C., Leu, M.C., Yin, Z., American Sign Language Alphabet Recognition Using Microsoft Kinect. Presented at the *Proceedings of the IEEE Conference on Computer Vision and Pattern Recognition Workshops*, pp. 44–52, 2015.

23. Geetha, M., Manjusha, C., Unnikrishnan, P., Harikrishnan, R., A vision based dynamic gesture recognition of Indian Sign Language on Kinect based depth images. *2013 International Conference on Emerging Trends in Communication, Control, Signal Processing and Computing Applications (C2SPCA)*, Bangalore, pp. 1–7, 2013.

24. Chai, X. *et al.*, Sign Language Recognition and Translation with Kinect, *IEEE Conf. on AFGR*. Vol. 655, 2013.

25. Ghotkar, A. and Kharate, G., Dynamic Hand Gesture Recognition for Sign Words and Novel Sentence Interpretation Algorithm for Indian Sign Language Using Microsoft Kinect Sensor. *J. Pattern Recognit. Res.*, 1, 24–38, 2015, 10.13176/11.626.

26. Yang, H.-D., Sign Language Recognition with the Kinect Sensor Based on Conditional Random Fields. *Sensors (Basel, Switzerland)*, 15, 135–47, 2014, 10.3390/s150100135.

27. Ravi, S., Suman, M., Kishore, P.V.V., Eepuri, K., Sign language recognition with multi feature fusion and ANN classifier. *Turk. J. Elec. Eng. Comp. Sci.*, 26, 2872–2886, 2018, 10.3906/elk-1711-139.

28. Nguyen, H.B.D. and Do, H.N., Deep Learning for American Sign Language Fingerspelling Recognition System. *2019 26th International Conference on Telecommunications (ICT)*, Hanoi, Vietnam, pp. 314–318, 2019.

29. Bilgin, M. and Mutludoğan, K., American Sign Language Character Recognition with Capsule Networks. *2019 3rd International Symposium on Multidisciplinary Studies and Innovative Technologies (ISMSIT)*, Ankara, Turkey, pp. 1–6, 2019.

30. Kendall, A., Grimes, M., Cipolla, R., PoseNet: A Convolutional Network for Real-Time 6-DOF Camera Relocalization. *2015 IEEE International Conference on Computer Vision (ICCV)*, Santiago, pp. 2938–2946.

31. Cao, Z., Hidalgo Martinez, G., Simon, T., Wei, S., Sheikh, Y.A., OpenPose: Realtime Multi-Person 2D Pose Estimation using Part Affinity Fields. *IEEE Trans. Pattern Anal. Mach. Intell.*, 43, 1, 172–186, 2019.

32. Kim, J. and O'Neill-Brown, P., Improving American Sign Language Recognition with Synthetic Data, in: *Proceedings of Machine Translation Summit XVII Volume 1: Research Track*, pp. 151–161, 2019.

33. Thongtawee, A., Pinsanoh, O., Kitjaidure, Y., A Novel Feature Extraction for American Sign Language Recognition Using Webcam. *2018 11th Biomedical Engineering International Conference (BMEiCON)*, Chiang Mai, pp. 1–5, 2018.

34. Lepetit, V., *Recent Advances in 3D Object and Hand Pose Estimation*, arXiv preprint arXiv:2006.05927. 2020.

35. Avola, D., Bernardi, M., Cinque, L., Foresti, G.L., Massaroni, C., Exploiting Recurrent Neural Networks and Leap Motion Controller for the Recognition of Sign Language and Semaphoric Hand Gestures. *IEEE Trans. Multimedia*, 21, 1, 234–245, Jan. 2019.

36. Kumar, A., Sastry, A.S.C.S., Kishore, P.V.V., Kiran Kumar, E., 3D sign language recognition using Spatio temporal graph kernels. *J. King Saud Univ.- Comput. Inf. Sci.*, 30, 2018.

37. Camgoz, N.C., Hadfield, S., Koller, O., Ney, H., Bowden, R., Neural Sign Language Translation. *2018 IEEE/CVF Conference on Computer Vision and Pattern Recognition*, Salt Lake City, UT, pp. 7784–7793, 2018.

38. Camgoz, N.C. *et al.*, Multi-channel Transformers for Multi-articulatory Sign Language Translation. European Conference on Computer Vision, Springer, Cham, 2020.

39. Bragg, D., Koller, O., Bellard, M., Berke, L., Boudrealt, P., Braffort, A., Caselli, N., Huenerfauth, M., Kacorri, H., Verhoef, T., Vogler, C., Morris, M., Sign Language Recognition, Generation, and Translation: An Interdisciplinary

Perspective, The 21st international ACM SIGACCESS conference on computers and accessibility, 2019.

40. Saunders, B., Camgoz, N., Bowden, R., Adversarial Training for Multi-Channel Sign Language Production, 2020.

Index

Printed and bound by CPI Group (UK) Ltd, Croydon, CR0 4YY

27/10/2024

14580126-0003